AUDIENCE ECONOMICS

AUDIENCE ECONOMICS

MEDIA INSTITUTIONS AND THE AUDIENCE MARKETPLACE

PHILIP M. NAPOLI

COLUMBIA UNIVERSITY PRESS
NEW YORK

COLUMBIA UNIVERSITY PRESS

Publishers Since 1893

New York   Chichester, West Sussex

Copyright © 2003 Columbia University Press

Library of Congress Cataloging-in-Publication Data

Napoli, Philip M.
    Audience economics : media institutions and the audience marketplace /
        Philip M. Napoli.
        p.   cm.
    Includes bibliographical references and index.
    ISBN 0–231–12652–2 (cl. : alk. paper) — ISBN 0–231–12653–0 (pa. : alk. paper)
    1. Television advertising. 2. Television advertising—United States. I. Title.

    HF6146.T42N364 2003
    659.14'3—dc21

                                                                2003040977

Columbia University Press books are printed on permanent and durable
acid-free paper

Printed in the United States of America

Designed by Lisa Hamm

c 10 9 8 7 6 5 4 3 2 1

p 10 9 8 7 6 5 4 3 2 1

References to Internet web sites (URLs) were accurate at the time of writing.
Neither the author nor Columbia University Press is responsible for web sites
that may have expired or changed since the articles were prepared

TO MY WIFE, ANNE

CONTENTS

ACKNOWLEDGMENTS

Although completing this book seemed to primarily involve sitting alone and staring at my computer, a number of individuals and organizations provided me with valuable assistance.

The National Association of Television Programming Executives (NATPE) provided me with a faculty development grant that allowed me to conduct the participant observation component of the research. In particular I want to thank Mike Donovan of the NATPE Educational Foundation for making the arrangements for such a fruitful research experience. The National Association of Broadcasters provided me with a faculty research grant that helped fund the quantitative analyses that are the backbone of chapter 2. Fordham University provided me with a faculty research grant that assisted me with the quantitative analyses that I describe in chapter 4. And the Fordham University Graduate School of Business Administration provided additional financial assistance for this project in the form of two summer research assistant grants and two summer research stipends.

Shelly Cagner at Arbitron deserves special thanks for giving me access to the radio audience data that I used in the quantitative analyses in chapter 4. I also want to thank Georgina Santilli of BIA Research for helping me to navigate BIA's research software.

I am grateful to have had the opportunity to present portions of this research at conferences, meetings, and seminars sponsored by a number of organizations, including the Pratt Institute, the National Cable and Telecommunications Association, the National Association of Broadcasters, the Turku School of Economics and Business Administration in Finland, the Association for Education in Journalism and Mass Communication, the

Quello Center for Telecommunication Management and Law at Michigan State University, and the Federal Communications Commission (FCC). With regard to the last, I am especially grateful to Robert Pepper, Jonathan Levy, and David Sappington of the FCC's Office of Plans and Policy for inviting me to take part in the Roundtable on Media Ownership Policies.

A number of other people provided useful information and feedback pertaining to various components of this project; they include Oscar Gandy of the University of Pennsylvania, Jay Isabella of Telerep, Adrienne Lotoski of WCVB-TV in Boston, David Gunzerath of the National Association of Broadcasters, and the anonymous reviewers who reviewed the initial book proposal and the completed manuscript. I also particularly benefited from the many interesting and informative panels organized in recent years by the Radio and Television Research Council in New York City. I also would like to thank Bill Livek of ADcom Information Services, Ken Wollenberg of Nielsen Media Research, Betty Frazier of WTVJ in Miami, and Beth Barnes of Syracuse University, all of whom graciously participated in a conference panel that I organized in the summer of 2002 on the economics of new audience measurement technologies. Many interesting ideas arose from their presentations and the lively discussion that followed.

I received valuable assistance from a number of excellent graduate research assistants, including Parmela Ramchandani, Joseph Brown, and Rachel Cheetham. They spent hours in the library and at the copy machine on my behalf and caught many errors that I otherwise would have missed.

I want to give special thanks to Steve Wildman and Jim Webster, who provided me with guidance and inspiration while I was a graduate student at Northwestern University. This book is an outgrowth of their combined influences.

Finally, I want to thank my dogs, Bella and Pablo, for providing a necessary distraction during those long days camped in front of the computer and, most important, my wife, Anne, for always being there for me, always patiently listening to my ideas, and for being a never-ending source of enthusiasm and support.

AUDIENCE ECONOMICS

INTRODUCTION

The media industries represent a unique component of the U.S. economy (Napoli 1997a). These industries are different from other industries in part because of the enormous amount of time and money that the public spends interacting with them. Recent data show that the average American spends more than five hours each day consuming some form of media. Consumer spending on communications and media products has been estimated at more than $150 billion for 2001 (Veronis, Suhler, and Associates 2001). Thus the prominence of the media industries in the U.S. economy has demanded the extensive attention and analysis that they receive.

The media industries also are different because of the profound social and political influence that they can have on the public (Napoli 1999b), affecting political and cultural attitudes (Lowery and DeFleur 1995), voting behaviors (Patterson 1980), and the propensity toward violence (Comstock et al. 1978; Hamilton 1998; Surgeon General 1972). Few, if any, other industries in the U.S. economy have the ability to affect the attitudes, beliefs, values, and behaviors of citizens across such a wide range of areas.

These unique attributes of the media industry are apparent even to casual observers of the role of the media in U.S. economic and political life; consequently, they have been the subject of extensive analysis (e.g., Dupagne 1997; Iyengar and Reeves 1997; Lowery and DeFleur 1995; McCombs 1972; Napoli 2001c; Page 1996; Son and McCombs 1993; Wood 1986). Less apparent, and less intensely analyzed, however, is a third unique characteristic of the media industries, the one that provides the impetus for this book. Specifically, media industries are unique in that they operate in what is best described as a dual-product marketplace. That is, media industries often offer simultaneously two distinct but interrelated products to two distinct sets of consumers (Napoli 2001b; Poltrack 1983; Shaver 1995).

The first—and most obvious—of the products that media industries provide is content. Whether it be news, entertainment, sports, or data, media industries produce a wide range of content for consumption by an audience. Sometimes they provide this content for a price, as is the case with most magazines, daily newspapers, cable television programming, videocassettes, DVDs, CDs, and some Internet sites (e.g., subscription-based sites). In other cases they provide this content for free, as is the case with some newspapers (e.g., local weeklies), as well as over-the-air radio and television broadcasts and the majority of Internet sites.

As many economists have noted, media content itself is a fairly distinctive product, with a number of important characteristics. For instance, the "public good" aspect of media content has been the subject of extensive analysis (e.g., Waterman 1987; Owen and Wildman 1992). As a public good, media content is not "used up" in consumption. Consequently, media firms can sell and resell the same media product indefinitely without incurring additional production costs. As many analysts have demonstrated, the economic implications of the public good aspect of media content are far reaching, affecting the budgeting decisions, distribution strategies, and pricing policies of media companies (Owen and Wildman 1992; C. Shapiro and Varian 1999; Waterman 1987; Werbach 2000).

Unfortunately, the second major product of media firms has not been subjected to a comparable degree of analysis, although its production is inextricably intertwined with the production of the first and it may have an equally profound effect on the media industries. This second product is audiences. Media firms produce content, then either give this content away or sell it in order to attract audiences. Media companies then sell these audiences to advertisers that are seeking the attention of potential consumers of their products or services.

Analysts of the media industries long have recognized this notion of the audience as economic product and the unique means by which this product is produced (Ang 1991; Bowman 1976: Gandy 1984; Jhally and Livant 1986; Meehan 1984; Nielsen 1988; Smythe 1977; Webster and Phalen 1997). As Rothenberg (1962) observed in the context of broadcast television:

The television market is quite different from that of most commodities. A television program presumably benefits the listening audience, yet the market transaction is one where the station or network sells the program not to this audience but to advertisers. The buyer benefits to the extent that the product (i.e., the program) gains the attention of third parties who are not themselves buyers of the program or even of any joint product of the program.   (46)

Although Rothenberg was writing in the context of free, over-the-air television, his 1962 observation is relevant for all media that derive at least part of their revenue from advertising. More recent observations by media professionals echo his point. As one television executive stated, "I can't think of another business that makes one product but sells a different product. . . . We make programs and put them on the air. We are not selling the programs, we are selling the people that watch the programs . . . so there is no direct correlation between that audience and that product that we are putting on the air" (Phalen 1996:76).

Most media firms operate simultaneously in both the content and audience markets, and what happens in one product market can significantly affect the other.[1] Consider, for instance, a cable television system. On the one hand, a cable television provider is trying to attract subscribers to its subscription-based service. Thus it is trying to sell content to audiences. In doing so, the cable provider is likely to offer a variety of service options and rate plans with multiple tiers of service (e.g., basic, expanded basic, premium, etc.). In addition, the provider is likely to offer different bundles of subscription channels (such as HBO, Showtime, and the like) at different prices.[2] The cable provider probably will also experiment with a variety of different program sources and channel offerings in an effort to attract and retain the largest subscriber base possible.[3]

While the cable provider is engaging in all these activities in the content market, it also is attempting to sell advertising time to local and national advertisers. Although the cable provider may not own any of the networks that provide content through its system, the cable provider retains and sells to advertisers a portion of the time on many networks. The amount of revenue that the cable provider can earn from advertisers depends upon the size and demographic composition of the audience attracted to the individual cable channels and programs. Thus although common terminology refers to the sale of advertising *time,* the time is worthless and meaningless absent the audience members whose attention the cable provider is capturing and then selling to advertisers. Thus the size and composition of the audience "product" are a function of the nature and appeal of the content "product" that the cable provider makes available.

Even services such as over-the-air broadcast television and radio, which do not charge for the programming they provide, operate simultaneously in both the content and audience markets. Unlike cable systems or cable networks, broadcasters collect virtually all their revenue from the sale of audiences to advertisers. However, although broadcasters collect all their revenue from the audience market, their success in this market rests upon their ability to compete successfully in the content market, because they must compete for audience attention (see Napoli 2001b). Thus both the broadcast and cable examples illustrate a key interaction between content and audience markets: Success in the audience market depends heavily upon a media organization's ability to capture the audience's attention in the content market.

A second important interaction involves advertiser demand for particular demographic groups. Advertisers frequently target specific demographic groups (see Turow 1997), some of which generally are more valuable to advertisers than others. Not surprisingly, these more valuable demographic groups become the target of an increasing amount of content, as content providers attempt to deliver these high-revenue audience segments to advertisers. For instance, recent years have seen a flood of television programming directed at teenagers and young adults. This trend is in response to the growth in the size and spending power of this segment of the population and the consequently greater value that advertisers are placing on younger audiences (Elber 1999). Thus here the supply-and-demand dynamics of the audience market affect the nature of the product supplied in the content market. In this book I will address these and other ways that the dynamics of the audience market affect the content that media organizations produce and distribute. My key objective at this point, however, is to illustrate the basic dynamics of the dual-product marketplace in which media firms operate.

Unfortunately, despite the wide recognition that the audience is a defining product of the media industry, detailed investigations of the audience marketplace have been relatively infrequent. Therefore, in contrast to previous analyses of the media industries (e.g., Noll, Peck, and McGowan 1973; Owen and Wildman 1992; Vogel 1998), my analysis focuses on the audience market and the audience product, not content. For just as media industries are unique in operating in a dual-product marketplace, they also offer a product that is unique: audiences. In selling audiences to advertisers, media firms essentially deal in human attention, and human attention represents a much more abstract, elusive, and intangible product than, say, steel, insurance, or legal services.

Human attention resists the type of exact verification and quantification that typify the transactions that take place in most other industries. Steel is weighed, insurance is expressed in specific dollar amounts of coverage, and legal advice generally is measured in terms of the amount of time spent producing and delivering it. Thus whether the measurement is in pounds, dollars, or hours, reasonably precise and stable measurement systems facilitate these transactions, and the products themselves are reasonably tangible.

But human attention is more difficult. As Ang has noted, "The audience for the mass media . . . is a much more elusive phenomenon" (1991:34). Verifying the presence or absence of human attention to media typically requires entering people's living rooms, bedrooms, and cars and monitoring their behavior. To be maximally effective such monitoring typically requires audience members' explicit permission, cooperation, and even participation in order to turn something as abstract as attention into tangible audience data that can then be bought and sold in the marketplace.[4] Thus Webster, Phalen, and Lichty have described the process of measuring an audience as an effort to "define the intangible" (2000:13).

Of course, monitoring the behavior of every audience member is impossible. Consequently, audience measurement firms generally measure audiences by compiling a sample of the population as a whole and measuring only the behaviors of this sample. Thus the behaviors of a select few individuals represent the behaviors of the entire population. That is why Smythe describes media audiences as "a strange type of institution. . . . a statistical abstraction" (1981:49). Even assuming that the measurement firm can obtain the cooperation and participation of an acceptable number of audience members, and that it can monitor their behaviors effectively, the firm cannot guarantee that the historical audience data that an advertiser receives will provide an accurate portrayal of how tomorrow's audience members choose to distribute their attention. In the chapters that follow, I will discuss these and other unique attributes of the audience as product.

Key issues that I address in this book are how media firms predict, measure, and value human attention and the challenges and implications of these activities. My ultimate goal is to provide readers with a deeper understanding of media audiences as an economic product and how the pursuit of this product affects the structure of media industries and the behavior of media organizations.

In focusing on media audiences as an economic good, I integrate the field of audience research with the field of media economics, as the book's title reflects. These two fields of research overlap in important ways, yet work in one area seldom has informed work in the other. Consequently, audience researchers often ignore or discount the economic dimensions and implications of audience behavior and audience measurement, whereas media economists often underestimate or neglect the complexities of audiences in the functioning of media industries.

The field of audience research traditionally has focused on documenting patterns in audience behavior, as well as on explaining audience motivations for media consumption and audience interpretations of media content, with much less attention devoted to the economic dimension of media audiences.[5] Thus the primary research questions that have guided audience researchers to this point have included what motivates media consumption (Blumler and Katz 1974; Frank and Greenberg 1980); how audiences consume and interpret media products (Biocca 1988; Hay, Grossberg, and Wartella 1996; Moores 1993; Radway 1984; Renckstorf, McQuail, and Jankowski 1996); how audiences "flow" across programming options (Barwise and Ehrenberg 1988; Goodhardt, Ehrenberg, and Collins 1975); and how new media technologies affect the behavioral patterns of audiences (Becker and Schoenbach 1989; Coffey and Stipp 1997; Becker, Dunwoody, and Rafaeli 1983; Heeter and Greenberg 1988; Levy 1989). Granted, these are all important questions that improve significantly our understanding of the dynamics of media consumption. However, most of this research has approached audiences as individual or aggregate consumers and interpreters of media products, whereas little of this research has approached media audiences from an economic standpoint, that is, as a product market with unique characteristics and significant points of interaction with media industries (for exceptions, see Neuman 1991; Webster and Phalen 1997; Ettema and Whitney 1994).

One might expect such an analytical perspective to be more prominent among media economists than audience researchers. However, media economics generally has focused on the behavior of media firms in the production and distribution of content (e.g., Busterna 1988b; Thomas and Litman

1991; Owen and Wildman 1992) and on structural analyses of various components of the media industry (e.g., Chan-Olmsted 1991; Compaine and Gomery 2000; Silk and Berndt 1993, 1994), to the neglect of the economic dimensions of audiences.[6] Efforts to define the field of media economics have focused on subject areas such as media ownership, institutional behaviors, and market structures (Gomery 1993). Basic texts on the subject typically focus on each of the various industry segments (e.g., radio, broadcast television, motion pictures, music, etc.), with little attention devoted specifically to the dynamics of the audience marketplace (e.g., Albarran 1996; Alexander, Owers, and Carveth 1998; Vogel 1998).

In the rare instances in which media economists have turned their attention to media audiences, their analyses have not incorporated the extensive theory and research that audience researchers have developed in regard to the dynamics of audience behavior. Instead, many economic analyses of media audiences are filled with an array of simplifying assumptions that often divorce such analyses from any reasonable approximation of the reality of audience behavior. Perhaps the best example of this disconnect between media economics and audience research is the extensive "program choice" literature developed primarily by media economists (e.g., Beebe 1977; Spence and Owen 1977; P. Steiner 1952). Research in this vein has attempted to model how radio and television programmers will program their channels under varying structural conditions and how audiences will distribute themselves across available content options. Thus the program choice literature represents a rare and important inquiry into the interaction between the audience marketplace and the content marketplace.

These theoretical models, however, assume behavioral tendencies that bear little resemblance to the behavioral tendencies that empirical audience research shows that audiences actually exhibit. For instance, early program choice models assumed that if an audience member's single favorite program type was not available, that person would turn off the radio or television (P. Steiner 1952). Audience behavior research repeatedly has demonstrated, however, that program type preferences are not an overwhelmingly strong predictor of media consumption (Ehrenberg 1968; Frank, Becknell, and Clokey 1971; Kim and Grant 1996; Kirsch and Banks 1962; Lehmann 1971; Rao 1975; Youn 1994). Most viewers or listeners will not turn off the television or radio if their favorite program type is unavailable. They simply will watch or listen to something else.

Later work relaxed the "single choice" assumption (e.g., Beebe 1977; Rothenberg 1962; Spence and Owen 1977; Waterman 1992; Wildman and Owen 1985) but perpetuated another inaccurate assumption regarding audience behavior—that audiences possess complete awareness of all the content offerings available to them and thus make perfectly informed choices regarding what they want to watch or listen to.[7] In reality, audiences have less-than-perfect awareness of all available content options (D. Ferguson and Perse 1993; Heeter 1985; Donthu 1994; Webster and Wakshlag 1983).[8] The relative extent of this awareness diminishes as the range of content options increases (Heeter and Greenberg 1988). Audiences generally cope with their expanding media choices by developing "repertoires" (D. Ferguson and Perse 1993; Heeter 1985)—subsets of available content options that they consume with some regularity. These repertoires typically represent a limited subset of the full range of content offerings; most research in this vein shows that as the number of content options increases, the proportion that an audience member consumes regularly in fact declines (D. Ferguson 1992; Heeter 1985). These repertoires also seem to reach comparable limits across media.[9]

These failures in the media economics literature to reflect the dynamics of audience behavior show that most analyses seldom, if ever, draw upon audience research in developing their theoretical models.[10] This tendency illustrates the general disconnect between audience research and media economics research that has persisted for years. As a result broad-based interdisciplinary inquiries into the interaction of the audience marketplace and media industries have been lacking.

Often, research that has approached audiences from the perspective of their interaction with media industries has been criticized for being "administrative," because its underlying purpose ultimately is to facilitate media firms' ability to maximize audience attention (Ang 1991).[11] In this book I intend to demonstrate that approaching audiences as economic products can have a broader purpose. Specifically, I will show how commercial media firms' unavoidable imperative to approach audiences from an economic standpoint affects the development of media industries and technologies, the distribution of revenues, and the availability of different forms of media content to audience members. Thus my goal here is not only to provide a basic understanding of media audiences as economic products but also to examine the broader implications of this perspective for the behavior and development of U.S. media institutions.

To these ends, I attempt to integrate audience research and media economics by taking a predominantly economic approach to audience research and the role of the audience marketplace in the functioning and development of media industries. In doing so, I approach the notion of media audiences fairly broadly, although my emphasis is on electronic mass media. Thus my analyses here primarily will focus upon television, radio, and the Internet. I will draw occasional points and examples from the magazine and newspaper industries, as well as the recorded music and motion picture industries. Indeed, my purpose in this book is to provide an understanding of media audiences that transcends traditional industry boundaries, given that the convergence of media technologies is disintegrating these boundaries (Baldwin, McVoy, and Steinfeld 1996; Dizard 1997).

However, television, radio, and the Internet are my primary focus for a number of reasons. First, research on audience behavior thus far has concentrated on the electronic media—particularly television (Webster and Phalen 1997). Thus much of the theory and research upon which I draw has developed within the context of electronic media. Nonetheless, many points that I make here will be relevant for all forms of media.

Second, most challenges, recent developments, and controversies regarding the audience marketplace are much more prominent within the electronic media than within other media forms, such as print or motion pictures. For instance, methodological and technological changes in audience measurement are much more frequent within the electronic media, and their consequences are often much more severe. Since the mid-1980s how electronic media audiences are measured has changed significantly (with additional changes on the horizon), and an entirely new field of electronic media audience measurement (Internet audience measurement) has emerged. These developments and their implications are central to understanding the role of the audience marketplace in the functioning of media industries.

I also want to emphasize that this book primarily is concerned with *advertiser-supported* media. One of my central objectives is to explore media audiences as products that marketplace participants (i.e., advertisers and media firms) buy and sell. Historically, the techniques and terminology associated with the buying and selling of audiences have proved to be remarkably similar across media (Leckenby and Hong 1998; Mandese 2001), often with the techniques and terminology of older media being applied to newer media in order to facilitate cross-media comparisons (Cannon 2001; Dreze and Zufryden 1998; Novak and Hoffman 1997; Webster and Lin 2002).[12] These commonalities provide the basis for this analysis. Given this analytical focus, nonadvertiser-supported media such as motion pictures and recorded music are of only occasional relevance to the analyses that I present here, because audiences do not represent a product that these industries attract *and* sell. Certainly, the media that do not sell audiences to advertisers still are deeply immersed in the process of understanding, measuring, and predicting the behaviors of the audiences that purchase their product (consider, for example, the motion picture industry's efforts to forecast movie attendance; see Albert 1998; Litman and Kohl 1989; Prag and Casavant 1994; Rosen 1981; Sochay 1994). Within these contexts I occasionally will integrate these nonadvertiser-supported media in my analyses.

This study of the audience marketplace draws data from a variety of sources and uses a variety of methodological approaches. I draw heavily from the relevant scholarly literature and media industry trade publications. I also used television and radio industry ratings, scheduling, and financial data to conduct quantitative analyses of the factors affecting the predictability (see chapter 2) and value (see chapter 4) of media audiences. Finally, I have integrated into each chapter observations drawn from the six weeks that I spent during the summer of 2001 as a participant observer in one of the television industry's largest "rep" firms.[13] This organization, which represents local television stations in the national advertising market and assists them with program acquisition and scheduling, provided unrestricted access to scheduling, sales, and research meetings; conference calls with stations, advertisers, and program producers; and a variety of presentations and seminars, including presentations of new syndicated programs from major program producers, meetings with Democratic and Republican political media buyers, orientation sessions with new clients, and presentations of the fall 2001 prime-time program schedules for five of the major broadcast networks (ABC, CBS, Fox, UPN, WB). During this period I informally interviewed some of the "rep" firm's senior executives in programming, sales, and research, as well as sales representatives from motion picture studios and television production companies. Finally, this period as participant observer also allowed me to gather and analyze more than one thousand pages of internal and external documents pertaining to various aspects of television advertising sales, research, promotion, and scheduling, including white papers, ratings reports, schedule analyses, orientation materials, and sales presentations. I have organized the analyses that I drew from these various data sources as follows:

Chapter 1 provides an overview of the audience marketplace and the audience product. I describe the key participants in the audience marketplace and how they interact with one another and then discuss the notion of the audience as a product, with a particular emphasis on the unique aspects of the audience product. In this chapter I also provide a detailed deconstruction of the audience product as three separate components: the predicted audience, the measured audience, and the actual audience.

Chapter 2 focuses on the relationship between the predicted audience and the measured audience. As I show in this chapter, purchasers of audiences typically must purchase predicted audiences. That is, they must purchase time or space within a particular media product before the audience has seen that product, under the assumption that the product will attract a particular size and type of audience. Consequently, audience forecasting—the process of predicting the behavior of media audiences—is a central component of the audience marketplace. I also examine the process of forecasting media audiences and the means by which participants in the audience marketplace attempt to improve their forecasting accuracy. I also focus on the inherent uncertainty involved in dealing in predicted audiences and how this uncertainty affects the behavior of media organizations, particularly in terms of their content decisions. I conclude by describing the results of a quantitative study that integrates audience behavior theory with decision-making theory in an effort to identify the sources of uncertainty—and hence the sources of inaccuracy—in the forecasts of audiences for new prime-time network television programs.

Chapter 3 focuses on the relationship between the measured audience and the actual audience. As I show in this chapter, the process of measuring audiences is fraught with uncertainty, yet measured audiences represent the coin of exchange in the audience marketplace. Advertisers buy ratings points as a proxy for audience attention, yet various segments of the media industry long have disagreed about the degree to which these ratings provide an accurate representation of the actual audience. This chapter reviews the primary methodological issues that contribute to this uncertainty and discusses how participants in the audience marketplace cope with this uncertainty.

In chapter 3, I also focus on the role of audience research (i.e., measured audiences) in the establishment and evolution of media industries and technologies. Audience measurement provides the economic foundation upon which advertiser-supported media develop. Consequently, changes or advances in the techniques and technologies of audience measurement can have profound ripple effects on the industries whose economic viability depends upon audience data. To illustrate the centrality of audience measurement to the economics of media industries, I discuss high-profile developments in the audience measurement field, such as the introduction of people meters by Nielsen Media Research (the primary source of television audience data in the United States) in the 1980s and the establishment and evolution of audience measurement systems for the Internet.

Chapter 4 focuses on the valuation of media audiences. Unlike the one-person, one-vote parity of the U.S. political system, in the audience marketplace one individual's attention to a particular media product can be worth much more than another individual's attention. Here I focus on the key factors that traditionally have affected the value of media audiences and on the logic underlying these valuations. In addressing these issues, I include a quantitative analysis of the factors that affect the valuation of radio station audiences. I also discuss how variations in the value of different components of the media audience affect the content that media organizations provide. Because advertisers value some audience segments more highly than others, content providers adjust their content offerings to attract these more valuable audience segments. As a result audience valuations are inextricably intertwined with the content options that media firms provide.

Chapter 5 focuses on how new technologies, in terms of both media and audience measurement, are affecting the audience product. In this chapter I argue that, despite continued efforts to increase the congruence between predicted and measured audiences, and between measured and actual audiences, technological changes in the media environment are threatening to undermine the quality of the audience product and consequently the vitality of the audience marketplace. The first of the key changes at issue is the increasing fragmentation of media audiences. As I show in this chapter, this is exacerbating many difficulties associated with effectively predicting and measuring media audiences. The second key technological shift involves the degree to which new media technologies are increasing "audience autonomy." Media audiences are gaining greater control of the media consumption process, which undermines existing systems of audience control and audience measurement. Improvements in the techniques and technologies of audience prediction and audience measurement are unlikely to offset the erosion of the quality of the audience product that results from increasing fragmentation and audience autonomy.

Chapter 6 explores how declines in the quality of the audience product might affect the economics of media industries and the nature of the content that they provide. Here I speculate that in the future alternative business models are likely to replace the traditional approach of inserting discrete advertising messages in media content and charging advertisers on the basis of presumed levels of audience exposure. Among the alternatives likely to become increasingly prominent are pricing structures based upon consumer behavior rather than exposure; business models that focus more aggressively on gathering and marketing the personal information of media consumers; and business models that increasingly rely upon audiences, not advertisers, to pay for media content. All these potential changes ultimately could have dramatic effects on the content that media institutions provide.

CHAPTER 1

THE AUDIENCE MARKETPLACE

The audience marketplace is a vital component of the U.S. economy. In 2001 the investment-banking firm of Veronis, Suhler, and Associates estimated that the media industries had earned more than $190 billion over the previous year through the sale of their audiences to advertisers. Before I examine the dynamics of the audience marketplace, a review of the key participants in this marketplace, their primary activities, and their relationships to one another is in order. This overview will help place later discussions about the nature of the audience product and the effects of changes in the predictability, measurement, and valuation of the audience product in the proper institutional context.

COMPONENTS OF THE AUDIENCE MARKETPLACE

The audience marketplace is comprised of four primary participants. In the first category are the media organizations—which I define as any type of media content provider that derives revenue from the sale of audiences—that provide the content designed to attract audiences. Thus this category includes, among others, television and radio stations and networks, cable systems and networks, Web sites and Internet service providers (ISPs), as well as newspaper and magazine publishers. The United States has approximately 1,300 VHF and UHF commercial television stations, 11,200 commercial radio stations, 280 cable networks, 10,000 cable systems, 11,800 magazines, 1,400 daily newspapers, 8,000 foreign-language and nondaily newspapers, and thousands of Web sites that derive at least part of their revenue from the sale of audiences to advertisers (Compaine and Gomery

2000; FCC 2002b; National Cable 2002). Thus advertisers have a nearly overwhelming number of outlets by which to reach audiences.

These raw numbers do not, however, provide an accurate picture of the level of competition in the audience marketplace. Like all markets for goods and services, the audience market is differentiated according to geographic markets and product markets. From a geographic standpoint, some media organizations (such as broadcast and cable networks) provide advertisers with access to a nationwide audience. Other media organizations, such as an individual radio station or metropolitan newspaper, generally provide access to a much more local audience. Reflecting this market segmentation, Arbitron has organized its radio audience measurement reports according to 286 distinct radio markets within the United States. Similarly, Nielsen Media Research has delineated 210 distinct television markets within the United States. Local television or radio stations do not often compete for the same advertising dollars as the broadcast and cable networks. Thus it is important to recognize that the audience market is not only national (and increasingly global) but that smaller, geographically defined local audience markets number in the hundreds.

Markets are defined not only geographically but also in terms of product characteristics. From an advertiser's standpoint one media outlet's audience is not necessarily a reasonable substitute for another media outlet's audience. Advertisers seek specific characteristics in the audiences that they try to reach: age, gender, income, and a host of other distinguishing factors (see chapter 4). Thus for most advertisers the audience for the Nickelodeon cable network (which targets children) is not likely to be an acceptable substitute for the audience for NBC's *Friends* (which targets young adults).

Media organizations differ in the extent to which their viability depends upon the sale of audiences to advertisers. In many instances they supplement revenue from the sale of audiences to advertisers with revenue from the sale of content to audiences. The revenue breakdowns for each major advertiser-supported medium appear in table 1.1. As the table shows, free over-the-air broadcast radio and television derive basically all their revenue from the sale of audiences to advertisers. In contrast, cable television systems rely heavily upon subscriber fees. Subscriber fees account for roughly 85 percent of cable systems' revenues, with advertising revenues comprising only about 15 percent. Cable networks, on the other hand, derive, on average, 60 percent of their revenue from the sale of audiences to advertisers and

40 percent from the sale of their content to cable and direct broadcast satellite systems. Consumer and trade magazines operate under quite different economic models.[1] Consumer magazines operate at a roughly 50–50 split between the sale of audiences and the sale of content. Trade magazines, on the other hand, derive roughly 90 percent of their revenues from the sale of audiences to advertisers. Newspapers receive roughly 70 percent of their revenues from the sale of audiences to advertisers and 30 percent from the sale of their content. In most cases the price that consumers pay for a daily newspaper does not even cover the costs of the paper and ink. These data provide an indication of how different media have taken different strategic paths in navigating the dual-product marketplace that characterizes the media industries.

TABLE 1.1 Revenue Breakdowns for Advertiser-Supported Media

MEDIUM	REVENUE SOURCE	
	AUDIENCE SALES	CONTENT SALES
Broadcast television	100%	0%
Cable television systems	15	85
Cable television networks	60	40
Broadcast radio	100	0
Newspapers	70	30
Consumer magazines	50	50
Trade magazines	90	10
Internet sites	Varies	Varies

Sources: National Cable 2002; Compaine and Gomery 2000; Veronis, Suhler, and Associates 2001.

Within each component of the media industry, many individual media outlets fall under the broad umbrella ownership of a few large, diversified media corporations (Bagdikian 1997; Compaine and Gomery 2000). Most of the largest media firms have expanded their reach across a variety of media technologies, suggesting that they realize certain economies by providing advertisers with access to audiences across a range of media types.[2] Although the issue of the growth of media conglomerates is largely beyond the scope of this book, this phenomenon is relevant to the extent that, among the primary rationales for media firms' efforts to expand their holdings is their desire to bring greater efficiencies to the sale of audiences to advertisers and to be able to offer advertisers what essentially amounts to one-stop shopping for all their audience needs.[3] The merger of CBS and Viacom was deemed a particularly shrewd strategic maneuver in this regard. The combined holdings of CBS-Viacom range from the Nickelodeon cable channel, with its predominantly preteen audience, to MTV, with its teenage and young adult audience, to CBS, with its predominantly over-50 audience. CBS/Viacom is using this combination of media properties to provide what its executives have called "cradle-to-grave" marketing opportunities to advertisers.[4]

In the second key category of participants in the audience marketplace are the audience measurement organizations, which provide quantitative data on audience attention. Both advertisers and media organizations purchase these data, which function essentially as the coin of exchange in the audience marketplace. Although audience measurement typically is discussed within the context of analyzing individual segments of the media industry, the measurement of media audiences is a significant industry in its own right, with its own distinguishing characteristics, historical progression, and enduring controversies (Beville 1988; Buzzard 1990; P. Miller 1994). Although audience measurement originated internally among media organizations, third-party firms long have dominated the process because of the obvious potential for bias if audience transactions were based upon data supplied by the media organizations (Beville 1988). Thus it is important to regard audience measurement firms as a separate participant within the audience marketplace.

Across all the advertiser-supported media are a number of firms that provide either specialized or comprehensive data about the distribution of consumer attention to various content options. These data can range from standardized syndicated reports that provide a broad overview of how audiences are distributing themselves across the entire range of content options to highly specialized, commissioned studies of the audiences for individual media products (P. Miller 1994). One defining characteristic of the audience measurement industry is that, although a number of different firms provide statistical representations of media audiences, only one firm tends to dominate the distribution of comprehensive audience data for each media technology. Thus Arbitron is the primary source for radio audience data,

Nielsen Media Research is the sole source for comprehensive television audience data, and the primary sources for detailed magazine audience measurement are Simmons and Mediamark Research, Inc., with general circulation data provided by the Audit Bureau of Circulations, which also provides circulation figures for the newspaper industry. The development of the Internet audience measurement industry is following historical precedent, in that two major competitors remain from the dozens of measurement firms that initially offered this service: comScore Media Metrix and Nielsen Net-Ratings. As Jim Spaeth, president of the Advertising Research Foundation, has noted, "There is a tendency toward monopolization in ratings services" (Thompson and Lake 2001:55).

The primary explanation for this phenomenon is that audience data function as the coin of exchange within the audience marketplace. Thus both the buyers and sellers of audiences subscribe to audience measurement services in order to be fully informed of the nature of the product that they are buying and selling. The introduction of a second measurement service essentially represents a second currency. New entrants in the field generally use measurement techniques or technologies that differ in either minor or significant ways from the incumbent's. Such deviations are a natural and logical effort by firms to differentiate themselves from the competition. The measurement techniques and technologies of the new competitor may even be of a substantially higher quality than those used by the incumbent. In any case, these methodological differences inevitably result in audience data that differ significantly from the data provided by the incumbent. Thus buyers and sellers in the audience marketplace are faced with two different accounts of, for example, how many people watched last night's episode of *CSI* or of how many people listened to the local classical music station. In such a situation participants in the audience marketplace naturally will seize upon those numbers that best reflect their best interests. When CBS is negotiating advertising rates, it is likely to rely upon the data from the service that shows a higher rating for *CSI*, while advertisers are likely to rely upon the service that shows a lower rating.

Thus the existence of competing measurement services substantially complicates the process of buying and selling audiences, as it introduces additional uncertainty into the nature of the product being bought and sold and introduces an additional negotiation factor. Marketplace participants generally see these additional complications as problematic because they slow down or discourage the process of buying and selling a product that is highly perishable.

Also important is that, with two competing currencies on the market, marketplace participants often must subscribe to both (Beville 1988). The obvious inefficiency here is that buyers and sellers of audiences are paying twice for depictions of the same product. The costs of this redundancy, combined with how the existence of multiple measurement systems complicates negotiation in the buying and selling of audiences, mean that both advertisers and media organizations tend to favor (or at least accept) the existence of a single audience measurement system for each medium. Thus competing measurement systems historically have found it difficult to establish and maintain a foothold against an entrenched incumbent (Beville 1988). For example, Arbitron (among others) attempted to compete with Nielsen in providing data about television audiences (see Buzzard 1990). In 1993, however, Arbitron abandoned its television operation because it had been unable to capture sufficient market share from Nielsen.

For these same reasons many analysts of the Internet industry saw the consolidation that has taken place in Internet audience measurement as inevitable (Thompson and Lake 2001). Ultimately, as the media researcher Erwin Ephron has noted, "This is not a business that lends itself to competition. You don't want more than one currency" (Bachman 2000a:7). This sentiment—and the trade-offs that it entails—is reflected in an analysis of the consolidation of Internet audience measurement: "For customers, there could be a silver lining. . . . Having one fewer ratings company may not result in the most accurate figures, but it will at least reduce confusion" (Thompson and Lake 2001:55).

As this statement suggests, these periods of competition lead to data of higher quality (Beville 1988; Buzzard 1990), just as competition in any product market typically results in higher-quality products at lower prices. As Rubens (1984) shows, competition between Nielsen and Arbitron led to a rapid expansion in the number of markets in which they deployed set-top meters. Similarly, competition from Audits of Great Britain in the 1980s accelerated the deployment of people meters (Rubens 1984).

Thus the audience marketplace illustrates two countervailing forces. On the one hand, the desire for better quality in audience measurement persists, because better measurement means a higher-quality audience product (something generally desired by both advertisers and media organizations). On the other hand, the audience marketplace wants a single parsimonious currency, something achievable only when the provider of audience data is a monopoly.

The third key participant in the audience marketplace is the advertisers. Advertisers are the consumers of the audience product. I am using the term *advertisers* broadly here to encompass both the providers of products and services seeking an audience of consumers to purchase their offerings, as well as the advertising agencies, media planners, and media buyers who act on their behalf to create advertising messages and place them within various media products (see Silk and Berndt 1993, 1994).

Table 1.2 presents the ten largest advertisers in the United States in 2000, along with the total amount that they spent on advertising in that year. As this table shows, these top ten advertisers represent more than $22 billion worth of advertising. Given that annual media advertising revenues exceed roughly $150 billion, clearly no one advertiser has monopsony power in the market for audiences. Further reinforcing this point is that the top one hundred advertisers represented only 48.3 percent of total advertising expenditures in 2000 (Endicott 2001). Thus although concentration levels among the sellers of audiences are of long-standing concern (see Napoli 2001b; Stucke and Grunes 2001), historically, concentration levels among the buyers of audiences have been of comparatively little concern.[5]

TABLE 1.2 Ten Largest Advertisers in the United States (By Expenditures).

CORPORATION	2000 ADVERTISING EXPENDITURES
1. General Motors Corp.	$3,934.80
2. Phillip Morris Cos.	$2,602.90
3. Procter & Gamble Co.	$2,363.50
4. Ford Motor Co.	$2,345.20
5. Pfizer	$2,265.30
6. PepsiCo	$2,100.70
7. DaimlerChrysler	$1,984.00
8. AOL Time Warner	$1,770.10
9. Walt Disney Co.	$1,757.50
10. Verizon Communications	$1,612.90
	Total: $22,736.90

Source: Endicott (2001:52).

Finally and perhaps most important are the consumers of advertised products and services, whose attention represents the foundation upon which the entire audience marketplace is based. I use the term *consumers* here as a reminder that the advertisers who drive the audience market are fundamentally concerned with reaching potential purchasers of the products and services that they have to offer. The central underlying assumption in the audience marketplace is that the audience product provides a meaningful representation of consumer attention to advertising messages. This attention should then influence consumers' purchasing decisions (see M. Ehrlich and Fisher 1982).

Certainly, the use of the term *consumers* here, instead of *audiences* or *potential audiences,* reflects a fairly limited view of the processes by which individuals interact with media. As many analysts of media audiences have pointed out, being part of a media audience and consuming media products are complex sociocultural phenomena containing numerous layers of meaning and multiple points of analysis (Ang 1991; Butsch 2000; Chang 1987; Moores 1993; Webster 1998). Audience consumption of media content certainly can be analyzed at levels that run deeper than mere exposure to content and its integrated advertising messages, addressing issues such as audience appreciation or interpretation of media content (e.g., Danaher and Lawrie 1998; Gunter and Wober 1992; Lindlof 1988). Indeed, this analysis of the audience marketplace, and the role that consumers/audience members play in this marketplace, takes as a given the frequent criticism that media organizations, advertisers, and measurement firms operate with a limited conceptualization of what it means to be part of a media audience (e.g., Ang 1991; Mosco and Kaye 2000). Much of what we know, or want to know, about the nature of—and processes associated with—media audiences is of no immediate concern to these marketplace participants.

However, given that the focus here is on the role and function of audiences within the economics of media industries, the analytical perspective toward media audiences narrows considerably. Indeed, from a strictly economic standpoint the "audience" is not a participant in the audience marketplace. As Ettema and Whitney note, individual audience members "do not exist in an institutional conception of mass communication" (1994:5). Only "institutionally effective audiences" (5) have any meaning or value within our commercial media system. This is why the complex and multifaceted concept of the media audience (Webster 1998) can, within the con-

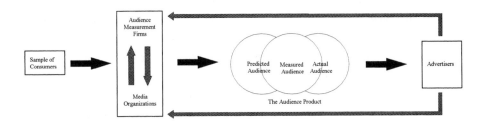

FIGURE 1.1. The Audience Marketplace

text of the model presented here, be stripped down to the more basic and unidimensional concept of the audience product, which participants in the audience marketplace conceptualize purely as a representation of consumer attention to advertising messages.

Figure 1.1 illustrates the processes by which each of these institutions participates in the audience marketplace, and the relationships that exist between them. To understand the basic flow of the audience marketplace, follow the model from left to right. The solid arrows represent the process of producing and selling the audience product. As the figure shows, the audience product is the output of a sample of consumers' simultaneous interaction with media organizations and audience measurement firms. Consumers are located at the far left, reflecting their position as the starting point of the process of producing the audience product. Consumers' interaction with media firms takes place in the form of the media consumption choices that consumers make. Consumers' interaction with audience measurement firms takes place when measurement firms monitor the media consumption habits of a small fraction of consumers. It is important to emphasize that the logistical and financial limitations of audience measurement typically mean that the firms measure the behaviors of only a few consumers and that the behavior of these few consumers then is projected to the population as a whole (see chapter 3).

The audience product is produced through consumers' simultaneous interaction with media organizations and audience measurement firms. This process is represented by the solid arrow leading from the media firms and measurement firms to the section labeled "audience product." The media and measurement firms are represented within the same rectangle to reflect that together they represent the industrial process that manufactures consumers (essentially the raw materials) into the audience product. Both institutions are essential to the process. Without media firms no audience exists to be measured. Similarly, without measurement firms no tangible audience data exist to sell to advertisers. The next step in the process (represented at the far right of the model) is when advertisers receive the audience product (in the form of exposure to advertising messages) that media organizations and audience measurement firms produce. However, as I discuss later in this chapter (and in chapter 2), it is important to recognize that advertisers typically purchase audiences *before* they are actually produced.

In addition to these direct production and distribution relationships, which are represented by the solid arrows in figure 1.1, a number of other important influence relationships (represented by the shaded arrows) need to be understood. The term *influence relationships* refers to the variety of influences that many participants in the audience marketplace are capable of exerting over other participants in the marketplace, thereby changing the institutional structures, behavioral patterns, or processes of these participants.

Note first the shaded arrow leading from advertisers to media organizations. This arrow represents the tremendous influence that advertisers can exert on the structure and behavior of media organizations. The most obvious examples involve the many instances in which advertisers' refusal to advertise in conjunction with content that they deem offensive, risky, in poor taste, or not in their best political or economic interests has led content providers to modify or eliminate such content (Baker 1994; Gitlin 1985) or has led to the demise of individual media outlets or organizations.[6] One well-known example involves the demise of *Ms.* magazine, which folded at one point largely because advertisers resisted the magazine's position on social issues (Shoemaker and Reese 1996).

Advertisers also occasionally have taken a proactive approach in developing content. Perhaps the most well-known example involves the the entire soap opera genre, which was developed first in radio and then transferred to television by Procter and Gamble in an effort to market its cleaning products to housewives (Greenstein 1999). More recently, major national advertisers have pressured the broadcast networks to air more "family-friendly" programming (Frutkin 2002b). Advertisers such as Ford, General

Motors, Johnson and Johnson, Kellogg, and Procter and Gamble established the Family Friendly Programming Forum in 1998 in an effort to work
with programmers to develop shows that satisfy advertisers' desires for programming that parents and children will watch together. To this end, the forum lobbies network executives, presents awards, and has established a
script development fund—all activities that suggest an active role for these
advertisers in the development of television content (Schlosser 2000). The
WB network's prime-time program *The Gilmore Girls* was one of the first to
emerge from the efforts of the Family Friendly Programming Forum
(Schlosser 2000). By the fall of 2002 the forum had four programs on broadcast network schedules (Frutkin 2002c).

At a broader level advertiser willingness to advertise in various media can
affect the direction and speed with which a medium develops. For instance,
Procter and Gamble, which has been one of the nation's largest advertisers
for decades, was central to the rapid growth and content characteristics of
both the television and radio industries (Greenstein 1999). Given Procter
and Gamble's traditionally enormous advertising budget, the company's
commitment to advertising in these media when they were in their developmental stages meant an enormous infusion of revenue for programmers.
This helped emerging media achieve financial stability while also promoting
greater investment in content, presumably leading to programming of higher quality (see Owen and Wildman 1992).

By the same token, advertisers may, for various reasons, transfer their advertising dollars away from a certain medium, which may undermine its financial viability. For instance, the introduction and rapid diffusion of television led many national advertisers to abandon radio as an advertising
vehicle (Baughman 1997; Dimmick and Rothenbuhler 1984). As a result the
overall structure and function of the industry changed dramatically. Radio
stations abandoned their efforts to appeal to broad diverse audiences, because television had become the mass-advertising vehicle of choice. Instead,
radio stations focused on appealing to narrow audience segments, thereby
cultivating relationships with smaller or more specialized advertisers seeking niche audiences. In doing so, radio station content changed dramatically, moving away from broad appeal to content with more narrow appeal
(Baughman 1997; Napoli 1998a). Thus today few radio stations attempt to
program to different audience segments at different times of the day or to
appeal to a broad audience base throughout the day. Instead, individual ra-

dio stations maintain the same, narrowly targeted program format all day (MacFarland 1997), which reflects their focus on delivering a narrow and specific audience demographic to advertisers. Television's appeal as a national advertising medium also led radio stations to focus more intensively on capturing local advertising dollars, rather than national advertising dollars, which had provided the bulk of radio industry revenues before the introduction of television (Dimmick and Rothenbuhler 1984). Thus the behavioral patterns of advertisers affected both the organizational practices and programming of the radio industry.

Finally, perhaps the most consistent and systematic means by which advertisers influence the structure and behavior of media organizations involves the nature of advertiser demand for audiences (see chapter 4). That is, advertiser demand for certain types of audiences systematically shapes the content that media organizations provide (Shoemaker and Reese 1996). At the heart of this relationship is that media firms will make content production decisions that will bring them the most revenue (Owen and Wildman 1992; Rust and Donthu 1988). Thus they will produce more content that targets those segments of the audience that advertisers value most highly (see Owen and Wildman 1992). This process is much less overt—but much more consistent—than the examples of advertisers' actively influencing content development that I discussed earlier.

The next key influence relationship is that between advertisers and audience measurement firms (represented by the shaded arrow connecting these two participants in figure 1.1). In many ways this relationship is similar to the relationship between advertisers and media organizations. Specifically, advertiser demand for specific types of data about media audiences can lead measurement firms to alter their measurement techniques or technologies in order to better serve the clients who purchase their products. For instance, measurement firms now provide detailed information about media audiences that extends well beyond media consumption patterns and demographic data. Psychographics and spending habits are an increasingly common part of the pool of data that measurement firms provide to advertisers, as advertisers seek more extensive data on their potential consumers (McAdams 2000a; Stockley and Farmer 2001; Turow 1997).[7] Advertisers' data demands and preferences also can lead to the rise of some measurement firms and the demise of others. The history of audience measurement is dotted with the carcasses of various measurement firms that fell out of favor with the advertising industry (Buzzard 1990). Thus just as advertiser demands affect the structure and behavior of the media industry, advertiser demands affect the structure and behavior of the audience measurement industry.

Finally, the model depicts a reciprocal influence relationship between media organizations and audience measurement firms. Media organizations influence the structure and behavior of measurement firms because, like advertisers, the media industries are major clients of audience measurement firms and are of course a major stakeholder in how advertisers value audience data. Consequently, when the media industry demands better or alternative approaches to measuring audiences, they too can wield significant influence in terms of how measurement firms measure their audiences or which measurement firms survive and prosper and which fail (Beville 1988; Buzzard 1990). Thus the media industry's displeasure with the nature of audience data frequently has influenced the structure and behavior of the audience measurement industry. For example, Arbitron recently instituted a service that aggregates radio listening shares across markets by county. This service was widely seen as helping large radio conglomerates (with their station holdings in many markets) capture more ad revenues from independent stations or smaller station groups (Bachman 2001c). Some industry analysts perceived the new service as a direct effort to please Clear Channel Communications, the nation's largest radio group. Clear Channel represents 22 percent of Arbitron's annual revenue and had been threatening not to renew its contract (Bachman 2001c). Speculation within the radio industry suggested that Arbitron's creation of the new audience reporting service was a condition of Clear Channel's eventual contract renewal (Bachman 2001c).

When a competing measurement system does arise, it often is a response to media industry displeasure with the service provided by the incumbent (see Beville 1988). Media organizations often will even provide funding to help launch the competing measurement system. Such actions suggest that these marketplace participants actually do value the existence of competition. In reality, however, these early indications of support for an upstart do not always represent a genuine interest in competition or even a desire to have the new measurement firm supplant the incumbent as the agreed-upon standard. Rather, the apparent show of support for a new measurement firm actually is an effort to compel the incumbent to improve or alter its measurement techniques or technologies. Typically, the incumbent responds to this threat, and the advertiser or media firm stops underwriting the new firm (Terranova 1998).

A classic example of this process occurred in television audience measurement in the 1990s, when broadcast network displeasure with the Nielsen system (see Jensen 1996) led the networks to invest more than $40 million in an alternative service called the SMART system (Systems for Measuring and Reporting Television), which was developed by the audience research firm Statistical Research, Inc. (Burgi 1997). The SMART service offered slight but significant technological and methodological differences from Nielsen. Specifically, the SMART system's measurement hardware was less obtrusive in terms of installation and maintenance (Edmondson 1997). From a methodological standpoint, the SMART system used a different definition of *viewing*, instructing participants to log in whenever they were in the room while the television was on, as opposed to logging in only when they were watching the television (Clancey 1994; Terranova 1998). Many audience researchers believed that this alternative definition of television viewing would positively affect broadcast ratings relative to cable ratings (hence the backing of the broadcast industry). Other significant differences involved data reporting and price structure. The SMART system made raw data available to subscribers for a flat monthly fee, enabling them to conduct their own specialized analyses when needed, rather than order expensive specialized studies from Nielsen (Burgi 1997). The networks eventually canceled their support for the upstart system in 1999 (Thompson et al. 2000), after Nielsen adopted some of the attributes of the SMART system (such as allowing subscribers to generate their own reports; see Mandese 1999). Statistical Research shut the SMART service down soon after.

Just as media organizations are capable of influencing the structure and behavior of audience measurement firms, measurement firms are capable of significantly influencing the structure and behavior of media organizations. When audience measurement firms change the techniques and technologies that they use to measure media audiences, the resulting data often can represent a significant departure from the data produced by the earlier measurement approach. In many instances these changes benefit some components of the media industry while hurting others. The introduction of the people meter (see chapter 3) is a classic example. In this case a drastic change in how national television audiences were measured produced a significantly different picture of the television audience, one in which many more viewers were watching cable television, as opposed to broadcast television. Needless to say, the cable industry's ability to compete for advertising dollars improved tremendously as a result of this measurement change, while the broadcast industry suffered. Thus changes in the behavior (i.e., measurement processes) of audience measurement firms can affect the competitive dynamics among the media organizations participating in the audience marketplace. This can lead to dramatic changes in the structure and content of the media landscape.

THE AUDIENCE PRODUCT

Thus consumers, media organizations, and audience measurement firms together produce the audience product that is central to the audience marketplace. This product has a number of distinct components (see figure 1.1). As the figure shows, the audience product has three distinct but interrelated components: the predicted audience, the measured audience, and the actual audience. Figure 1.1 depicts the audience product as three overlapping spheres. This representation reflects the disconnects that can exist between each component of the audience product. Thus as the figure suggests—and as I will demonstrate—the difficulty inherent in controlling and predicting audience behavior means that a perfect convergence of the predicted audience and the measured audience never exists. Similarly, limitations in the measurement of audience behavior mean that the measured audience provides an imperfect representation of the behavior of the actual audience.

THE PREDICTED AUDIENCE

An audience transaction typically begins with predicted audiences. That is, contracts between the buyers and sellers of audiences generally are based on agreed-upon forecasts of the likely size and composition of a particular media product's audience. These contracts are signed before the media product is available, but until the media outlet presents a media product and the audience data are available, nobody knows for certain the size or composition of the audience that the advertiser has purchased.

This situation represents an unusual marketplace arrangement, one in which the exchange of goods is based upon what essentially are educated guesses about the size and composition of the product. Buyers and sellers get together, each with their own assessment of the probable audience that a particular media product will deliver. Not surprisingly, the sellers' forecasts of the audience typically are a bit more optimistic than the buyers' forecasts. Ultimately, however, they manage to agree on an anticipated audience, and the transaction takes place (see Phalen 1996).

Audience forecasting is central to the process of buying and selling audiences, partly because the audience product comes from raw materials that the media organizations and audience measurement firms cannot effectively control. As the economists Berry and Waldfogel note within the context of radio broadcasting, "The production process . . . is unusual in that the primary inputs, listeners, are not purchased by the firm but rather make a free choice about listening to radio" (1999:399). Thus when considering the audience product, "output is determined by listener behavior rather than a traditional production function" (399). Thus an understanding of audience behavior, be it listening, watching, or reading, is essential to an understanding of the audience marketplace and the audience product. Because the manufacturers do not control the production of audiences, any efforts to bring predictability and rationality to the process of producing audiences must draw upon a sophisticated understanding of the essentially uncontrollable yet (fortunately) somewhat predictable behavior of media audiences. Of course, understanding the behavior of media audiences and being able to control the behavior of media audiences are two separate things. Control essentially is impossible, but a strong understanding can result in an increased likelihood of producing or purchasing the desired audience.

Another reason that predicted audiences are central to the audience marketplace is the inherent perishability of media audiences. Unlike media content (the other product that media firms produce), which has a virtually unlimited shelf life and can be sold and resold indefinitely (Owen and Wildman 1992), the shelf life for media audiences is exceptionally short, lasting only for the period in which a media product is consumed (Bogart 2000; Poltrack 1983). Thus Ang has described audiences as "very fleeting products: they become obsolete almost instantly" (1991:61). Beville (1988) provides a useful description of this important characteristic of the audience product:

> Any discussion of rating usage must be connected to a fundamental aspect of the broadcast media (radio, TV, cable)—the perishability of electronic communication. Once a program is aired, the audience and po-

tential commercial time it bears are gone forever, never to be regained. Like the airline seat, empty when the jet takes off, or the ticket still in the box office after Sunday's pro football game, these unsold units are down the drain—there's no chance for revenue recovery by stockpiling or sale pricing at a later date.   *(185)*

Thus the central challenge inherent in the audience product is that, while media audiences must be sold before the product has been distributed and consumed, the size and composition of a media product's audience cannot be determined until after the product has been consumed, when buying or selling that audience no longer is possible. Thus the perishable nature of media audiences, combined with the time it takes to establish their size and composition (and hence their value), means that the buying and selling of audiences must take place largely on the basis of predictions about the probable audience for a media product.

Predicted audiences, then, represent the first component of the audience product. The accuracy of the predicted audience then is verified against the audience measurement data obtained after the media product has been presented. The greater the congruence between the predicted audience and the measured audience, the more efficient the transaction. Consequently, buyers and sellers in the audience marketplace devote much time and effort to forecasting audiences and maximizing the degree to which these forecasts correspond to the subsequent measurement data (see chapter 2).

THE MEASURED AUDIENCE

The data used to verify the accuracy of the predicted audience represent the measured audience, that is, the audience as represented by audience measurement firms. As much as the predicted audience is a vital component of the audience product, and is in fact the starting point for any audience transaction, the measured audience represents the primary coin of exchange among buyers and sellers of audiences and thus represents the central component of the audience product (see figure 1.1). Predicted audiences are used in the initial stages of an audience transaction; however, the actual quality of this transaction ultimately is confirmed against the audience measurement data produced after the fact by measurement firms. These data are used to determine the estimated size and composition of the audience reached and to determine exactly how much an advertiser ultimately spent to reach a particular size and type of audience. Thus the measured audience, as represented by audience data, is the primary tool for assessing any audience transaction.

These data provide the basis for allocating advertising dollars, as well as the criteria for deciding the particular mix of content to provide. Television programs live and die by their Nielsen ratings. Programs whose measured audiences do not meet certain thresholds of acceptability are likely to be canceled or at least moved to a different place in the schedule in the hope that audience delivery will improve (Adams 1993; Adams et al. 1983; Atkin and Litman 1986). Radio programs similarly live and die by the Arbitron ratings, and Nielsen NetRatings or comScore Media Metrix data increasingly are a key factor in the decision to shut down content-focused Web sites. Thus the measured audience, as represented by ratings data, is central to the decision making that determines the content mix that audiences receive. This is, of course, because these data also are central to how advertisers choose to distribute their advertising dollars. Media products that deliver small audiences relative to their competition are less likely to be desirable to advertisers seeking to maximize consumer exposure to their messages.

As this discussion suggests, the past performance of media products generally is seen as a primary indicator of future performance (see chapter 2). Thus the measured audience, which always is a historical representation of audience behavior (Webster, Phalen, and Lichty 2000), often provides the analytical foundation for the predicted audience. However, past performance does not guarantee future results; thus, as I noted earlier, the measured and predicted audiences are not always in perfect congruence.

The centrality of audience measurement data to the buying and selling of audiences provides a primary reason why I use the term *audience product* here, rather than the simpler term *audiences*. Although it is common industry parlance to say that media firms deal in audiences, this notion needs to be taken one logical step further. As Meehan (1984) notes, the notion of the audience as product is in some ways too broad. Instead, "the commodity produced, bought, and sold is constituted solely by ratings" (Meehan 1984:216). Ratings points, as a representative measurement of audiences, are really what advertisers and media firms are buying and selling. Thus, as Pekurny (1982) states in regard to television, "Ratings are the basic mechanism which rationalizes the television industry" (133). Pekurny's point is relevant to the entirety of the audience marketplace, because all audience transactions are based on measurement data intended to provide an estimation of audience attention.

Thus the measured audience represents the central economic currency in the audience marketplace. Therefore within this context the processes, principles, and dynamics of audience measurement become inextricably intertwined with the economics of media industries. As Ang (1991) notes, "Audience measurement bears an economical meaning in so far as it produces the necessary standard through which advertising rates can be set" (53).

Once we accept the notion that the measured audience represents the central product of the audience marketplace, it becomes clear, as the media researcher Gale Metzger once noted, that "in advertising-supported services, the medium is only as good as the measurement because the measurement is what is bought and sold" (Schiavone 1988:RC-13). For this reason the industry has an ongoing imperative to improve the process by which the measured audience is created. The demand for improved accuracy stems both from advertisers' concerns that their messages are actually reaching the size and type of audience that they are paying to reach and from media organizations' concerns that their product is being measured in a way that maximizes its value to advertisers. Measurement firms always are seeking to improve the representativeness of their samples and the accuracy and ease of use of their measurement techniques and technologies, often under pressure from advertisers and media firms. Thus participants in the audience marketplace face challenges in maximizing the congruence between the predicted audience and the measured audience and between the measured audience and the actual audience.

THE ACTUAL AUDIENCE

The audience marketplace always is plagued with uncertainty that the measured audience, while certainly more tangible and concrete than the predicted audience, still is fundamentally different than the true audience. Arbitron data may tell an advertiser that thirty thousand males aged 18 to 34 were listening to a particular radio station when the advertiser's ad was broadcast. However, thirty thousand is a projection based upon a much smaller sample of listeners. A variety of sources of error, ranging from the representativeness of the sample to the response rates of the sampled participants to the ability of the participants to recall accurately their listening behaviors could mean that the actual audience for the advertisement was only fifteen thousand or perhaps as high as fifty thousand (see chapter 3).

Given that no one knows for certain exactly how accurate or inaccurate a particular measurement technique is, the actual audience essentially represents the invisible ideal in the audience marketplace. Although the actual audience essentially is unknowable, it is still an important component of the audience product, given that advertisers and media firms frequently evaluate the measured audience in terms of their own perceptions or assumptions about the actual audience. In addition, as the means of producing measured audiences become more sophisticated and less prone to error, participants in the audience marketplace assume that the new and improved measured audience represents a closer approximation of the actual audience. Thus it is safe to say that the measured audience gives us a substantial degree of insight into the nature of the actual audience, yet the full truth about the behavioral patterns of the actual audience is not completely capturable by the techniques and technologies of audience research.

The actual audience also is subject to very different interpretations. Different participants in the audience marketplace have quite different perceptions of the nature of the actual audience. Thus television broadcasters may see a change in the Nielsen measurement techniques or technologies as widening the gap between the measured audience and the actual audience, while the cable industry may view this same change as narrowing the gap (see chapter 5). Of course, these perceptions typically correspond to how the different stakeholders are affected economically by any changes in the process of producing measured audiences. Thus the broadcast industry is likely to view as distortions of the measured audience any measurement changes that produce greater audiences for cable and vice versa.

Ultimately, the actual audience is largely unknowable. Its ambiguous nature makes it a highly contestable component of the audience product. Yet it has relevance because all participants in the audience marketplace do, at various points, compare the measured audience to their own assessments of the actual audience. If, for instance, advertisers believe that measured audiences for a particular medium are deviating significantly from actual audiences, they have reason to believe that they are not spending their advertising dollars effectively and that they are not getting the product that they paid for. In such instances, advertisers are likely to seek out other media options, where they perceive a greater correspondence between the measured and the actual audience.

Although such questions arise frequently, it is important to recognize that in terms of the day-to-day functioning of the audience marketplace, buyers and sellers generally treat measured audiences as accurate representations of actual audiences. As Gitlin (1983) notes, once participants in the audience marketplace "agree to accept a measure, they act as if it is precise" (53), primarily because of the added complexities and difficulties that would arise from treating the measured audience otherwise. Consequently, participants in the audience marketplace deal primarily in measured audiences and only seldom confront in a meaningful way the question of whether the measured audience significantly corresponds to the actual audience. Should participants in the audience marketplace begin to seriously question the quality of the audience product, the audience marketplace could be affected dramatically.

CHAPTER 2

THE PREDICTED AUDIENCE-MEASURED AUDIENCE RELATIONSHIP

Forecasting media audiences is rife with uncertainty. Given that they cannot control the behavior of media audiences, buyers and sellers in the audience marketplace always face the possibility that the predicted audience upon which a transaction is based will not match the measured audience that ultimately is produced by measurement firms. How does the inherent uncertainty in this relationship between the predicted audience and the measured audience affect participants in the audience marketplace? How do participants attempt to cope with—and reduce—this uncertainty? Reducing this uncertainty is central to the audience marketplace. Because the buying and selling of audiences can take place only when buyers and sellers have a tangible and reasonably reliable product to exchange, "uncertainty about the audience must . . . be combated at all costs" (Ang 1991:54).

In addressing these issues, this chapter includes a study in which I have attempted to identify specific sources of uncertainty in the marketplace for broadcast television audiences. I looked at forecasts for new prime-time network programs and integrated decision-making theory with audience behavior theory in an effort to reach a better understanding of the factors affecting accuracy in the forecasting of television audiences.

BUYING PREDICTED AUDIENCES

The central danger involved in buying and selling predicted audiences is that the measured audience that a media product ultimately delivers could prove to be quite different from the predicted audience upon which the transaction was based. Such disparities are handled differently by the various segments of the media industry and according to the type of purchase involved. Network television, syndication, and cable sometimes supply "make-goods" when a program does not deliver its predicted audience (Phalen 1996). That is, programmers will provide additional commercial time free of charge to advertisers in order to make up for the shortfall in audience delivery. Generally, a program has to underdeliver by more than 10 percent for programmers to provide make-goods (Webster, Phalen, and Lichty 2000).

Make-goods, however, are not available in all contexts. For instance, in the "spot" television market (time purchased on short notice), stations typically do not guarantee make-goods to their advertisers (Phalen 1996).

The Internet represents a slightly different situation because two distinct models of audience exchange have emerged. The first is based on the traditional cost-per-thousand (CPM) approach: Advertisers purchase space on a Web site in accordance with an estimate of the number of audience members who are going to view the advertisement. As with television and radio, such an approach involves making a deal based upon a forecast of the likely audience size for a Web site. And, as with television, in some contexts the advertiser can negotiate make-goods if a Web site does not deliver an audience of an agreed-upon size. However, the interactive nature of the Internet has allowed another model to emerge, one in which basic audience exposure is no longer the coin of exchange. Specifically, advertisers pay according to a cost-per-action (CPA) model in which the only audience members who count are those who "click through" the advertiser's banner ad and then are transported to the advertiser's Web site or who visit the site and actually purchase the advertiser's product. This approach requires maintaining logs of click-throughs and/or purchasing behaviors, and the advertiser pays a set price for each click-through recorded or a set percentage of the revenue from each sale. Clearly, this approach takes much of the risk out of on-line advertising, as the exchange between buyers and sellers of audiences is not predicated to any significant degree upon the anticipation of a certain level of traffic. However, if a Web site takes longer than the desired time to deliver a desired number of click-throughs, the predicted audience has not equaled the measured audience within a particular time frame.

The current Internet advertising environment is one in which CPM-based deals are more prominent than CPA-based deals, with hybrid deals (involving both CPM and CPA) becoming increasingly prominent (see Mack 2000:M52). The obvious appeal of "pure performance" deals is that they reduce the importance of audience forecasting—and its associated uncertainty. Content providers, however, have resisted pure performance-based models (see Kerschbaumer 2001), given that they are able to charge for only a small percentage of the total audience that visits their sites (the average click-through rate for a banner advertisement is less than .5 percent; see Gugel 2001; Media Dynamics 2001a). For these reasons the Internet's ability to accommodate such performance-based pricing has been described as "both the curse and the blessing of the Internet" (Kerschbaumer 2001:44).[1]

As this discussion suggests, some types of audience purchases offer greater risk to the purchaser than others. When "make-goods" are available, it may even seem that the purchaser incurs virtually no risk at all. This is not the case. From the advertisers' perspective "make-good" slots may not fit the initial media plan as well as the original placements (Rust and Eechambadi 1989). Indeed, these slots may represent the leftover, least-desirable placements. These slots may not deliver the demographics that the advertiser wants and thus may be of little overall value. Or the make-good slots may not coincide with the optimum time period for the advertising campaign. For instance, if the ad placements for a new motion picture underdeliver, make-goods available weeks after the film's release probably are not as desirable to the advertiser as spots airing in the week before the film's release. Consequently, advertisers want initial forecasts that are as accurate as possible and that give the advertisers a sense of the likelihood that a media product will deliver its projected audience.

Make-goods also negatively affect the sellers of audiences, because they must give away audiences that they could have sold to other advertisers. In cases of extreme inaccuracy make-goods can represent tens of millions of dollars in free advertising time (Adams 1994). In contrast, when network programs, for example, meet or exceed their projections, the leftover inventory is available to be sold in the "scatter" market (Consoli 2000c). Thus overestimating audiences can adversely affect both buyers and sellers in the audience marketplace.

Underestimation represents a somewhat different dynamic. Generally, if a particular media product overdelivers on its projected audience, advertisers do not pay additional compensation to content providers. On the surface it may seem that such a situation represents a pure benefit to advertisers. However, this may not always be the case. Advertisers allocate their budgets across media and markets on the basis of specific audience-reach goals. Consequently, as Poltrack (1983) suggests, "If the [media] buyer over-achieves the goal of the advertiser by a substantial amount, the client has misallocated dollars to that market. These dollars probably could have been used more effectively elsewhere. . . . Ideally, the schedule would deliver audiences identical to the buyer's projections" (187). From the seller's standpoint underestimation means that the seller failed to capture all the revenues it could have received for a particular media product's audience. For this reason sellers of audiences are unlikely to underestimate in their audience projections, erring instead on the side of overestimation.

This seemingly one-sided relationship, in which advertisers sometimes are compensated when media products underdeliver but need not provide additional payment when a media product overdelivers, is best understood as a reflection of the high level of uncertainty—and therefore high level of risk—involved in purchasing audiences. The key point of this discussion, however, is that the forecasting of media audiences is a central component of doing business in the audience marketplace and that accurate forecasts are vital to both the buyers and sellers of audiences.

PREDICTING AUDIENCES: COPING WITH UNCERTAINTY

Uncertainty is a key factor in any economic transaction. Traditionally, economists have assumed that all participants in a transaction are rational actors with all the information necessary to make the correct decision. Since the 1970s, however, economists have increasingly recognized that marketplace participants seldom have all the information necessary to make the optimal decision; rather, most economic transactions involve some level of uncertainty (e.g., Simon 1976; Williamson 1985). Uncertainty is particularly prominent in the audience marketplace (Gitlin 1983; Pekurny 1982; Phalen 1996, 1998). Analysts of media industries long have recognized that media organizations face tremendous uncertainties regarding the behavior of their audiences and that these uncertainties affect the behavioral practices and institutional structures of media organizations (McQuail 1969). Indeed, Phalen has described audiences as "the key uncertainty" affecting the economics of the media industries (1996:169).

Much work in the field of organizational decision making has focused on the processes by which organizations cope with uncertainty when making decisions (e.g., March 1994; Stinchcombe 1990). Typically, *uncertainty* is defined within decision-making theory as "imprecision in estimates of future consequences" (March 1994:178). The key point that comes from this body of literature is that decision quality generally is inversely related to uncertainty and that uncertainty is reduced by the availability of information (March 1994; Stinchcombe 1990). Thus the less information that is available, the less likely it is that the decision will be of high quality. As Stinchcombe says, "Uncertainty is reduced through news; then finally the residual uncertainty is transformed into risk and people make their bets" (1990:5).

Stinchcombe's statement provides an accurate summary of the process of forecasting media audiences. When predicting audiences for media products, forecasters face a highly uncertain decision-making scenario. Whenever possible, they rely on historical data to guide their predictions, such as measured audience data for existing programs, stations, or formats.

In the case of new media products, forecasters can only draw upon the track record of the organization or individual producing the media product (Gandy 1984; Gardini 2001) or that of the product's genre or format (Gitlin 1983; Pekurny 1982). Of course, past performance is no guarantee of future performance, as content quality, audience tastes, and competing media options, to name only a few factors, can change rapidly. Consequently, forecasters also use their own assessments of the product's audience appeal, scheduling or distribution factors, and the relative strength of the competing media products (Wakshlag, personal communication, 1998). Ultimately, forecasters draw on a combination of social science research, professional judgment, and gut instincts. It is not surprising, then, that forecasting media audiences has been described as both science and art (Webster, Phalen, and Lichty 2000:55).

PRETESTING MEDIA PRODUCTS

One prominent way that participants in the audience market attempt to cope with uncertainty is by pretesting content on "sample" audiences and then using the feedback to generate predictions of the media product's performance. For instance, the magazine industry conducts audience simulations for yet-to-be-published magazines (P. Miller 1994). These simulations involve developing circulation numbers by using such data as the new magazine's publishing philosophy, target audience, and the circulation numbers for similar magazines in the marketplace (P. Miller 1994).

Television programmers have for years conducted "pilot testing" for their new programs. In many instances the data derived from these tests are a central factor in determining whether a program makes it on the air (see Schlosser 2001). Pilot tests involve showing the first episode of a new program (the pilot) to audiences and then recording their reactions, typically through theater testing or in-home cable testing. Theater testing involves recruiting a reasonably representative sample audience to attend a theater screening of a program. After the screening the programmer uses questionnaires and focus groups to record the audience's reaction to the program. Theater testing also uses what is known as "dial testing." In dial tests audience members use a device that allows them to register their level of satisfaction with the program while they are viewing it. Viewers turn the dial in one direction if they are enjoying what they are seeing and the opposite direction if they are dissatisfied. These individual responses are then aggregated to produce what looks like a minute-by-minute electrocardiogram of the program. Newer versions of the dial-test technology even include a "tune-out" button, which audience members can press to register the specific point at which they no longer wish to view the program (Greene 2000). These data can be used not only to decide whether to air a program but also to edit out or reshoot poorly received scenes or to drop or recast entire characters, if their appearance on screen coincides with low levels of satisfaction among the audience members (Gitlin 1983; Greene 2000).

Dial testing of media products dates to the late 1930s, when the first "program analyzer" was developed by Frank Stanton, then head of audience research for the CBS radio network, and Paul Lazarsfeld, then the director of Princeton University's Office of Radio Research (Levy 1982). In those early days the program analyzer was used primarily to test radio programs. During World War II the program analyzer was used to test army training films and war propaganda (Levy 1982). Today advanced variations of the original program analyzer are used to test a variety of media products, including advertisements, theatrical motion pictures, and even political speeches (Millard 1992).

Despite its prominence as an analytical tool for programmers, theater testing is not without its flaws. First, the degree to which a small theater audience recruited off the street accurately represents the viewing audience as a whole has major limitations (Gitlin 1983). Interestingly, researchers have found that Las Vegas, with its mix of families, young singles, retirees, and conventioneers from all over the country, provides them with the best opportunity for constructing a geographically and demographically representative test audience (Consoli 2001a).[2] Nonetheless, representativeness remains a major limitation. In addition, many critics have noted that theater tests do not reflect the typical media consumption environment. That is, watching a program in a theater with a group of strangers is fundamentally different from watching a program in the comfort of one's own home, with friends or family. Consequently, whether theater test audiences are watching and responding to programs in a frame of mind that accurately reflects how they watch—and respond to—television programs at home is questionable.

In-home cable testing involves recruiting a sample of viewers and instructing them to watch a particular cable channel at a particular time. In conjunction with the local cable system, the programmer then transmits the test program at the designated time. After the broadcast, testers interview the participants by telephone to get their reactions to the program (Stipp and Schiavone 1990).

Cable testing addresses some weaknesses of the theater testing approach but also has unique shortcomings. Unlike theater tests, cable testing does allow viewers to watch and evaluate a program within the comfort of their own home. In addition, cable testing permits construction of a much larger viewing audience than is possible using theater testing. However, representativeness is once again an issue, given that roughly 30 percent of the television audience does not subscribe to cable. These viewers are thus unreachable via the cable testing method. In addition, not all cable systems are willing to participate, which introduces the possibility of further distortions in the geographic and demographic mix of participants.

Other methods have been developed to test television programs in recent years. For instance, the media consulting firm Frank Magid Associates has used in-home VCR testing. This method involves sending recruited audiences a VHS tape of the program being tested. After viewing the program, the testers interview the audience members by telephone. Given that VCR penetration is roughly 90 percent in the United States, VCR testing offers a better opportunity for a representative sample than cable testing (Greene 2000). Other firms are beginning to use computers and the Internet. As video-streaming technology improves, the Internet offers the opportunity to test programs with a large audience and receive immediate feedback at a relatively low cost. Of course, with Internet penetration hovering at about 50 percent of U.S. households (only a fraction of which have the high-speed Internet access necessary to view streaming video), achieving a representative sample of the television audience once again is a problem (Greene 2000).

Radio uses similar pretesting techniques. Researchers use a variety of methods to pretest the appeal of individual songs. One approach, called "call-out" studies, involves playing small segments of songs (called "hooks") over the telephone to a random sample of respondents and collecting their feedback (see Fletcher 1991; MacFarland 1997). "Call-in" studies involve contacting participants by mail, then having them phone in to a designated number to listen to a series of hooks and provide feedback by either mail or telephone. The criticism of these approaches is that the telephone represents a much lower level of sound quality than radio (Fletcher 1991; MacFarland 1997). Radio researchers overcome the issue of sound quality by using auditorium studies, in which participants are recruited to a theater or auditorium to listen to a series of songs or hooks. However, the trade-off for providing better sound quality is that auditorium studies generally are too time consuming and too expensive to gain feedback from as many participants as is possible with call-in or call-out studies. Radio researchers also test the appeal of individual radio formats when a new station is entering the market or when an existing station is considering a change in format. Format research involves obtaining feedback from audience members (using both survey and focus group methods) about whether they are likely to listen to each of any number of format options (Hanson 1991).

MODELING AUDIENCE BEHAVIOR

Audience researchers develop sophisticated predictive models that frequently integrate these various means of assessing the audience preferences for media products. While many of these models remain proprietary (Rust, Kamakura, and Alpert 1992), a number of published studies provide insight into how it is possible to predict the behavior of media audiences by using quantitative modeling (although these published models generally do not use the pretesting data that are incorporated in the proprietary models). Much of this research has focused on television.

It is important to note that while the audience size and composition for an individual media product often are difficult to predict accurately, overall levels of media consumption generally are quite predictable. For instance, a study by Barnett and colleagues (1991) found that seasonal factors such as temperature, precipitation, and hours of daylight could reasonably explain variations in the overall level of television viewing. Similarly, overall television audience levels are consistent in terms of the time of day and the day of the week. Generally, television viewership gradually increases throughout the morning, levels off at approximately 30 percent of households during the early and midafternoon, and then increases rapidly in the late afternoon. During prime time (8 to 11 P.M.) viewership levels are at their highest, peaking at about 10 P.M., when almost 70 percent of television households are likely to be watching. After 10 P.M. viewership levels begin to decline sharply. This pattern is repeated with remarkable consistency each weekday (the pattern is somewhat different during weekends). Day-to-day patterns are quite consistent as well. The highest levels of prime-time television viewing almost always occur on Sunday evenings, when the largest numbers of people are at home, while the lowest levels occur on Friday and Saturday evenings (Media Dynamics 2001b; Nielsen Media Research 2000), when many people are out for the evening. Demographic variations within these viewing patterns are reasonably predictable as well. For instance, on Friday and Saturday evenings the television audience contains a larger proportion of elderly and very young viewers than normal. During the weekday afternoon hours the television audience contains a large proportion of children and teenagers (see Webster and Phalen 1997).

These relatively stable and predictable patterns in audience availability allow television programmers to schedule their lineups accordingly. Programmers are able to take advantage of the relative certainty that certain sizes and types of audiences are going to be available at certain periods and construct schedules that reflect these viewing patterns. Thus Friday and Saturday evenings see much programming targeted at either the very young or the elderly.[3] Sunday evenings inevitably are when programmers air their most expensive or high-profile programming (e.g., the Superbowl, a miniseries), in order to take advantage of the large audience available on those evenings.

Radio demonstrates similar consistency in overall audience availability. The highest usage period is from 6 to 9 A.M., when almost 40 percent of the population is listening to the radio (see Webster, Phalen, and Lichty 2000). This time period, labeled "morning drive" within the industry, is when listeners are commuting to work, reflecting the large proportion of radio listening that takes place in automobiles. Not surprisingly, radio stations invest most heavily in their programming during the morning drive period. As with television, radio has predictable demographic variations. Radio listening among teenagers, for instance, is at its highest in the morning (reaching about 30 percent of the teenage population) but also maintains a relatively high level throughout the late afternoon and evening, with about 20 percent of the teenage population listening to radio between 4 and 10 P.M. In contrast, radio listening among men aged 18 to 64 is near its lowest levels (5 to 10 percent) in the evening hours (Webster, Phalen, and Lichty 2000).

Even the Internet is beginning to demonstrate fairly predictable variations in audience availability. In terms of at-home usage during a typical workday, the percentage of people with Internet access who are on line at any given time generally is quite low (peaking at about 5 percent), particularly when compared to television and radio usage levels. The general pattern is one of a steady increase in Internet use throughout the day, with peak usage occurring between 7 and 10 P.M. (closely corresponding to prime-time television). Usage then declines steadily into the late-night hours. Again, demographic differences in Internet use are consistent and stable, with usage by children and teenagers peaking in the late afternoon and usage by adults peaking in the evening (Media Dynamics 2001a).

When trying to ascertain how audiences are going to distribute themselves across a medium's content options at a particular time, prediction becomes more difficult. Forecasters have had some success, however, in developing predictive models (e.g., Weber 2001). These models generally take as their bases the relatively stable and predictable levels of audience availability. Thus audience forecasting has been described as a two-stage process; the first stage is estimating the available audience, and the second is predicting the distribution of this available audience across content options (see Webster, Phalen, and Lichty 2000).

Webster and Phalen (1997) have established two primary categories for the various predictive factors that can influence a media product's audience size: audience factors (characteristics of the audience) and media factors (characteristics of the media environment). They further subdivide each of these factors into two categories: structural determinants and individual determinants.[4] They define structural determinants as macro-level factors that are characteristic of the mass audience, whereas individual determinants are micro-level variables that are descriptive of a person or household. Thus, for example, a structural media factor would be the number of channels available on a cable system, whereas an individual media factor would be a person's cable channel subscription package. In contrast, a structural audience factor would be the overall level of audience availability at a particular time period, whereas an individual audience factor would be a particular person's preferences among program types (see Webster and Phalen 1997). Webster and Phalen drew their categories from a fairly extensive literature devoted to identifying the factors that aid in the prediction of audience exposure patterns (e.g., Eastman 1998; Walker 1988; Webster 1985; Webster and Newton 1988; Webster and Wang 1992).

Structural media factors figured prominently in some of the earliest research in this vein. One early study found that shares for individual television programs were a function of the characteristics of the individual stations, such as frequency assignment (UHF versus VHF), network affiliation, and the number of stations in a market (White 1977).[5] Another study, which focused on overall levels of audience exposure to advertising schedules, also emphasized the importance of structural factors, such as network and daypart (Headen, Klompmaker, and Teel 1979; see also Sabavala and Morrison 1981). A third study used seasonal variations in television viewing, as well as ratings histories for programs and time slots, to develop a predictive model of audience sizes for prime-time network programs (Gensch and Shaman 1980). Like the other predictive models developed during this period, this third study did not include variables related to audience characteristics or program content. Similarly, a study that took a rare look beyond prime-time network programming found that structural media factors, such as the ratings for the program's lead-in and lead-out, were a good basis for predicting ratings for syndicated television programs (R. Cooper 1993).[6] That these models demonstrated substantial predictive power despite the absence of individual audience and content variables provides an important indication of the importance of structural factors in predicting audience behavior.

Other studies have focused on individual-level audience factors, such as audience members' perceptions of the attributes of television programs and the effect of these factors on viewing preferences (Lehmann 1971). One study found that channel and program type preferences could explain almost 75 percent of the variance in audience members' television-viewing patterns (Darmon 1976). More recent research found that audience members' decisions to view individual programs were significantly related to the viewers' program type preferences and a variety of demographic factors, including age, income, education, and region of the country in which they lived (Rust, Kamakura, and Alpert 1992).

Individual factors also were a prominent component of a series of studies conducted primarily during the 1960s and 1970s that focused almost exclusively on the effectiveness of program type preferences in predicting television-viewing behavior. Generally, these studies were inconsistent in terms of the degree to which they showed that program type classifications effectively differentiate viewer preferences (Ehrenberg 1968; Frank, Becknell, and Clokey 1971; Kirsch and Banks 1962; Lehmann 1971; Levin 1980; Rao 1975). However, in assessing the entirety of this body of research, Webster and Wakshlag (1983) concluded that traditional classifications of program types are systematically related to program preference. This conclusion is supported in more recent research that demonstrates that program type categories are significant predictors of audience ratings (Kim and Grant 1996). Research also has shown that, as the number of channel options available to a television viewer increases, program type preferences become an increasingly powerful predictor of viewer behavior (Youn 1994). Among cable subscribers, about 50 percent of all program consumption coincided with program type preferences, compared to approximately 25 percent for nonsubscribers (Youn 1994). An important implication of these results is that as the number of channel and content options available to audiences increases, audiences will take advantage of the increasing availability of their preferred program type, rather than take advantage of the greater diversity of program types available in the expanded channel environment.[7] Thus the expanding media environment may favor individual, not structural, factors as the most useful determinants of audience behavior (Adams 1993; Eastman 1998).

It is important to emphasize, however, that much of the day-to-day forecasting of audience behavior that takes place in the audience marketplace primarily relies on previous audience exposure data. Particularly in the United States, systematic audience measurement seldom looks beyond exposure to media content to more qualitative factors such as audience members' assessments or levels of appreciation of the content. Some analysts of the media industry have argued that a more sophisticated understanding of audience behavior could arise from such qualitative assessments (Adams 2000, 2001;

Gunter 1993; Gunter and Wober 1992; Livingstone 1993; Schlosberg 1993), perhaps thereby increasing the accuracy of predictions of audience behavior. However, efforts to launch such qualitative audience research services in the United States generally have proved unsuccessful (see Mitgang 2000).[8]

In sum, whether for new or existing media products, the information gleaned from pretesting and modeling allows forecasters to reduce, but not eliminate, the uncertainty surrounding the predicted audience. Thus people who forecast media audiences are "boundedly rational" (Simon 1976). That is, they make rational decisions but do so without all the information necessary to make the optimal decision.

IDENTIFYING "UNCERTAINTY VARIABLES": THE CASE OF PRIME-TIME NETWORK TELEVISION

Given the uncertainty that both buyers and sellers face in dealing in predicted audiences, it is essential, as March (1994) points out, that decision makers form estimates of the amount of risk present in any individual decision-making situation. Thus investigating whether particular factors affect the degree of risk (uncertainty) surrounding individual forecasts is essential. Although, as I have shown, research has advanced our understanding of the factors affecting the size of a program's measured audience (e.g., Adams 1993; R. Cooper 1993; Headen, Klompmaker, and Teel 1979; Henry and Rinne 1984; Horen 1980; Wakshlag and Greenberg 1979), analysts have paid little attention to the factors affecting the accuracy of the predictions. Investigating this question can provide insights into the factors that affect the congruence between the predicted audience and the measured audience.

In order to explore this dimension of the audience forecasting process, I will integrate decision-making theory, which often has focused on the role of uncertainty in the decision-making process, with audience behavior theory, which often has focused on the factors that affect the behavioral patterns of media audiences.[9] I will then apply this integrated theoretical perspective to a case study of the forecasting of new prime-time network television programs. The linkage between these seemingly disparate bodies of literature makes it possible to identify programming conditions with higher levels of uncertainty in decision making, which therefore lead to higher levels of inaccuracy in audience forecasts. The basic assumption that guides this analytical approach is that the magnitude of forecasting error for new prime-time network television programs is related to the amount of uncertainty surrounding the programs.

The introduction of new prime-time network television programs represents one of the most challenging and most visible displays of the audience-forecasting process. Each spring advertising agencies and media buyers purchase roughly 75 to 80 percent of the broadcast networks' ad inventory during the "up-front" period (Mandese 1995). This spending includes purchases of advertising time for new programs that have yet to air a single episode. Of course, whether a program is new or returning, advertisers are still purchasing anticipated audiences; however, in the case of new programs, the situation is more extreme.

In the case of new prime-time broadcast network programs, forecasters generally construct their predictions on the basis of pilots, clips, descriptions, and competitive scheduling (Mandese 1995). That is, on the basis of their assessments of the probable audience appeal of the program and the perceived audience appeal of the competition, forecasters develop a predicted audience for the new program that becomes a central factor in the planning of ad schedules (DeCoursey 1995). The obvious question that arises from this scenario is whether the new programs that air in the fall will fulfill the projections that guided the audience purchases.

In fact, these audience forecasts have been described as notoriously inaccurate (Rust and Eechambadi 1989:13; see also Forkan 1986). For example, an analysis of the 1997–98 television season found that advertising industry forecasters incorrectly predicted the audience shares of twenty-two new prime-time programs and accurately predicted the audience shares for only five (Wells 1997).[10] Typically, these forecasts overestimated, rather than underestimated, the performance of the new programs.

On the surface it may appear that all new programs have an equal amount of uncertainty, given that none of them ever has aired. However, it may be possible to identify variations in the level of uncertainty for individual programs. That is, some new programs may pose greater amounts of uncertainty than others, in which case the predictive tools and experience available to advertising industry forecasters should be less effective in some situations than others. Identifying these sources of uncertainty would enable forecasters and the consumers of forecasts to identify "high risk" decision-making situations and invest their resources accordingly.

INHERITANCE EFFECTS

Research on "inheritance effects" focuses on the effects of the lead-in and lead-out on on a program's audience size. Generally, both the size of a program's lead-in audience and the size of its lead-out audience are significant predictors of a program's audience size, given that viewers have a tendency to remain with a single channel throughout an evening (Barwise and Ehrenberg 1988; Webster and Phalen 1997). Generally, the lead-in effect is more powerful than the lead-out effect (R. Cooper 1993), although these effects have diminished over time (particularly the lead-out effect) as programming options have increased (Eastman 1998).[11] Regardless, from a decision-making standpoint, knowledge of the past performance of the lead-in and lead-out is useful for predicting the performance of a new program. Consequently, if a program's lead-in or lead-out is new, less information is available to forecasters when they make their predictions. This leads to the following hypotheses:

h1: *Programs with returning lead-ins will have lower forecasting error than programs without returning lead-ins.*

h2: *Programs with returning lead-outs will have lower forecasting error than programs without returning lead-outs.*

COMPETITIVE SCHEDULING AND COUNTERPROGRAMMING

Audience behavior research has demonstrated that the size of a program's audience also is partially a function of the programming available on competing channels (e.g., Horen 1980). The common strategy of "counterprogramming" (placing a program that appeals to a different audience segment opposite another program; see Eastman 1998) grows from the fact that the audience size for any given program cannot be understood purely in terms of the appeal and merits of that particular program (and its lead-in and lead-out). Rather, programmers should approach any program's audience size in terms of how that program is likely to fare against its competition. Thus network programs scheduled to run against extremely popular network programs typically are expected to have small audience shares, given the difficulty that they are likely to encounter in drawing the available viewing audience away from these programs.

From a decision-making standpoint, accurately taking into account the effects of competitive scheduling on a new program's audience size becomes more difficult as the amount of information about the competing programs declines. Thus a program that is scheduled against primarily new programs poses a greater level of uncertainty to forecasters than a program that is scheduled against returning programs. This leads to the following hypothesis:

h3: The greater the percentage of competing network time occupied by new programs, the greater the forecasting error will be.

NEW PROGRAM QUANTITY AND DECISION MAKING

When the time available for making a specified number of decisions is constant, we should expect better decision-making quality as the number of decisions decreases. When an analyst has fewer decisions to make, the analyst can devote more time to information gathering and processing for each decision. As the number of decisions that the analyst needs to make in that period increases, the amount of time available for information gathering and processing for each decision decreases. Subsequently, the uncertainty level for each decision increases, and decision quality should decrease.

Applying this logic to television audience forecasting, those seasons in which more new programs are introduced impose greater information-gathering and -processing burdens on forecasters than those seasons in which fewer new programs are introduced. As Phalen (1998) has demonstrated, those who work in audience markets encounter difficulty both in processing all the available pertinent information and in obtaining the information they need. Given that the time from program schedule introduction to forecast generation remains relatively constant, the introduction of more new programs should result in greater levels of uncertainty and thus greater levels of forecasting error. This leads to the following hypothesis:

h4: The greater the number of new prime-time network programs introduced in a new program's debut season, the greater the forecasting error will be.

AUDIENCE BEHAVIOR THEORY AND
THE NEW MEDIA ENVIRONMENT

The enormous changes taking place in the media environment have complicated the process of predicting the behavior of television audiences (Eastman 1998; see also chapter 5). Developments such as the remote control device, the VCR, and the enormous channel capacity of cable television have made it more difficult for programmers to attract and retain audiences using traditional programming strategies and for forecasters to anticipate how viewers are likely to be distributed across their program options (see Walker 1988). Recent additions to the media mix such as direct broadcast satellite (DBS), personal video recorders (PVRs; also commonly referred to as digital video recorders), and the Internet further complicate the process of predicting audience behavior. As the media marketplace has grown and become more complex, it seems that accurately predicting audience behavior has become increasingly difficult (Kirkham 1996). For instance, Lin (1994) found that the viewing behavior of cable television subscribers was much less predictable than the behavior of viewers who received only broadcast television, with its much more limited channel offerings. These findings led Lin to conclude that "the more advanced a technology environment is, the more difficult it is to predict or define viewing patterns" (36). Similarly, interviews conducted by Blumler (1995) with television professionals about the implications of the increasing channel capacity of the contemporary television environment revealed a common theme—that "uncertainty about the likely audience to all individual program offerings has been heightened" (102). These increasing complications, and the associated uncertainty about exactly how they are likely to affect viewing behavior, lead to the following hypothesis:

h5: Forecasting error for new prime-time network television programs will increase over time.

PROGRAMMING HISTORY AND AUDIENCE HOMOGENEITY

Given that this analysis focuses on the predicted audience shares for the Big Four networks' new prime-time programs, it is important to recognize that the Fox network has some fundamental differences that may affect forecasting outcomes. First, Fox is comparatively new, having begun broadcasting in prime time only in 1987. The network still does not present a complete prime-time programming lineup (leaving the 10 P.M. slot to the local affiliates). As a newer network, with less of a programming record for forecasters to draw upon in their decision making, Fox appears to present a greater level of uncertainty than the traditional Big Three (ABC, CBS, and NBC). In addition, the time period that I studied (1993–98) represents a period of much greater volatility for Fox than for the other three networks. That is, Fox was still very much in its developmental stages, particularly in terms of expanding its program offerings and establishing affiliates. Thus the status of the Fox network changed more substantially from year to year than the status of the Big Three networks. In addition, throughout its history Fox has been more likely to experiment with unconventional or mixed genres (Bielby and Bielby 1994), which have less of a track record upon which to base predictions. Together, these factors suggest greater uncertainty for predicting the audiences for Fox programs.

However, there also is reason to expect lower levels of forecasting error for Fox programs. Research by Tavakoli and Cave shows that "viewing variation tends to increase with the age of the viewers" (1996:78). Specifically, as viewers age, they tend to consume a greater diversity of program types and become more difficult to associate with particular program type preferences. This pattern suggests that the viewing behavior of younger viewers presents less uncertainty and should be easier to predict than the viewing behavior of older viewers. Given that Fox always has targeted a younger audience than the Big Three (Consoli 2000a), predicting audiences for Fox programs may pose lower levels of uncertainty than predicting audiences for the other networks' programs. These competing logical approaches lead to the following research question:

rq1: Will Fox programs exhibit more or less forecasting error than Big Three programs?

METHODOLOGY

In order to investigate the relationship between uncertainty variables and forecasting error, I collected data on the predicted and measured audience shares for new prime-time network television programs for the broadcast seasons of 1993–94 through 1997–98. I included only the four major broadcast networks (ABC, CBS, NBC, and Fox) in this analysis, given that the newer networks (UPN and WB) began to offer a significant competitive presence only during the last two seasons for which I gathered data.

For each season I compiled predicted audience shares by using the annual advertising industry survey published in *Broadcasting and Cable,* the major trade publication for the television industry. Until recently, each summer *Broadcasting and Cable* published the results of a survey of the nation's major national advertising agencies. The survey included the mean national audience share predictions for both new and returning prime-time network television programs. Thus this annual survey essentially represented the advertising industry's consensus regarding the likely performance for each show in the prime-time network programming lineup.

I gathered measured national audience shares from weekly Nielsen Media Research reports published in *Broadcasting and Cable.* It is important to note that this analysis focuses on the relationship between the predicted and measured audience in terms of national audience shares (the primary focus of published forecasts, as well as much of the "horse race" coverage presented in the trade press), although television programming and audience analysis frequently focus on particular audience segments (particularly viewers aged 18 to 49; see chapter 4). With the necessary forecasting and ratings data, it is possible to build upon my model to conduct comparable analyses that focus on particular audience segments.

In order to generate a measure of a program's actual performance, I gathered national audience share data for the first four broadcasts (excluding the premiere) in which the program aired in its scheduled time slot, against its scheduled competition, and with its scheduled lead-in and lead-out. I excluded the premiere to reduce variability caused by significant differences in the amount of preseason promotion and because the premieres of many new programs run longer than their normally scheduled length. As one media-buying report has noted, "Premiere performance is rarely an accurate predictor of overall season performance" (Consoli 2000d:6).

Share forecasts are based in part upon an assessment of the likely effects of scheduling factors on audience shares (Wakshlag, personal communication, 1998). Consequently, forecasting error must be derived from broadcasts that accurately reflect the programming conditions that the forecasters assumed would exist. In some instances the trade press has published analyses of forecast accuracy by comparing initial predictions and each program's mean share during the season, regardless of relevant scheduling changes (e.g., Gelman 1997). A program that performs in close accordance with forecasters' preseason projections after being moved to a completely different time slot provides no real indication of the forecasters' accuracy, given that the program is performing in a competitive and scheduling environment that the forecasters never actually assessed.

This situation makes it difficult to obtain at least four acceptable broadcasts. Given the increasing volatility of the broadcast network schedules (Adams 1993; Eastman 1998), not all new programs ever even receive four regularly scheduled broadcasts.[12] Rescheduling of the program, its lead-in, lead-out, or competition often can occur within a month. The addition of special sporting events such as the World Series each fall adds further volatility to the schedule. Indeed, obtaining four regularly scheduled broadcasts for a new program often necessitated consulting ratings reports well into December and January of the broadcast season. In many instances (fifty-two cases) I could not obtain a full four regularly scheduled broadcasts because of the schedule volatility. However, I included these programs in the analysis in order to avoid biasing the data set against programs that performed poorly (and subsequently were removed from the lineup or rescheduled). It is important to also note that when I excluded from the analysis those programs with one to three regularly scheduled broadcasts, I found virtually no difference in the overall explanatory power of the model or in the direction or magnitude of the relationships between the independent variables and the dependent variable. One weakness of this approach is that it does not capture effectively the possibility that, midway through the season, a new program could catch on with an audience and experience significant share increases. However, the increasing speed with which the networks reevaluate and reorganize their schedules (see Media Dynamics 2001b) makes it unlikely that a program could find an audience late in the season within a programming context that reflects the programming conditions under which the initial forecast was generated.

From these data I created a measure of forecasting error (ERROR). I calculated this measure as follows:

$$\text{ERROR} = |(P_i - A_i)/A_i| \times 100,$$

where P_i equals the predicted share for program i and A_i equals the actual share for program i. This equation produces a percentage measure of the degree to which each program's predicted share deviated from its measured share. I used a percentage measure rather than an absolute measure to account for the greater accuracy of a forecast that is off by 1 share point for a program with an actual share of 20 than a forecast that is off by 1 share point for a program with an actual share of 10. Thus in the first example the forecasting error would be 5 percent, whereas in the second example the forecasting error would be 10 percent. Also, the dependent variable is measured as an absolute value, given that no theoretical rationale exists for anticipating the direction of the forecasting error (i.e., overestimating versus underestimating) on the basis of identifying sources of uncertainty.

In some instances programs that were part of the schedule when the forecasts were generated were removed from the fall broadcast schedule. I did not include such programs in the data set. In other instances programs that were scheduled in one time slot when the forecasts were generated were moved to a different time slot before the season commenced. I also excluded these programs from the analysis, given that their predicted shares were not based on the competitive situation that the programs actually faced when they aired. Finally, in other instances a new program never actually ran against the competitive lineup that it was scheduled to face or never ran with its scheduled lead-in or lead-out. These situations often arose because the network quickly removed the program, one or more of its competitors, or its lead-in or lead-out from the schedule or moved it to another time slot. I also removed these programs from the analysis, because the published advertising industry forecasts are based in part upon assessments of how the program will perform against its regularly scheduled competition. As a result of these conditions I could not use seventeen programs, leaving a total of 140 programs.

In order to investigate hypotheses 1 and 2, I created dummy variables for whether each new program's lead-in and lead-out were returning network programs (RLEADIN; RLEADOUT; 0 = No; 1 = Yes). Some new programs started or concluded a network's prime-time lineup (e.g., a starting time of 8 P.M. EST; 7 P.M. EST on Sunday; or concluding program that began at 10 P.M. EST, or 9 P.M. EST for Fox), in which case they lacked either a network lead-in or lead-out. To account for this distinction I created additional dummy variables for each new program that had *any* network lead-in or lead-out (LEADIN; LEADOUT; 0 = No; 1 = Yes).

In order to investigate hypothesis 3, I calculated the percentage of competing network time occupied by new programs (PERCNEW) as follows: first, I added up the total number of half-hour blocks of Big Four network broadcast time that encompassed the time of the new program. Then I calculated the total number of those blocks occupied by new programs. I then divided this number by the total number of half-hour network broadcast blocks. This can be represented as follows:

PERCNEW = $(B_i^N/B_i^{N+R}) \times 100$

where B_i^N equals the total number of program i's competing half-hour blocks comprised of new programming, and B_i^{N+R} equals the total number of program i's competing half-hour blocks (new and returning).

Thus if a program aired at 8 P.M. (when all the Big Four networks broadcast) and ran for half an hour, the total number of competing network broadcast blocks was three. If one of the competing network programs airing during this half hour was new, PERCNEW was 33 (1/3 x 100). If a program aired at 10 P.M. (when only ABC, CBS, and NBC broadcast) and ran for an hour, this produced a total of four competing network broadcast blocks (two half-hours on each of the two competing networks broadcasting at that time). If one competing network was broadcasting a new hour-long program during that time period, PERCNEW was 50 (2/4 x 100).

This measure of competing programming accounts for only broadcast network programming. Certainly, competing cable programming can affect network audiences as well. However, only recently have individual cable programs begun to perform well enough relative to broadcast programs to warrant their inclusion in forecasts of broadcast program audiences. Indeed, broadcast programmers tend to focus on the programming lineups of the competing broadcast networks in their scheduling decisions (Eastman 1998), and advertisers often consider cable programming in the aggregate in terms of its effects on the size of broadcast audiences (Wakshlag 1998).[13] In any case, however, it is important to recognize that the scope of this analysis is limited to how competing Big Four broadcast network programs might affect the forecasting error for Big Four programs.

In order to investigate hypotheses 4 and 5, I recorded the total number of new programs to be introduced each season (NEWSEAS), as well as the year that each program was introduced (YEAR). Finally, in regard to research question 1, I recorded the network designation for each program. As I noted earlier, my primary concern was whether the program aired on the Fox network. I created a dummy variable (FOX), by which I coded those programs airing on Fox as a 1 and those programs not airing on Fox as a zero. Table 2.1 presents descriptions of all the variables.

TABLE 2.1 Variables

VARIABLE NAME	DESCRIPTION
ERROR (DV)	Absolute value of forecasting error (%).
LEADIN	Does the program have a network lead-in (0 = No; 1 = Yes)?
RLEADIN	Does the program have a *returning* network lead-in (0 = No; 1 = Yes)?
LEADOUT	Does the program have a network lead-out (0 = No; 1 = Yes)?
RLEADOUT	Does the program have a *returning* network lead-out (0 = No; 1 = Yes)?
PERCNEW	Percentage of competing network time occupied by new programs.
NEWSEAS	Total number of new programs airing in program's debut season.
YEAR	Year program was introduced.
FOX	Program aired on Fox network (0 = No; 1 = Yes).

RESULTS

Table 2.2 presents statistics that describe the nature of the forecasting error for the data set. The top portion of table 2.2 presents the mean forecasting error as well as the mean absolute value of forecasting error. As the table shows, on average forecasters overestimated the performance of new programs by about 15 percent (note that a negative mean would have reflected a tendency toward underestimation). This tendency is somewhat surprising, given that advertisers ultimately must negotiate ad rates with the networks on the basis of these forecasts. However, the results presented here conform with the results of previous research, which showed a tendency among advertising industry forecasters toward overestimating the performance of prime-time network programs (see Wells 1997). Perhaps this optimism is partly a result of forecasters' failure to account adequately for audience erosion by cable in their forecasting models (Wakshlag 1998) or owes to forecasters' need to base their predictions in part on viewing pilots of new programs. These pilots often exhibit higher production values than regular season episodes, which may lead forecasters to overestimate their prospects. When forecasting error is expressed in absolute value terms, the mean is more than 21 percent.

The lower portion of table 2.2 displays the mean forecasting error (in absolute value terms) according to network. As the table shows, the traditional Big Three networks have forecasting error means of 20 to 25 percent,

TABLE 2.2 Means for Forecasting Error (N = 140)

VARIABLE	MEAN	STD. DEV.
Percentage of error (difference/actual share)	15.23*	24.84
Absolute value of percentage of error (ERROR)	21.35	19.78

MEAN ABSOLUTE VALUE OF PERCENTAGE OF FORECASTING ERROR BY NETWORK

NETWORK	MEAN	N	STD. DEVIATION
NBC	20.48	36	21.84
ABC	23.84	39	22.41
CBS	25.11	36	19.26
Fox	14.38	29	11.11

Note: F = 1.90 (p > .05).

FOX VERSUS BIG THREE

NETWORK	MEAN	N	STD. DEVIATION
Fox	14.38	29	11.11
Big Three	23.16	111	21.14

Note: F = 4.65 (p < .05).

*Note: Positive sign indicates that on average forecasts overestimated, rather than underestimated, audience shares for new network programs.

whereas Fox programs have a mean of roughly 14 percent. When Fox programs are compared to Big Three programs, the difference in the mean forecasting error is statistically significant ($F = 4.65$; $p < .05$). These results suggest that a greater congruence exists between the predicted audience and the measured audience for Fox programs.

Table 2.3 presents the results of the multiple regression model. The adjusted R^2 for the model is .19 ($p = .00$). RLEADIN, RLEADOUT, and YEAR are all statistically significant in the expected direction, providing support for hypotheses 1, 2, and 5. As the table shows, programs with a returning lead-in exhibit less forecasting error than programs without returning lead-

TABLE 2.3 Summary of Simultaneous Regression Analysis for Variables Predicting Forecasting Error ($N = 140$)

VARIABLE	B	STD. ERROR	ß
LEADIN	9.29	5.21	.20
RLEADIN	-13.80	4.25	-.35**
LEADOUT	9.18	5.80	.17
RLEADOUT	-9.42	3.76	-.24*
PERCNEW	-.08	.06	-.10
NEWSEAS	.51	.51	.08
YEAR	3.49	1.17	.26**
FOX	-5.76	4.06	-.12
Constant	-6960.01	2334.86	

Note: Adjusted R^2 = .19 (p = .00).

** $p < .01$.

* $p < .05$.

ins ($ß = -.35$, $p < .01$). Similarly, programs with returning lead-outs exhibit less forecasting error than programs without returning lead-outs ($ß = -.24$, $p < .05$). Neither of the dummy variables designed to account for programs without network lead-ins or lead-outs (LEADIN, LEADOUT) was significant at the .05 level. The significant positive coefficient for YEAR ($ß = .26$; $p < .01$) shows that forecasting error has been increasing over time.

The coefficients for NEWSEAS and PERCNEW were not significant at the .05 level, thus providing no support for hypotheses 3 and 4. Neither the number of new programs introduced in a season nor the percentage of competing network time composed of new programs was significantly related to forecasting error. In terms of research question 1, although Fox programs exhibited significantly lower mean forecasting error than Big Three programs, the Fox dummy variable was not significant within the multivariate analysis ($ß = -.12$; $p > .05$).

OBSERVATIONS

This exploratory study represents a first step toward a greater understanding of the factors that affect the predictability of television audiences and the relationship between the predicted audience and the measured audience. I found that the presence of returning network lead-ins and lead-outs is significantly related to lower levels of forecasting error for new prime-time network programs. Just as lead-ins and lead-outs affect the size of program audiences, they also appear to affect the predictability of program audiences. These results suggest that returning lead-ins and lead-outs significantly reduce the amount of uncertainty that forecasters face, enabling them to better predict the performance of new programs.

Given forecasters' tendency to overestimate the audience shares for new programs, the absence of returning network lead-ins or lead-outs is more likely to lead to overestimates of a program's audience. As I said at the outset, such overestimates can undermine the effectiveness of an advertising campaign, even when broadcasters supply make-goods to cover the difference between the predicted and measured audience. This analysis also showed that forecasting error is increasing significantly over time, suggesting that the dynamic and increasingly complicated media environment has made the task of predicting audiences more difficult. I discuss the implications of this phenomenon in chapter 5.

Other hypothesized uncertainty factors, such as the percentage of competing network time occupied by new programs and the number of new programs airing in a program's debut season, were not significantly related to forecasting error. The insignificance of the number of new programs airing in a particular season may be the result of a lack of variability in this measure, given that the number of new programs per season ranged from twenty-seven to thirty-six during the years that I studied.

The insignificance of the percentage of competing time occupied by new programs may mean that structural factors, such as competitive scheduling, are decreasing in importance in terms of understanding the distribution of television audiences (see Adams 1993). As the number of program options increases, viewers are increasingly likely to base their decision on program type preferences (Youn 1994). Cable television obviously is central to this transition; however, my study did not account for how cable program schedules might influence forecasting error. Specific variations in cable programming schedules can certainly affect the performance of individual broadcast network programs. Future research in this vein should include cable programming and other emerging structural complexities (e.g., DBS and emerging networks such as WB, UPN, and PAX) of the television environment.

In regard to whether Fox programs exhibit more or less forecasting error than Big Three programs, means comparisons showed significantly lower levels of forecasting error for Fox programs. However, in the multivariate analysis the Fox dummy variable was not statistically significant. The significant difference between the means does, however, suggest important avenues for future research. Recall that the reason for expecting lower forecasting error for Fox programs was the greater ease in predicting the viewing behavior of younger audiences. The results presented here provide some support for such a possibility, given that the network with the youngest audience—Fox—exhibited the lowest forecasting error, and the network with the oldest audience—CBS—exhibited the highest forecasting error (see table 2.2).[14] However, recent discussion within the broadcast industry has advocated the opposite perspective, with younger viewers (particularly teenagers) characterized as increasingly unpredictable because of their taste for novelty, low levels of brand/channel loyalty, and the increasing number of program options available to them (Salamon 2001). Given that ratings analysis is growing less concerned with overall audience shares than with shares of particular demographic groups, future research should investigate whether predictability varies in accordance with demographic factors. Fournier and Martin (1983) found that advertisers will pay a premium for audiences whose predicted size more closely matches their actual size. Consequently, the possibility of associating "predictability" with certain demographic characteristics could introduce an important factor that could affect the valuation of particular audiences.

PREDICTED AUDIENCES AND MEDIA CONTENT

The uncertainty inherent in dealing in predicted audiences has a significant effect on the content production decisions of media organizations. Specifically, the inability of media organizations to confidently anticipate the audience size and composition of individual media products compels these organizations to duplicate content that already has proved successful. Thus media organizations rely upon successful genres, formats, and formulas in an effort to maximize the likelihood that their offerings will succeed (see Bielby and Bielby 1994; Hirsch 1972). In this regard reliance upon established "formulas" essentially functions as a risk reducer (Nord 1980). Thus it is not surprising that, for example, within the context of prime-time network television, when a specific genre is particularly successful in one season, the number of programs in that genre on the network schedules the following season increases (Frankel 2001; McDonald and Schechter 1988). A recent example of this pattern can be seen in the flood of game shows and "reality" programming that followed the success of ABC's *Who Wants to Be a Millionaire?* and CBS's *Survivor.* Moreover, proposed programs that attempt to either break with traditional genre boundaries or to combine genres have a much lower likelihood of gaining a spot in the prime-time schedule (Bielby and Bielby 1994).

During pitch meetings for new syndicated programs that I attended during the participant observation component of this study, the sales reps typically were pitching new versions of old game shows and variations on court programs. Perhaps the most common phrase spoken by the sales reps was, "We're not reinventing the wheel here." This statement reflects the centrality of the reliance on established genres and formats in the program production and sales process. Efforts by programmers to bring greater certainty to their audience forecasts also explain why remakes and spinoffs have remained common in television programming and why the same producers, performers, and genres often are used repeatedly (Bielby and Bielby 1994; Kennedy 2002; Pekurny 1982).[15] Although the assumption that a producer's or genre's past performance is a useful predictor of future performance has not held up under empirical scrutiny (Bielby and Bielby 1994; Gardini 2001; Kennedy 2002), it remains a standard practice in television programming.

The statement of a sales representative for a major production company illustrates the force of this economic imperative and its relationship to efforts to combat uncertainty. When asked about the viability of unique or original program ideas or formats, she said: "Who could sell something new? Everyone would say, 'Give me an up-front guarantee.'"[16] Thus, as this statement suggests, in an environment in which uncertainty runs high, the risk perception associated with new or unique ideas is likely to be considered too high for such a program to be considered economically viable. An advertising industry researcher, who was assessing the state of syndication, recently echoed this perspective: by saying, "When you only have so much money to produce a slate of shows, you're going to try to hedge your bets, and a lot of times that means going with a formula" (Frutkin 2002a:11).

Such reliance on the familiar is not confined to television. Radio stations are notoriously hesitant to play music by new artists because radio executives don't know whether such music will appeal to audiences (Peterson 1994). Magazine executives increasingly are armed with detailed data about the sales figures that individual celebrities generate when they are featured on the cover. Thus editors place certain celebrities on the cover with greater frequency, with a certain degree of confidence that these celebrities can and will deliver an audience of a particular size. Ultimately, as Gitlin (1983) notes, "to build certainty, the 'science' of numbers has to be joined to the 'art' of hunches—consisting mostly of noting previous hits" (63).

The key point here is that media organizations must deal in predicted audiences and these audiences remain exceptionally difficult to predict, which has a significant influence on the nature of the content that these media organizations provide. The general pattern across media industries, of duplicating and recycling popular formats and genres, and of relying upon a fairly narrow range of performers and producers—even in the absence of compelling evidence that such strategies are successful—is a direct response to the persistent difficulties associated with predicting the audiences for individual media products. This pattern supports Stinchcombe's argument that "the introduction of an innovation involves a higher level of uncertainty than do the production and marketing of goods that have been on the market for a long time" (1990:25). Consequently, the unpredictability of the audience leads to greater predictability—and less diversity—in the content that media organizations provide.

CHAPTER 3

THE MEASURED AUDIENCE–ACTUAL AUDIENCE RELATIONSHIP

Just as incongruities exist between the predicted audience and the measured audience, so there are significant incongruities between the measured audience and the actual audience. Most important, these incongruities, and the efforts undertaken to reduce them, have important effects on the structure and behavior of the media institutions participating in the audience marketplace.

Regardless of the medium at issue, the ability of measurement techniques and technologies to accurately capture an audience's media consumption patterns is far from perfect. In this chapter I examine the processes by which measured audiences are created, emphasizing the weaknesses in contemporary audience measurement and the implications for the audience marketplace. Because purchasers of audiences ultimately purchase measured audiences, they always are left with the possibility that the measured audience that they purchased did not match the actual audience that saw the advertisement. This inconsistency of course raises the possibility that the advertising message was delivered to fewer people than the advertiser paid to reach and/or to a different demographic group.

I also will explore the linkages between the process of audience measurement and the structure and behavior of media institutions. Changes in the techniques and technologies of audience measurement can have a significant effect on the economics of media industries (because these changes can affect advertiser behavior), the relative economic health of various segments of the media industry, and the nature of the content that media organizations provide. Thus the process of audience measurement is inextricably intertwined with the competitive dynamics within the media industries and the evolution of media institutions.

PRODUCING MEASURED AUDIENCES

The continuing challenge in measuring audiences is to present a statistical representation of audience behavior, derived from a small sample of audience members, that portrays the behavior of the entire media audience as accurately as possible. Audience measurement firms first must construct a sample of willing participants that accurately reflects the composition of the population as a whole as closely as possible. They also must develop and use an accurate means of measuring the behavior of these participants. Failures or shortcomings in these areas introduce error into the final product, undermining the degree to which the measured audience accurately reflects the actual audience and diminishing the value of the audience product. As one analyst noted in regard to Internet audience measurement, "if the pillar of traffic ratings were cast into serious doubt, confidence in the Internet Economy could crumble" (Thompson et al. 2000:188). This statement (made before confidence in the Internet Economy did in fact crumble) illustrates the vital linkage between systems of audience measurement and the economics of advertiser-supported media.

THE SAMPLING PROCESS AND THE PRODUCTION OF AUDIENCES

Given that measured audiences are the product of a small sample of the total population of consumers, it is essential that this sample reflect the demographic and behavioral characteristics of this population as accurately as possible. If it is inaccurate, advertisers will have substantial doubts as to whether their campaigns are reaching their intended audience, and media organizations will be uncertain about the defining characteristics of the product that they are attempting to sell. The two key sampling factors affecting the congruence of the measured audience and the actual audience are sample size and sample representativeness. Numerous roadblocks stand in the way of producing sufficiently large and representative samples of consumers for the process of audience measurement. These roadblocks work against achieving congruence between the measured audience and the actual audience.

SAMPLE SIZE

Any measured audience must be derived from a sample that is sufficiently large to represent the population as a whole. Samples that are too small cannot account adequately for the diversity of types of individuals within a given population and therefore cannot provide an accurate representation of the population as a whole. A basic rule of sampling is that the adequacy of a sample's size is a function of the complexity of the population being measured (see Webster, Phalen, and Lichty 2000). More complex populations require larger samples, so that a sufficient number of participants represent each disparate category of audience member. Otherwise, measurement firms run into the possibility that their sample contains, for example, only a few men aged 18 to 24, yet the firms are extrapolating from these few the media consumption habits of all 18-to-24-year-old men in the country—and one or more of this small group may have unique and idiosyncratic media consumption habits. The overall effect of such individual idiosyncrasies on audience data is reduced when audience estimates are drawn from a larger sample of the population. For this reason, when measurement firms seek to measure the media audience in greater detail, they need a larger sample size. This larger sample facilitates dividing the mass audience into narrower segments. Thus when Nielsen Media Research moved from simply providing data about television households to providing demographic data about individual television audience members, the company had to use a much larger sample in order to account effectively for the increased level of detail (see Beville 1988; Buzzard 1990).

Within the context of media audience measurement, the adequacy of a particular sample size also is a function of the nature of the medium being measured. Specifically, the greater the number of content options available to any measured audience member, the greater the sample size that is necessary to measure the distribution of audiences across these content options. Thus measuring a medium such as 1960s-era television, in which the average household could receive four or five television stations, required a smaller sample than measuring the contemporary television environment, in which the average household can receive over seventy channels. Similarly, measuring audiences for a medium such as the Internet, with its hundreds of thousands of advertiser-supported Web sites, requires a larger sample than does measuring audiences for radio or television, where the number of available content options is much smaller.

Media with greater "channel capacity" create greater opportunities for the measured audience sample to be spread out across a wider range of content options. The fewer the number of participants from which the measured audience for a particular media product is derived, the less likely it is that the measured audience accurately reflects the actual audience for that media product (den Boon 1994). Consequently, media environments that offer more content options require a larger audience sample.

The current state of Internet audience measurement provides an extreme example that helps illustrate the measurement challenges posed by a media environment with enormous channel capacity. Nielsen NetRatings, one of the major Internet audience measurement firms, monitors a sample of roughly seventy thousand U.S. Internet users (more than 200,000 worldwide) in an effort to measure traffic to individual Web sites. The audience projections for many Web sites are estimated from the attention of only a handful of participants in the measurement process, given the wide range of content options available to the measured sample. These small numbers undermine the ability to project from this audience to the population as a whole (see Thompson et al. 2000). Other Web sites, which may be receiving thousands of visitors a day, will not even appear on the measurement radar, because the measurement participants, facing so many content options, visited none of those sites. In an effort to address this measurement challenge, comScore has assembled a panel of 1.5 million Internet users, in an effort to provide more reliable data on a broader range of Web sites and to facilitate more detailed demographic analyses (Hallford 2000). However, even with a panel of 1.5 million Internet users, there are still more Web sites than there are measured audience members, meaning that the majority of Web sites—if they show up in the data at all—are getting audience estimates that are based on a small number of participants in the measurement process.

SAMPLE REPRESENTATIVENESS

A central tenet of sampling is that a large sample does not guarantee a representative sample, that is, a sample whose demographic and behavioral characteristics reflect those of the population as a whole. Reasonably representative samples can be achieved by sampling a small portion of the overall population so long as the sampler uses rigorous sampling techniques.[1]

Any flaws in the sampling process can have serious repercussions for the quality of the audience data, producing data that provide a distorted picture of the broader population and its media consumption patterns. As Kent notes, "Systematic error arises where the sampling procedures used bring about systematic over or under-representation of certain types of people or types of households" (1994:11). Thus any sampling process that overrepresents or underrepresents certain demographic groups will produce data that provide a distorted picture of the actual media audience. Such distorted samples (and their associated distorted data) may be the result of a wide range of shortcomings, the most common of which are flawed selection procedures and refusals by selected participants (see Kent 1994).

Looking first at the issue of selection procedures, it is essential that all members of the population have the opportunity to be included in the sampling frame. A sampling procedure that neglects certain regions of the country—or certain types of households or individuals—will not provide an accurate picture of the population as a whole. For this reason audience measurement firms use such techniques as random digit telephone dialing (almost every household in the country has a telephone) and drawing random samples of housing units from census data to construct samples from which almost every individual in the country has an equal chance of being selected (Nielsen Media Research 2001c:3). It is important to emphasize, however, that even a perfect random sample will contain deviations from the population as a whole, as no sample is, by definition, a perfect representation of the broader population.[2]

Refusals among individuals or households sampled represent perhaps the biggest problem in audience measurement. An accurate and reliable sample depends upon the initial response rate. The more people in the sample agree to participate, the more that sample will reflect accurately the population as a whole. Thus two systems may each measure 50,000 households; however, if system A needed to approach 200,000 households (a 25 percent response rate) about participating, whereas system B needed to approach only 75,000 households (a 67 percent response rate), system B's data are inherently more reliable (assuming all other aspects of the measurement processes of the two systems are identical). This is because the type of people who are more likely to refuse to participate in the measurement process have characteristics, in terms of age, income, geographic location, or media consumption habits (see Bolton 1999a; Rubens 1989), that are different from those who are more likely to agree to participate (Poltrack 1988).[3] High refusal rates therefore bias the data in the direction of particular types of audience members. For this reason audience measurement firms usually will make repeated attempts to get the selected panelists to change their mind and agree to participate (see Media Metrix 2001).

Refusals have become a particular concern in recent years, as most measurement systems have seen their response rates drop. Probable reasons for this decline include increased concerns about personal privacy, increased telemarketing activity (which makes potential audience measurement participants more hostile to calls requesting participation), and the widespread use of telephone-screening technologies such as answering machines, voice mail, and Caller ID (see Gunzerath 2000). According to recent estimates, less than 40 percent of households approached to become part of the Nielsen Television Index agreed to participate (Ephron 2000). This response rate raises obvious questions about the representativeness of the Nielsen sample, and the drop in response rates (though they improved somewhat in 2001–2002) has led some to question the long-term viability of Nielsen's measurement system (Ephron 2000). Before being acquired by comScore, Media Metrix (2001) reported response rates in the 30 to 35 percent range for its sample of workplace participants in its Internet audience measurement system, though difficulties in obtaining permission to monitor Web usage in a workplace setting have resulted in workplace samples that are significantly smaller (roughly one-fifth the size) than at-home samples. Measurement firms use a variety of techniques in order to maximize the acceptance rates among those asked to participate, including token financial compensation, free merchandise, coupons, and sweepstakes (see Appel 2001; Hallford 2000). However, such incentives have had only a modest effect on the increasing unwillingness among consumers to participate in the audience measurement process.

Of particular concern to audience measurement firms is that certain demographic groups are less likely to participate than others, resulting in data that systematically misrepresent the media consumption patterns of these demographic groups. For instance, Nielsen Media Research has encountered substantial difficulties in achieving response rates among ethnic minorities that are comparable to the response rates within the broader population. Partly because of this pattern, in 1992 Nielsen instituted a separate Hispanic American television measurement service and associated samples and uses bilingual recruiters, diaries, and interviewers in an effort to bolster response rates within this demographic group (Nielsen Media Research 2001b).

MEASUREMENT TECHNIQUES AND TECHNOLOGIES

The challenges associated with generating an accurate sample are only the first in a series of challenges associated with maximizing the congruence between the measured audience and the actual audience. Measurement firms also must develop and implement measurement systems that accurately capture audiences' media consumption patterns. Doing so requires a system that can capture the full range of audience behaviors, with minimal input and responsibilities required of the participant, and that is not prohibitively expensive. A brief review of the evolution of electronic media audience measurement techniques and technologies illustrates these various concerns.[4]

Electronic media audience measurement began with the advent of radio broadcasting in the 1920s. Early pioneers in radio audience measurement, such as C. E. Hooper and Archibold Crossley, used such methods as telephone recall and telephone coincidental surveys (see Buzzard 1990). Recall surveys involved phoning a sample of households and asking respondents which programs they had listened to the previous day. Coincidentals, on the other hand, asked respondents to report which program they were listening to at the time of the call. These methods were limited by the extent of telephone penetration at the time. Recall surveys were further limited by the number of individuals who were at home to answer the phone. This was not a problem for coincidentals, as anyone not at home was not listening to the radio (listening to a car radio was not yet an issue, given the size of early radios). Coincidentals were limited by acceptable calling hours, as researchers could not phone households at midnight to determine whether anyone was listening to the radio.

Over time, telephone survey methods were replaced by other approaches, such as the audimeter and the paper diary, which were deemed more accurate and/or more cost effective (see Buzzard 1990).[5] The term *audimeter* in this case refers to a device that was connected to a radio and could record the channel to which the radio was tuned and compile a log of all set-tuning activity. The audience member then mailed the log to the measurement firm. After purchasing the rights to the audimeter from members of the faculty of the Massachusetts Institute of Technology in 1936, A. C. Nielsen began offering metered audience data to clients in 1942 (Buzzard 1990). Audimeters, while costly, provided a high level of accuracy in terms of radio set tuning. However, they could not provide demographic information about radio listeners. Paper diaries, in contrast, were less expensive and could record demographic information. The diary method initially became prominent in the 1950s (Buzzard 1990) and has remained the primary method of radio audience measurement to this day (see Arbitron 2001a). Both diaries and meters also went on to become significant components of television audience measurement.

The current system of radio audience measurement, as structured by Arbitron, the nation's primary source for radio audience data, works as follows: The firm uses random digit dialing to recruit participants. Households that agree to participate receive a separate diary for each household member aged 12 and older. Given that radio is predominantly a local medium, Arbitron measures audiences primarily at the local level, constructing separate samples for each of the 286 radio markets in the United States.[6] The sample sizes in each market vary in accordance with population size. Arbitron measures small markets with samples numbering in the hundreds and uses samples in the thousands to measure larger markets.[7] It measures large markets for twelve-week periods four times a year but measures smaller markets only twice a year. During these twelve-week periods the service expects participants to compile and return diaries that record one week's worth of radio listening. Participants must record the times at which they listened to radio (in fifteen-minute increments), the station names or call letters, and the place (home, work, car) where listening occurred (see Arbitron 2001a). Paper diaries are widely considered an inaccurate and outdated system of measuring media audiences (see "Fragmentation Face-off" 2001; Weiss 2001), and this system has changed little since in the 1950s.[8] However, as I discuss in chapter 5, substantial changes in the technology of audience measurement may be on the way.

As I noted earlier, in the 1950s television adopted many developments in radio audience measurement, such as the personal diary and audimeter (Buzzard 1990). Diaries and audimeters remain a prominent component of television audience measurement to this day. Television audience measurement also has seen the introduction of a more advanced audimeter. Dubbed the "people meter," this more advanced set-top device can measure not only the program to which a set is tuned but also the number and demographic characteristics of those watching the program (see Stoddard 1987). Unlike audimeters, people meters have individual buttons that are assigned to each member of the household. Each time family members start and stop watching television, they are supposed to log in and log out by using their personal button. Each family member's demographic data already are recorded, thereby allowing Nielsen to compile data on the size and demographic composition of the audiences for individual television programs.

Audits of Great Britain developed the first people meter in 1981. The meters first were installed in television households in the United Kingdom and Italy in 1984 and in Ireland in 1985 (Gane 1994), before the meters replaced audimeters for measuring national television audiences in the United States in 1987. Under the current system national television audiences are measured by placing people meters in a random sample of five thousand television households (about thirteen thousand people). Nielsen uses audimeters in conjunction with paper diaries to measure local television audiences. In fifty-five of the largest television markets, a random sample of four hundred to five hundred households (separate from the national sample) receives an audimeter. Nielsen augments set-tuning data at least four times a year with demographic data obtained from paper diaries kept by separate households (larger markets are measured more often than smaller markets). Together, the diary and audimeter data provide the basis for audience estimates in these large markets. In the remaining 155 television markets, Nielsen obtains viewing data only four times a year, by using paper diaries. Selected viewers use these diaries to record their viewing for the months of November, February, May, and July (the "sweeps" periods) (see Nielsen Media Research 2001c).

The variety of measurement techniques and technologies currently used to measure television and radio audiences all have clear strengths and weaknesses. Paper diaries, while slow to process, do have the benefit of being relatively inexpensive. They also are capable of capturing out-of-home radio and television consumption, which is particularly important for radio, given that a substantial amount of radio listening takes place in the workplace and in automobiles. This may help explain why radio audiences recorded by using diaries can be more than 30 percent larger than audiences recorded by telephone interviews (Menneer 1992). Diaries, however, require a high level of commitment and diligence on the part of the participant and thus are quite an obtrusive measurement system. Consequently, they also offer ample opportunity for error, in terms of both recall error and intentional misrepresentation.

Audimeters require little, if any, input by the selected participants, which is both a strength and a weakness. On the one hand, participants cannot misrecord or misrepresent their media consumption; on the other hand, audimeters cannot determine whether any audience members are actually seated in front of a television or radio that is turned on and tuned to a particular channel. Nor can audimeters provide any data regarding the number or types of individuals consuming a program. People meters require a bit more of participants than do audimeters, namely, that participants remember to log in and log out, but they do allow the measurement company to compile demographic data. Of course, people meters—along with audimeters—are much more expensive than diaries. In addition, they cannot record out-of-home media consumption, although Nielsen is trying to address this by installing meters in vacation homes and college dorms (Consoli 2002b). Unlike diaries, however, both audimeters and people meters can provide data quickly.

The continued use of so many different measurement techniques and technologies for television audience measurement is a reflection of the overall value of different segments of the television audience. That is, Nielsen has enough clients and revenues for national television audience data and audience data in large markets to justify the expense of installing and maintaining meters. In the smaller markets, where the overall revenue potential for the data is not as great, Nielsen uses less expensive methods such as paper diaries.

However, widespread displeasure with the diary method ("Fragmentation Face-off" 2001) and compelling evidence that diary data are less accurate than people meter data (Soong 1988) have compelled Nielsen to begin deploying "local people meters" (see Bachman 2001a; Lotoski 2000, 2001; see also chapter 5).[9] Currently in use only in the Boston television market, local people meters are identical technologically to the people meters used at the national level. However, they may replace the audimeter–paper diary hybrid system now used to measure local television audiences. Depending upon the results in Boston—and client receptivity to the new system—local people meters may be used in more large markets. However, it is highly unlikely that they will completely replace the diaries and audimeters any time soon, given the high costs of doing so.

Clearly, the quality and comprehensiveness of audience measurement systems are not limited solely by available knowledge and technologies. Market and financial considerations come into play as well (see P. Miller 1994; Rubens 1989). However, there is a bit of a chicken and egg issue here, as the quality of the audience data available affects the revenue potential for individual television markets. Markets measured entirely by diaries are less appealing to advertisers. As one advertising executive noted regarding the spot television market, "We can't put more money in spot unless we have 52-week data. I can't do it with a diary four times a year" (Bachman 2001a:7). As this statement suggests, the measurement system can negatively affect the revenue potential of an individual audience market.

The brief history of Internet audience measurement provides further illustrations of the technological and methodological challenges confronting measurement firms seeking to maximize the congruence between the measured audience and the actual audience. Even in its brief history, Internet audience measurement, like other electronic media measurement systems, has seen an evolution in the predominant measurement approach. The predominant measurement approach in the earliest days of the medium involved the analysis of server records, the internal records that Web site servers keep of traffic. Server records provide information about the number of total "hits" a site receives, the number of different systems or browsers that visit a site, and which links visitors to a site follow.

In recent years, however, Internet audience measurement has focused instead on user-based systems, which rely on monitoring software placed on the hard drives of a sample of the population of Internet users (see F. O'-Connell 2002; Media Metrix 2001). These systems are similar to the meter system of television audience measurement in that they require participants to log in appropriately and in that they can download and compile data on a daily basis.[10] The monitoring software that these services use can record a wide range of computer and Internet use activities, including Web page viewing, network file requests (e.g., advertisements, graphics, audio, and streaming media files), and which software application is "in focus" (i.e., which application is in use, as opposed to those that are open but minimized at the bottom of the screen). The companies measure use at the personal computer user's home and office, though workplace measurement is more difficult, given that many employers refuse to have the measurement software installed on their terminals. The measurement company downloads the data over the Internet or, in some instances, has the computer user store the information on disk and return it via conventional mail (see Media Metrix 2001).

This shift away from server records and toward user-based systems is a result of important limitations in the data derived from server records. First, server records provide no demographic data (see Lake 2000) and no information about the characteristics of the individuals visiting particular Web sites (Dreze and Zufryden 1998), though in some cases the data do yield the geographic location of visitors to the sites.[11] In addition, the degree to which server records can distinguish individual users is limited. Server records provide only a record of the visits of individual machines to particular sites, not the activities of individual members of the Internet audience. Thus server records can allow researchers to distinguish between individual computers visiting a site (through the use of cookies or IP addresses); however, they cannot distinguish between multiple individuals using the same terminal.[12] By the same token, when individuals visit a Web site from a number of different terminals—or from a number of different Web browsers or Internet service providers (ISPs)—the result can be an overestimation of the number of unique visitors to that site (Kalyanam and MacEvoy 1999; Media Metrix 2001).[13] In addition, server records do not record visits to Web sites that have been "cached" on the viewer's hard drive (Dreze and Zufryden 1998) or when sites have been cached locally by ISPs and visited by those ISPs' subscribers (Media Metrix 2001). Given that the most popular Web sites tend to be those most frequently cached by ISPs, this weakness tends to affect the more popular Web sites more significantly than the less popular sites.[14]

However, the server record approach also has strengths (see FitzGerald 2002). An important characteristic of server record data is that the data are not projections from any type of sample; rather, they are a rough count of the actual number of visitors to a Web site. As such, they are free of the problems associated with using a sample audience and ensuring viewers' compliance with the measurement process. Server records account for audiences worldwide, whereas user-based systems provide data only about the audiences within the countries in which the system is in operation (Media Metrix 2001; Nicholas and Huntington 2000). Similarly, server records can capture traffic from institutions and public terminals (such as schools, libraries, kiosks, and Internet cafes), whereas user-based systems generally capture only home and workplace usage. Perhaps most important is that user-based systems, with their limited sample sizes, cannot effectively measure the audiences for many Web sites, given the enormous number of Web sites. Consequently, for many Web sites, server record data are the only meaningful source of audience data available to them or to advertisers considering advertising on sites that have audiences smaller than the reliability threshold for user-based systems. Thus although the major Internet audience measurement firms are using user-based approaches, server record data continue to play a prominent role in the market for Internet audiences (Collins and Bhatia 2001; Lake 2000).

It is important to note that these different approaches to measuring electronic media audiences generally result in quite different portraits of the audience. For television, research has shown that when a market switches from the diary system to a diary-audimeter hybrid, HUT levels (the percentage of television households using television) generally increase. These HUT-level increases do not, however, affect all programmers, dayparts, or programs equally. Affiliates of the newer networks generally experience gains in audience share, as do independent stations. HUT levels for some dayparts can increase as much as 85 percent over diary-measured levels.[15] Game shows as well as many talk shows exhibit declines in overall household viewership, as well as declines within many demographic segments, after a market makes the transition to a diary-audimeter hybrid system (*Introducing Meters* 2000). All these changes ultimately can affect how and where advertisers spend their dollars as well as the decisions that program schedulers make.

For the Internet, estimates of unique visitors based on server log file data can range from two to five times that of the user-based approaches (Media Metrix 2001). One study found that significant discrepancies in site rankings generally begin after the top three to six sites and that discrepancies between the two systems generally are larger for sites with less traffic (Kalyanam and MacEvoy 1999). Thus the particular measurement system used can have significant ramifications for the portrait of the measured audience for individual Web sites. The existence of such discrepancies ultimately undermines the confidence of all participants in the audience marketplace in the validity and reliability of the data that provide the basis for audience transactions. For this reason there always is pressure within audience marketplaces for a single system of audience measurement that is subscribed to, and accepted, by both the buyers and sellers of audiences (see chapter 1).

AUDIENCE COOPERATION IN THE MEASUREMENT PROCESS

Any system of audience measurement depends upon the participants in the process to interact with the system in an appropriate manner. This issue refers not to the percentage of individuals or households sampled who agree to participate but to the percentage of participants who accurately and conscientiously record their media consumption activities. Even a highly advanced measurement system (such as the people meter) is dependent upon the participants to use the technology conscientiously and appropriately. Otherwise, the data will not reflect the behaviors of the actual media audience.

Unfortunately, just as consumers' general willingness to participate in the measurement process has declined, so too has the cooperation level of those who do agree to take part. For instance, the percentage of those who agree to keep a diary who actually return their diary to Nielsen or Arbitron dropped throughout the 1990s (Downey 2001). Nielsen has seen some improvement recently (largely as a result of methodological improvements and increased financial incentives), although not so much that concerns about the accuracy of the data have disappeared. As I noted earlier, low levels of participation at any stage in the process create biases in the data and undermine congruence between the measured audience and the actual audience. As with the initial decision to take part in the measurement process, levels of cooperation among willing participants often vary along demographic lines. Arbitron, for instance, finds that 18- to 24-year-old blacks and Hispanics, as well as nonethnic men of the same age group, are particularly unreliable about returning diaries. For this reason Arbitron typically offers higher cash premiums to these groups in the hope of increasing cooperation rates.

In addition to the problem of underparticipation is the problem of inaccurate participation. Diaries, in particular, require quite a bit of diligence from participants. Participants must record accurately each day's television or radio consumption, recalling details such as the time they spent viewing or listening, the channel they watched or listened to, and the name of the particular program. The opportunities for error in this process are many, particularly if (as research shows) many participants opt to fill out their entire diary—which records a week's worth of television or radio consumption—the evening before they must return the diary to the measurement firm for tabulation. Obviously, inaccurate or incomplete participant recall becomes a significant factor affecting the extent to which the measurement data reflect actual audience behavior.

Even the people meter, which was intended to alleviate nonparticipation and participant-induced error, has encountered accuracy problems. The biggest problem involves participants who fail to log in and out of the system appropriately (McKenna 1988; Milavsky 1992). One study found that, on average, about 10 percent of participants exhibit some form of noncompliance with the people meter system at any time (e.g., logged in but not viewing, viewing but not logged in, etc.).[16] Noncompliance varied according to demographic factors such as age and income, with lower compliance levels for older and lower-income viewers (Danaher and Beed 1993).[17]

The possibility for straight-out lying also exists, and this is something that not even the people meter can protect against. Participants may misrepresent their media consumption habits—or even the number of people consuming a particular media product—in an intentional effort to distort the data. They may feel uncomfortable revealing their true media consumption habits, or they may seek to promote favorite programs or stations, even when they are not viewing or listening. An extreme example of such behaviors occurred in 1997 and involved an Albany, New York, television station. In this case an enormous spike in the station's ratings ultimately was attributed to a station employee who was among the Nielsen participants.[18] This employee had falsely reported that nine adults had each watched an average of 13.5 hours of television per day, most of it on the employee's station (Fine 1998).

As this discussion shows, the cooperation (or lack thereof) of those participating in the measurement process is a key source of error in the production of measured audiences. As some audience researchers have noted in regard to television, "The ideal television-audience-measurement system would use an automatic measurement method that required no active involvement on the part of the people living in sampled homes" (Lu and Kiewit 1987:9). Researchers have investigated a variety of sophisticated measurement technologies, some of which are now being tested, in an effort to further limit the extent to which active and conscientious participation is necessary. The key implication of these tests is that, in addition to the challenges associated with sampling audiences and developing technologies for measuring audiences, audience measurement firms must maximize the degree to which measured audiences properly participate in the process. Lack of participation and improper participation are additional factors that work against the congruence between the measured audience and the actual audience.

CONTENT AUDIENCES VERSUS ADVERTISEMENT AUDIENCES

As should be clear from this review of the predominant audience-measurement systems used in the United States, audience measurement typically focuses on measuring the audience for a particular piece of media content, not on measuring the audience for the advertisements embedded within the media content. Media planners generally distinguish between "vehicle exposure" (the number of people exposed to the media content) and "advertising exposure" (the number of people exposed to the media content who also are exposed to the advertisement) (see Ephron et al. 2001). It is important to recognize that these two audiences can, in fact, be quite different. Audience members who logged in to a people meter or who recorded in their diaries that they watched a particular program, or listened to a particular station, may have left the room during commercial breaks or briefly switched to another station. One study found that 38 to 43 percent of prime-time television viewers leave the room during commercial breaks (see Ephron et al. 2001). Similarly, an individual who acknowledges having read a particular issue of a magazine did not necessarily flip through every page and see every ad. Researchers estimate that 15 percent of the average issue's readers do not see the average page (Media Dynamics 2001a).

These are just some means by which content audiences and advertisement audiences will diverge. However, because most audience measurement systems are oriented toward measuring content audiences, not advertisement audiences, content audiences generally are the currency of exchange.[19] Not surprisingly, advertisers would prefer measurement systems that accurately measure advertising exposure. Such systems would provide a more accurate picture of the number of audience members actually exposed to an advertising message and would facilitate pricing accordingly. The American Association of Advertising Agencies recently formed a task force to push for industry-wide implementation of television commercial ratings (Consoli 2001b). However, systems oriented toward measuring and reporting vehicle exposure persist, primarily because of the (well-founded) fear within the media industries that a shift in measurement systems would undermine existing pricing systems (Ephron et al. 2001).

COPING WITH UNCERTAINTY IN AUDIENCE MEASUREMENT

The high level of uncertainty regarding the degree to which measured audiences provide an accurate and reliable reflection of actual audiences affects the behavior of participants in the audience marketplace. Generally, participants must devise means of coping with the uncertainty. The decision-making processes and buying and selling patterns of marketplace participants reflect these coping mechanisms.

Consider, for instance, the process of buying and selling cable television audiences, and recall that the reliability of audience data generally increases with the size of the sample. The data for media products with large audiences generally are more reliable than the data for media products with small audiences. Within the cable television industry the ever-growing number of channel options means that individual channels or programs often receive minuscule ratings. The cable industry and its advertisers cope with the high levels of uncertainty inherent in these small ratings by aggregating ratings across programs or time periods. Thus an advertiser will not purchase time on a single program but on a number of different programs, thereby reducing the random variation (Phalen 1996).

Similarly, in the syndicated television marketplace, where programs often air five times a week, buyers often will purchase time during the entire week rather than on a single broadcast. The volatility and unreliability of small-audience syndicated programs also has led syndicators to increase the degree to which they overestimate the audience size for a program. According to interviews with advertising and television industry professionals conducted by Phalen, syndicators use overestimation of ratings as a means of compensating for the smaller ratings and larger margins of error for these programs (1996:85).

Perhaps, however, the most prevalent, and most important, mechanism for coping with the inherent unreliability of the measured audience is an almost irrational willingness to accept the data as accurate. Indeed, although many advertisers, media organizations, and media planners are aware of the limitations of audience measures, they seldom consider these limitations in day-to-day practice. As long as all participants in the transaction treat the data as accurate, the inherent unreliability of the data has no significant effect on the exchange. The marketplace conveniently overlooks the estimated nature of all measures and instead perceives and treats them as the "truth" (Gitlin 1983). One critic of audience ratings has gone so far as to call measured audiences a "fictive entity" (Ang 1991:60) that participants in the audience marketplace embrace in an effort to bring order and objective rationality to the highly complex and subjective process of audience interaction with media. Lewis has described television advertising, in particular, as "a science based on specious data" (2000:11–12). As Gitlin noted in regard to network television, "When Nielsen publishes its figures . . . it reminds subscribers of the standard errors, but executives functionally forget what they were taught in elementary statistics: That all survey statistics are valid only within predictable margins of error. . . . Once managers agree to accept a measure, they act as if it is precise. They 'know' there are standard errors— but what a nuisance it would be to act on that knowledge" (1983:53). To facilitate this sort of acceptance of unreliable data as reliable, participants in the audience marketplace often operate under the assumption that the errors are relatively constant and that the figures will therefore at least accurately reflect change over time (Phalen 1996).[20]

Because participants in the audience marketplace generally treat the measured audience as a reliable representation of the actual audience, a program with a rating of 11.5 typically will be able to charge higher advertising rates than a program with a rating of 11.3, although this difference in ratings may fall well within the margin of error. The program with the 11.3 rating may actually have had a larger audience than the program with an 11.5. Similarly, programmers generally will regard a change in a program's rating from 11.3 one week to 11.5 the next week as a sign of improvement, although the second week's audience may indeed have been smaller (see Gitlin 1983).[21] Marketplace participants use similar practices in coping with the inconsistencies between content audiences and advertisement audiences. As Ephron and colleagues (2001) note with regard to the television industry, "Current practice is to assume that the average-minute program audience and the average commercial audience are the same" (2001:206).

Thus participants in the audience marketplace often cope with the incongruities between measured audiences and actual audiences by generally choosing to ignore the problem. Given that the audiences being bought and sold remain a statistical abstraction throughout all stages of the transaction, as long as both buyers and sellers agree to accept these abstractions as valid, the inconsistencies do not undermine the value of the audience product or the efficiency of the audience marketplace.

However, when major participants in the audience marketplace begin to call the accuracy of these measurements into question, the value of the audience product and the vitality of the audience marketplace are in jeopardy. For instance, many advertisers question the accuracy of Internet audience data, which has a negative effect on the overall value of Internet audiences (Fattah 2000). However, instances of participants' actually focusing on the differences between the measured and actual audiences and allowing these differences to affect their behavior in the audience marketplace are relatively rare. Instead, the more common tendency is for all participants in the audience marketplace to treat the measured and actual audiences as congruent, although they know better. This tendency is central to what happens when changes in the techniques and technologies of audience measurement affect the structure and behavior of media institutions: All participants in the audience marketplace internalize and accept the new system's revised depiction of the measured audience and change their behaviors accordingly.

AUDIENCE MEASUREMENT, MEDIA COMPETITION, AND MEDIA EVOLUTION

The dynamics of the process of audience measurement do not affect only how participants in the audience marketplace assess and purchase the audience product. Audience measurement also has profound effects on the structure and content of the media institutions participating in the audience marketplace. A central relationship in the audience marketplace is that between audience measurement and the competitive dynamics, institutional arrangements, and content decisions of media organizations. Changes in the techniques and technologies of audience measurement significantly affect the structure and behavior of media organizations and media industries, as well as their relative economic vitality. Indeed, audience measurement plays a central role in the economics and evolution of media industries (see generally Donato 1996).

First, it is important to note that the very presence of an audience measurement system is central to a medium's efforts to gain legitimacy and financial stability relative to other media. Any new medium that receives all or part of its revenues from the sale of audiences to advertisers has little or no economic viability until an established, accepted, and perceived-to-be reliable system of audience measurement is in place. In this most basic way audience measurement provides the lifeblood for any new or developing medium. Turow has described the introduction of such systems as "the watershed for a developing medium" (1997:170).

As Ang notes in regard to the early days of radio:

When the economic foundation of broadcasting in the United States was being established, advertisers were sceptical about the use of radio as a medium that could enhance sales of consumer products. What needed to be demonstrated was the very existence of an audience. Clues for radio's grip on people were available, for example, in the nationwide nightly suspension of "normal life" during the broadcast of the comedy series *Amos 'n Andy* at 7 P.M., and in the enormous amount of fan mail for radio stars and programmes. . . . But these impressionistic cultural indications of radio's popularity were not satisfactory to the advertisers: they wanted systematic and objective evidence. (1991:55)

That was why the advertising industry underwrote the first system of radio audience measurement (Beville 1988; Buzzard 1990). Only after this measurement system was established and accepted by both advertisers and programmers was radio able to establish a financial foothold in the audience marketplace (Spalding 1963–64).

We see a similar pattern in the development of cable television. As the cable industry developed in the 1980s, it became clear that the existing system of television audience measurement could not capture adequately the intricacies of the highly fragmented cable television audience (see Rubens 1984). This kept many advertisers from considering cable television as a legitimate advertising vehicle (Barnes and Thomson 1994). As one advertising executive noted, "For cable to achieve its potential as an advertising medium, it must move swiftly to establish more credible and accurate reporting of audience measurement" (Benvenuto 1987:72). As I will discuss later, only with the introduction of the people meter did cable television become well established as a legitimate advertising medium, because of the people meter's ability to provide more accurate and reliable data regarding the cable television audience (Barnes and Thomson 1994).[22]

New media technologies, such as satellite radio and the Internet, currently are seeking legitimacy as means of selling audiences to advertisers. The satellite radio broadcasters XM Satellite Radio and Sirius Satellite Radio contracted with the radio research firm Statistical Research, Inc., to provide measures of satellite radio audiences in an effort to "establish satellite radio as a bonafide advertising medium" (Bachman 2000b:10). The continued lack of an accepted standard for Internet audience measurement, along with evidence of severe disparities among the different measurement techniques (see Kalyanam and MacEvoy 1999), has contributed to severe advertiser suspicion regarding the reliability and accuracy of these data and a consequent hesitancy to invest in Internet advertising (Dreze and Zufryden 1998; Fattah 2000; V. O'Connell 2001; Taylor 2002). Although this problem is quite severe in the United States, it is even more severe in international markets, where systems of audience measurement are even less developed (Helft 2000). A good example of the continued resistance to the Internet as an advertising medium is data showing that although the Internet represents 12 percent of U.S. media consumption, it represents less than 3 percent of overall U.S. advertising expenditures (Lefton 2001). As history demonstrates, until advertisers feel confident that Internet audience measurement data are providing a reasonably accurate and reliable picture of Web site audiences, the Internet will be unable to establish itself as a significant supplier in the audience marketplace (Dreze and Zufryden 1998).

Advertisers are not the only group that relies on audience measurement data to determine its level of commitment to a new medium. The investment community relies heavily upon these data as well (Thompson et al. 2000), because audience ratings provide a useful index of the revenue potential for a particular media outlet or media organization (Webster, Phalen, and Lichty 2000). Research focusing on the factors affecting the valuation of Internet companies illustrates this point. One study found that Web site traffic data accounted for 77 percent of the variation in the acquisition prices paid for forty-two Internet firms, with acquiring firms paying an average of $167 for each monthly visitor. This study also found a significant positive relationship between audience traffic and stock prices (Rajgopal, Kotha, and Venkatachalam 2000). A similar study also found significant correlations between audience size and stock prices, with a Web site's overall reach (i.e., number of unique visitors) and stickiness (i.e., average time a viewer spends at a site) as the particular traffic measures of significance (Demers and Lev 2000).[23]

Thus audience data clearly provide the economic foundation for advertiser-supported media. What is of particular importance to this discussion, however, is how the nature of the audience measurement process affects the structure and behavior of media institutions. At the most basic level media always have responded to the dictates of the measurement process. Some television stations end their 10 P.M. news broadcasts at 11:03 P.M. so that the sports segment (the final segment of the broadcast and, apparently, the least popular) will not negatively affect the station's ratings for the final quarter hour of prime time.[24] Broadcast television networks traditionally air their most expensive and/or most appealing programming—and remove (either permanently or temporarily) underperforming programming—during each of the four one-month "sweeps" periods (November, February, May, and July), in an effort to boost the performance of their local affiliates while their audiences are being measured (Flint 2001; Weiss 2001). Local stations also alter their content during sweeps; the most obvious example is the extent to which local newscasts generally focus on more sensational topics during sweeps periods (M. Ehrlich 1995; Moritz 1989). In addition, local stations increasingly use "stunting," which involves using promotional gimmicks such as contests and cash giveaways, to inflate viewership during sweeps periods (Murphy 2001), despite Nielsen rules prohibiting such activity.[25] Obviously, such abnormal programming practices are likely to provide a distorted view of the typical audience size for individual programs (Weiss 2001), particularly given that, in most markets, the data obtained during the four one-month sweeps periods are the only data available to advertisers for the entire year. As one advertising researcher has noted, "Advertisers buy time on stations 365 days a year, yet we have no idea what ratings are for most of the year when there aren't those hyped, big-event programs" (Weiss 2001:2). One advertising industry study has estimated that stunting can increase a station's sweeps period audience as much as two ratings points over its nonsweeps period audience (Murphy 2002). For this reason buyers often will demand discounts from the rates established by sweeps data (McClellan 2002).

Radio stations engage in similar tactics to take advantage of the dynamics of the radio audience measurement process. Arbitron reports radio audiences in quarter-hour increments but requires that a listener listen to a station for only five minutes to be included as a listener for a particular quarter hour. Consequently, stations often will schedule no commercials for the first five minutes of each quarter hour. This tactic is intended to maximize the station's quarter-hour audience, even if many listeners actually switched to another station once the commercials started (McDowell and Dick 2002).

Similar efforts to manipulate audience ratings are emerging on line, where "pop-up" ads are being used to inflate traffic numbers for Web sites. The uncertainty about whether such measured exposures warrant being counted as such is reflected in the different decisions that Nielsen NetRatings and Jupiter (now comScore) Media Metrix made in 2001 regarding the legitimacy of Web site audiences obtained through pop-up ads. Jupiter Media Metrix counted all pop-up ad exposures as exposure to the Web site, and Nielsen NetRatings did not (Thompson 2001).[26]

Media organizations also will aim their programming and marketing only at those audience members taking part in the measurement process. As Meehan notes in regard to broadcasting, "It would be irrational for broadcasters to program for any viewership other than the fixed and semi-predictable sample" (1984:223) measured by the ratings services. A similar point has been raised regarding Internet audiences, with one executive stating that at company strategy meetings "people discuss 'how do we target our ad buys to be sure that we reach people monitored by Media Metrix' when we should be saying, 'How can we more effectively target our ads to reach business buyers?'" (Thompson et al. 2000:183). As one radio industry consulting firm emphasizes to its clients, "Your ratings are based on an unusual percentage of the population. Learn how to market to them, and your hard earned marketing budget will become a powerful weapon in the world according to Arbitron" (Bolton 1999b:2; see also Bolton 1999a). In other words, programming for the *actual* audience is a less prudent strategy than programming only for the *measured* audience.

A few examples illustrate the implications of the distinction. Consider, for instance, the constant repetition of radio stations' call letters throughout the broadcast day. This is not primarily a device to help general audience members recall the station so that they are more likely to listen to that station next time. Rather, the primary function of this repetition is to assist those audience members who are part of the Arbitron sample so that they later fill out their listening diary correctly (MacFarland 1997:67).[27]

Consider also recent controversies involving television stations that aired promotional spots targeted specifically at viewers who were part of the Nielsen sample. One short promotional spot, aired by WSAV in Savannah, Georgia, during its 6 P.M. newscast, stated simply, "You're watching News 3 at 6 on WSAV. If you have a ratings diary, please write it down now" (McClellan 2000:12). The station ran similar spots during its broadcasts of *Oprah* and *Today*. A Hattiesburg, Mississippi, station ran longer spots featuring the station's news personalities that told viewers: "If you're keeping track in a television diary which programs you are watching this week, write us down. . . . Without you, we wouldn't be able to continue providing 22 Daily News at 5, 6 and 10 P.M. So if you've got a television diary or know someone who does, make sure, write us down, talk us up; we always want to be here for you" (McClellan 2000:12). As a result of the increasing incidence of these flagrant attempts to affect the behavior of the measured audience, Nielsen Media Research instituted a new policy: Stations that promote directly to measured households receive a warning for their first violation and are deleted from the relevant quarter's ratings book for their second violation (McClellan 2000; "Nielsen Chastises KSWB-TV" 2000).

Arbitron has similar policies for radio stations that engage in activities such as "rating distortion" or "rating bias" (Arbitron 2001b). The company defines rating distortion as any "station activity that Arbitron believes may affect the way diarykeepers record their listening, so that recorded listening differs from actual listening" (Arbitron 2001b:5). Examples of rating distortion include soliciting diary keepers to misrepresent their listening behaviors or engaging in promotional activities that encourage such misrepresentation.[28] Rating bias is any "announcement, statement, or activity that may differentially prompt listeners to a particular station to participate in Arbitron's survey (relative to listeners to other stations)" (Arbitron 2001b:7), such as announcements regarding an upcoming measurement period or indirect appeals encouraging listeners to participate in the measurement process. As these examples show, the patterns and processes of audience measurement clearly affect media organizations' programming and marketing strategies.

The processes of audience measurement also affect competitive dynamics within the media industries. For instance, the audience measurement process can systematically favor some categories of media organizations or the production of some forms of content over others. For instance, for years television industry researchers assumed that Nielsen's system of television audience measurement was biased in favor of broadcast viewing and against cable. As I noted earlier, before the introduction of the people meter, Nielsen measured national network television audiences by using both paper diaries and audimeters. The audimeters recorded household viewing data, while the diaries yielded the demographic data. Nielsen placed audimeters in a sample of fourteen hundred U.S. homes and used them in conjunction with the data from a comparable number of diaries (Barnes and Thomson 1994). Cable television audiences were measured in a similar manner, combining audimeter data with diary data gathered from 100,000 local market diaries distributed during the sweeps periods.

This system was thought to favor broadcast television for several reasons. First, the diaries contained inadequate space for listing all cable channels. In addition, the diaries did little to overcome viewer confusion in recalling and differentiating among the large number of cable channels (see Beville 1988). According to Soong, given that diaries rely on recall, they have a tendency to "understate certain programs of low salience (such as independent stations, public television stations, and cable channels) and to overstate certain programs of high salience" (1988:54). One cable industry–sponsored study estimated that the diary system underestimated cable audiences by an average of 37 percent (Cable Television Advertising Bureau and Nielsen 1983). Perhaps most important, the small sample of audimeters used to compute cable ratings was widely considered insufficient to reliably and accurately capture the increasingly fragmented cable audience. Thus the system measuring television audiences that was in place until the mid-1980s effectively was biased against channels targeting small, homogeneous niche audiences and in favor of channels targeting traditional mass audiences (i.e., larger, demographically diverse audiences). Niche programmers suffered until the introduction of the people meter in 1987 brought greater precision to the measurement of small audiences and to the measurement of audience demographics.[29]

A similar problem plagues Internet audience measurement, where sample sizes (of about seventy thousand) used by the major measurement firms generally are deemed insufficient for accurately and reliably capturing the distribution of U.S. audiences across the enormous range of content options available on line, as well as for providing reliable data on the demographic composition of the audiences for individual Web sites (see Hallford 2000). Even with panels of sixty to seventy thousand people, it is essentially impossible to analyze the traffic of Web sites that receive fewer than 200,000 unique viewers per month (Hallford 2000). Thus under the existing system of Internet audience measurement, only the audiences for the most popular Web sites can be measured with any degree of reliability (Foan 2001; Hallford 2000; Leckenby and Hong 1998). Consequently, content providers seeking to take advantage of the Web's virtually unlimited channel capacity and serve a narrow niche audience will find that, regardless of the value of that particular audience segment to advertisers, the lack of audience data means that such an enterprise is not as financially viable as an effort to target a broader audience. As both the television and Internet examples suggest, the smaller niche content providers suffer disproportionately as a result of the limitations of the measurement process.[30]

Audience researchers frequently have documented a phenomenon known as double jeopardy. Content options with small audiences (jeopardy factor 1) also suffer from having audiences that are less loyal than content options with larger audiences (jeopardy factor number 2) (see Barwise and Ehrenberg 1988; Sabavala and Morrison 1977; Waterman 1986). These audiences are less loyal because of such factors as lower levels of awareness and appreciation (Danaher and Lawrie 1998; Donthu 1994). Thus the notion of the "small but loyal" audience is largely a fallacy. Instead, content that appeals to a niche audience faces not only the inherent economic handicap of its small audience but also the handicap of audiences' lower levels of commitment and sustained interest. The challenges of measuring media audiences suggest that expanding this double jeopardy concept to the level of triple jeopardy might be appropriate because the systems of audience measurement further undermine the economic prospects for content with narrow audience appeal.

Audience measurement systems, once established, are not static. Audience measurement systems evolve and improve, and these changes in the techniques and technologies of audience measurement can have significant economic repercussions for the media organizations whose content is being measured. It is widely understood that changes in the behavior or composition of media audiences (see Bower 1985) are likely to result in changes in media content, as media organizations attempt to account for—and capitalize upon—these changes in their content production decisions. Thus it is not surprising that television genres that are particularly successful in one season are more abundant in the following season (McDonald and Schechter 1988). Nor is it surprising that, for example, as the composition of the daytime television audience changed from primarily housewives to a mix of housewives and college students (as more women entered the workforce), the content of daytime soap operas changed to reflect these younger demographics (Cantor and Cantor 1986). Similarly, as this country has grown more ethnically diverse, more minority-focused media outlets and programming have developed (Wilson and Gutierrez 1985). However, the point I am making here is fundamentally different—specifically, that changes in the process of measuring media audiences—separate from whatever audience behavior or composition changes are taking place—can produce substantially different portraits of the behavior and/or composition of media audiences that media organizations then respond to in their content production decisions. Thus given that media organizations respond to measured audiences that can vary in the extent to which they reflect actual audiences, changes in audience measurement alone can produce changes in the structure and behavior of media organizations.

Changes in the system of television audience measurement in the 1980s provide a useful case in point. In the fall of 1987, when Nielsen introduced the people meter, the company also increased the national sample from fourteen hundred homes to four thousand homes. At the most basic level the introduction of the people meter improved cable's status as an advertising medium relative to broadcast by bringing greater statistical reliability to cable data because of the larger sample size.

Other effects of the people meter were even more profound. The people meter produced a portrait of the television audience that was substantially different from the one produced by the old approach. Specifically, the people meter showed that the television audience had more men, children, and teenagers than the earlier methods had indicated (see Ang 1991; Soong 1988). This is because these demographic groups, in particular, had lower levels of compliance with and participation in the diary method.

The introduction of the people meter also facilitated an expansion in the number of demographic classifications that Nielsen could use, given the larger sample size. Greater detail in the demographic delineations among the television audience facilitates greater targeting by advertisers and hence greater content specialization among programmers. Thus the increasing channel capacity provided by cable television would not necessarily have resulted in the increasingly demographically specific programming that we see today had it not been accompanied by a measurement system able to accurately and reliably capture increasingly narrow demographic distinctions (see Barnes and Thomson 1988).

Finally, the people meter presented a substantially different picture of how television audiences were distributed across available content options. Specifically, the introduction of the people meter coincided with an overall decline in prime-time broadcast network television audiences of roughly three ratings points—beyond the gradual pattern of decline that had been exhibited until then—and a comparable increase in cable television audiences (Adams 1994; Milavsky 1992). The people meter alleviated the difficulties associated with the diary, in terms of accurately recalling and recording cable television viewing, and led to a drastically revised view of the distribution of audiences across cable and broadcast program options.

Research suggests that these changes in the nature of the measured audience, in terms of both audience demographics and distribution—produced by changes in the process of audience measurement—significantly affected the competitive dynamics between the cable and broadcast television industries. After the introduction of the people meter, cable became a much more attractive medium to advertisers (Clarkin 1990). As one executive noted three years after the introduction of the people meter, "In the past, when the information we had on cable was limited, we were more likely to buy a certain daypart or run a schedule. . . . Once people meters started being used and we've had better and more timely reports, we've been able to look at program-by-program information, not just in terms of age and sex, but also income, family size and other market descriptions" (Clarkin 1990:48). Research by Thomson (1990) found that the introduction of people meters contributed to an increase in what specialized cable networks such as ESPN and CNN could charge advertisers for their audiences. Overall, the revenues for specialized cable networks (which benefited most from the revised measurement approach) increased an estimated 22 percent in the wake of the introduction of the people meter. Thus changes in the system of television audience measurement facilitated the rise of one media technology (with its associated content characteristics) and the decline of another by altering the playing field in terms of the quality and reliability of the audience data available for each medium and by altering the accepted wisdom regarding the size and composition of the measured audiences for each medium.

Such interactions between audience measurement and media evolution are not unique to electronic media. Barnes and Thomson (1988, 1994) document similar patterns within the magazine industry. They attribute the rise of highly specialized magazines and the decline of mass-circulation magazines such as *Life* and *Look* not only to the rise of television (the conventional wisdom) but also to the development of sophisticated methods of providing more detail on the demographic composition of magazine audiences. Of particular importance was the increasing power and affordability of computers in the 1960s and the associated ability of advertising agencies to process and analyze more data in more sophisticated ways (Barnes and Thomson 1988, 1994). Again, the central point is that audience measurement techniques and technologies achieved the means to satisfy advertisers' natural demand for highly specific demographic data; consequently, media products could then develop that were not only financially viable but thrived because they presented content that appealed to—and attracted—narrow audience demographics. Thus media content again changed in response to the means by which audiences were measured, with the measurement system's ability to provide a more detailed demographic picture again serving as the key mechanism for change.

In the radio industry the increasing format diversity that has characterized the industry is largely a product of "increasingly sophisticated ratings reports that included more detailed demographic information" (MacFarland 1997:73). Once advertisers and programmers could more reliably and accurately identify these smaller, more homogeneous audience segments, developing more narrowly focused programming that appealed specifically to these newly visible demographic niches became viable.

As a final example of the processes by which audience measurement changes can affect the structure and behavior of media organizations, consider how changes in the system of measuring recorded music audiences affected the content provided by the recorded music industry and its associated industries (radio and music television). While this example takes us outside the realm of advertiser-supported media to a certain degree, it is relevant to the extent that it illustrates the central process at issue here—the process by which changes in audience measurement create associated changes in the structure and behavior of media institutions. As Peterson (1994) notes, in 1991 *Billboard* magazine stopped measuring records' popularity by using reports from a sample of retail store managers and instead began using sales data automatically reported by an electronic system installed in record stores. According to Peterson, "With this new reporting system, the sales of country and rap records were shown to be much greater than reported by the old system, and Garth Brooks, a country music performer, was shown to be outselling such hot acts as Guns 'n' Roses, Nirvana, Def Leppard, Michael Jackson, Kris Kross, and Hammer" (1994:172).

On the surface it may be difficult to see how changes in how *Billboard* magazine composed its popularity charts could affect content decisions in the music industry, given that the record companies' sales and inventory data no doubt made clear the popularity of rap and country performers. However, when we extrapolate the probable consequences of this change, the effects on the structure and content of the music industry become clear. First, the sudden appearance of these genres and artists at the top of the charts no doubt generated substantial publicity and an associated bandwagon effect (i.e., people purchasing a product in which they previously had no interest because it has become popular) that is common in consumer behavior (Biddle 1991). Additional "multiplier effects" that affected sales included the price discounts and preferential displays given to albums on the charts (Shandler 2001). Thus sales for these genres benefited from their appearance at the top of the charts. Next, consider the probable behavior of associated advertiser-supported media, such as music video television channels and radio stations, which became more inclined to play this music, given documented evidence of its popularity (particularly given that many of these outlets rely on the *Billboard* charts in determining their playlists). Indeed, the increased air play of rap and country music since the 1990s could be attributed in part to this more public evidence of their popularity. The increased television and radio play for these genres no doubt provided an additional boost to sales. Thus these genres became a more lucrative market segment, inspiring record companies to produce more content of these types. These logical cause-and-effect relationships suggest that changes in the measurement system for recorded music audiences probably had a profound effect on content production decisions and format variety in the radio and recorded music industries.[31]

In sum, all these examples illustrate a central point made by Barnes and Thomson, that "the *measurement* of audience behavior, not audience behavior per se, changes the media" (1994:78). Absent a system of audience measurement that provides perfect congruence between the measured audience and the actual audience, the competitive dynamics and evolution of media institutions will continue to be a function of the process of audience measurement.

CHAPTER 4

AUDIENCE VALUATION

An increasingly important characteristic of the audience marketplace is that advertisers place different values on different members of the media audience. Advertisers seek to place their messages within content whose audiences represent the most likely consumers of their product. These presumptions regarding the probable consumers of certain products have a significant influence on how much advertisers are willing to pay for different audience segments. Audiences that are more likely to purchase the advertised product will be more expensive than audiences that are less likely to purchase the advertised product.

Typically, these presumptions about probable purchasing habits are based on various demographic factors, such as age, gender, and income. While this logic seems relatively straightforward, the factors that affect the valuation of media audiences are more extensive and more complex than is commonly realized. Audience demographics are only one of many factors that affect the value of media audiences. Other relevant factors include marketplace structure, the value that audiences place on media products, and technological and structural characteristics of the media.

Given that advertisers value different media audiences differently, it stands to reason that content providers factor these valuations into their content decision making. Thus at the most basic level content providers will, to a certain degree, focus on producing media products that appeal to the most highly valued, and therefore most lucrative, audience segments. However, here again the process and its implications are more extensive and complex than often is realized. The specific effects that these differential audience valuations can have on content can have wide-ranging social and political implications, involving issues such as media violence, the political functions of journalism, and the overall source and content diversity of the media system. Underlying all these issues is that the nature of advertiser valuations of the media audience can contribute to a media system that provides exceptional service and a wide range of content options to highly valued segments of the audience while largely neglecting less valued segments. Unfortunately, these neglected segments of the audience tend to be those who consume media most frequently and/or those who would benefit most from content directed at their particular interests and concerns.

The issue of audience valuation and its effect on media institutions is increasing in importance, given that the increased fragmentation of the media system and the increased sophistication of audience measurement systems have—to this point—enhanced media organizations' abilities to target and monetize narrow homogeneous audience segments. Increased channel capacity of course increases the degree to which audiences can be distributed across a wide range of content options according to their particular demographic makeup. When this increased channel capacity was coupled with measurement systems such as the people meter (see chapter 3), the extent to which advertiser valuations of different audience segments could drive content decisions increased.

In eras of fewer media options and lower channel capacity, extensive audience segmentation was not technologically or economically feasible. Consequently, despite their desire to target narrow demographic groups, advertisers were forced to rely on the more basic metric of raw audience size in their efforts to reach their target demographics. In such an environment audience value was almost exclusively a function of audience size (see Peterman 1971). As a result content decisions were not as heavily based on questions of which media products would attract the desired audience demographics. Thus it is important to recognize that the evolution of media and audience measurement technologies increased the degree to which audience valuations affect the structure and behavior of media institutions and—most important—the nature of the content they provide.

FACTORS AFFECTING AUDIENCE VALUE

Policy concerns typically have driven research on the factors affecting the value of media audiences.[1] Policy makers seeking to preserve and enhance competition and diversity within the media industries frequently have found it necessary to investigate the audience marketplace and how various marketplace and institutional factors affect the value of media audiences. As I noted in the introduction, advertiser-supported media operate in a dual-product marketplace, comprised of both content and audience markets. Success or failure in the audience market is dependent upon success or failure in the content market and vice versa. For this reason traditional media policy objectives, such as enhancing and protecting competition and diversity of sources and content within the media industries (see Napoli 2001b), can be affected by how various market and institutional factors affect what media organizations are able to charge for their audiences (e.g., Besen 1976; Fisher, McGowan, and Evans 1980; Ofori 1999; Peterman 1971). When media organizations fail to remain viable in the audience marketplace, their failure can lead to fewer sources of information, less diversity of content, and a marketplace of ideas that is less dynamic. Thus the long-standing goals of preserving competition and diversity in the marketplace of ideas (i.e., the content marketplace; see Napoli 1999b) and preserving competition in the audience marketplace (see Peterman 1971) are linked in important ways.

MARKET FACTORS

The dynamics of the particular market in which media audiences are being bought and sold affect their value. As I noted in chapter 1, geography and product characteristics define audience markets. From a geographical standpoint audience markets can be local (e.g., local television or radio markets) or national (e.g., national cable and broadcast networks). From the standpoint of product characteristics, various demographic classifications delineate the different audience markets. For instance, MTV and CBS do not, for the most part, participate in the same product market, given the different demographic compositions of the audiences that they attract and sell (although some advertisers would be interested in reaching both older adults and teenagers and young adults).

However particular audience markets may be defined, the structural characteristics of individual audience markets—particularly the level of competition within them—can have a significant effect on the value of the audiences being bought and sold. Thus an audience sold in a highly competitive market, which would have a large number of suppliers of audiences, is likely to be valued less than an identical audience (in terms of size and composition) sold in a less competitive market. Thus, for instance, analyses of the factors affecting the value of local broadcast television audiences frequently have taken into account competitive conditions such as the number of television stations in the market (e.g., Bates 1983, 1991; Besen 1976; Wirth and Wollert 1984), the number and/or circulation of newspapers (Poltrack 1983), and levels of cable penetration (Bates 1991; Wirth and Wollert 1984). Such factors provide an indication of the degree to which advertisers purchasing broadcast television audiences have other options available to them, both within broadcast television and within other media. Generally, the prominence of competing media has a negative effect on the value of broadcast television audiences (Bates 1991; Poltrack 1983; Wirth and Wollert 1984). This pattern suggests that audiences delivered by one medium can, to a certain degree, be substituted for audiences delivered by another medium. Although the empirical research that has addressed the issue of audience substitutability across media directly is relatively sparse (Seldon and Jung 1993), a number of studies have found varying levels of substitutability across the audiences delivered by different media (e.g., J. Ferguson 1983; Reid and King 2000; Smith 1995, 1998).[2]

Another market factor that has received far less attention than the dynamics of competition is the nature of the measurement system within a particular market. Some markets are measured more thoroughly and reliably than others. For instance, the larger local television markets are measured with a combination of audimeters and paper diaries, whereas smaller markets are measured only with diaries. Moreover, the ongoing transition to local people meters (see chapter 5) is likely to occur only in the largest television markets, increasing the quality gap in audience data between small markets and large markets. Similarly, as on-line measurement services attempt to globalize their service, their initial service in foreign markets has focused first on those markets with the highest levels of computer penetration and the most developed economies. As a result the Internet audience data in some countries is of a much higher quality than in other countries. Arbitron measures larger radio markets more frequently than it measures smaller markets, which means that more recent data are available for advertisers purchasing audiences in larger markets.

Such disparities in measurement systems are an outgrowth of how much revenue the measurement firms think they can bring in from each market (see chapter 3). The key issue at this point, however, is that lower levels of accuracy, timeliness, and reliability of data in certain markets can drive down the price that advertisers are willing to pay for audience members in these markets. Webster and Phalen (1997) demonstrated that advertisers will pay more for television audiences in markets where audimeters are used than for markets measured only by diaries. This finding is consistent with the assumption that audiences in markets with lower-quality audience measurement systems represent higher levels of risk and uncertainty in terms of estimated audience reach. This, of course, ultimately means a lower level of presumed congruence between the measured audience and the actual audience.

MEDIA FACTORS

The characteristics of individual media outlets or content options to which audiences are exposed also affect the value of media audiences. At the most basic level the market may value different media audiences differently on the basis of its perceptions of the differences in the effectiveness of messages delivered by the different media (Boivin and Coderre 2000; Cannon 2001). For instance, for 2000–2001 the cost-per-thousand for men aged 18 to 34 ranged from an average of $77.35 on prime-time network television to $10.70 on network radio to $26.60 in weekly newsmagazines to $52.05 in daily newspapers (Media Dynamics 2001b). Thus the cost of reaching one thousand demographically similar viewers can vary significantly across media. Of course, other factors can come into play in affecting these cross-media variations (such as average income levels, etc.); however, advertisers' assessments of the strengths and weaknesses of various media for delivering different types of messages (see Media Dynamics 2001b) do enter the calculus in determining the value of different audiences (see Surmanek 1996).

Differential valuations based upon technological characteristics can occur not only across media but within media. For instance, UHF television stations traditionally have earned less for their audiences than VHF stations (Bates 1983; Besen 1976; Fisher, McGowan, and Evans 1980). While the transmission characteristics of UHF stations limited their audience size relative to VHF stations, the lower value for UHF audiences persisted even when controlling for audience size (Fisher, McGowan, and Evans 1980)— the poorer reception quality of UHF signals made UHF stations less appealing to advertisers than VHF stations. The "UHF handicap," which encompassed the limitations that UHF transmission technology place on both the size and value of UHF audiences, became a major policy concern because it undermined policy makers' efforts to increase the number of television outlets and the range of content options available to citizens (see Besen 1976; Park 1971, 1972).[3] Today the UHF handicap has been reduced significantly by the penetration of cable television, which eliminates any signal quality distinctions between UHF and VHF stations for the subscriber and expands the audience reach of many UHF stations.[4]

A comparable situation exists in radio, where the superior sound quality of FM broadcasts relative to AM broadcasts generally has enabled FM broadcasters to earn more on a per-audience-member basis than their AM counterparts, all other things being equal. In many markets today AM stations are facing economic hardships reminiscent of those faced by early UHF broadcasters. The inability of AM broadcasters to charge as much for their audiences as FM broadcasters can undermine their ability to invest in programming and compete effectively in the audience marketplace.

Nontechnical media factors also can affect the valuation of media audiences. Perhaps the most important example involves differences in ownership or affiliation characteristics across media outlets. For instance, although it long has been recognized that network-affiliated stations are more lucrative than independent stations (Besen 1976)—because the affiliates attract larger audiences and receive payments from the networks to air their programming—evidence also exists that network affiliates earn more on a per-audience-member basis than independent stations (Bates 1983; Wirth and Wollert 1984). Further, some evidence suggests that group-owned television stations may be able to charge more for their audiences than independent stations (Wirth and Wollert 1984), although stations that also own radio stations or newspapers in their market have not been shown to be able to charge more (Peterman 1971; Wirth and Wollert 1984). In print media evidence exists that chain-owned newspapers are able to charge more for their audiences (controlling for other factors) than independent papers (Busterna 1988a). Possible explanations for this phenomenon include greater information available to chain newspaper managers to use in setting prices and the market power that chain-owned newspapers may achieve and use to exact higher rates from national advertisers (Busterna 1988a).[5]

Finally, characteristics of individual content options can affect what advertisers are willing to pay for audiences for those products. For example, levels of audience appreciation for certain media products or the levels of attentiveness or involvement that they command frequently are associated with variations in advertising effectiveness, because an audience's appreciation or attentiveness is likely to affect its recall of an advertisement or perceptions of the advertised product (see Lynch and Stipp 1999). For instance, one recent study found that advertisements placed immediately after exciting television programs scored higher in terms of audience attitudes toward the advertisement (McGrath and Mahood 2001). This process, labeled *excitation transfer* (see Mattes and Cantor 1982), suggests that advertisers can improve their effectiveness by considering the nature of the program into which their ad is placed. Similar studies have found that ad recall is stronger for advertisements placed in comedy programs than in suspense programs (Kennedy 1971) and that more positive evaluations of advertisements were associated with ads placed in programs with upbeat themes or comedic situations (Goldberg and Gorn 1987; Petty et al. 1993). The most obvious manifestation of such findings in advertiser behavior is some advertisers' unwillingness to advertise on news broadcasts, given the possibility that a downbeat story will lead into a commercial break (Beatty 2001b).[6]

Attentiveness and involvement figured prominently in Nielsen Media Research's controversial "Quad Study" which analyzed a sample of broadcast and cable programs and segmented their audiences in terms of overall frequency of viewing and time spent viewing. Thus viewers who watched a program frequently and who generally watched a large portion of each episode were designated "Gold Card" viewers.[7] Broadcast programs generally had larger proportions of Gold Card viewers than cable programs. This led broadcasters to argue that programs with greater proportions of Gold Card viewers were more valuable because the audience was paying more attention (and hence would have greater advertisement recall) and were likely to be associated with greater loyalty and commitment to particular programs (see Weissman 1999). Not surprisingly, the cable industry disputed such interpretations, arguing that such data did not effectively gauge viewers' states of mind, that the segment definitions were arbitrarily constructed, and that different interpretations of the viewing data were possible (Cable Television Advertising Bureau 1999; Weissman 1999).[8]

Similar issues have arisen in the print media, where what constitutes an audience member for a print publication has been controversial. Traditionally, the Audit Bureau of Circulations (ABC) counted as paid circulation only those magazines sold for at least half the cover price. The underlying assumption is that consumers who receive a publication for free, or for a very low price, are less likely to read the publication and be exposed to the advertisements or to read the publication as intently. Consequently, advertisers should not be required to pay for such audience members. Copies sold for less than half the cover price traditionally have not been included in the calculus that publications use in determining their advertising rates. However, in 2001 the ABC adopted a "paid at any price" rule, which allows any magazine not distributed for free to be included in circulation totals (M. Miller 2001). The ABC instituted a similar rule change for the newspaper industry. For newspapers the ABC changed the old cutoff of 50 percent of the cover price to 25 percent (Granatstein 2000, 2001). The ABC also requires publishers to report the net average price paid for the product. Publishers are concerned that such data could factor into negotiations in the audience market. As one publishing executive noted, "The concern is that buyers will use this [information] as a way of negotiating beyond what they already use. . . . You'll have Chrysler sitting there saying it looks like a third was sold for less than a dollar, so we'll only pay you for two thirds [of the rate]. . . . But that's ridiculous because you don't do that with TV. A pair of eyeballs is a pair of eyeballs" (Granatstein 2000:44). In such a scenario the price paid for the publication essentially would be used as a measure of attention, and the valuation of audiences would vary in accordance with the extent to which they paid the full price for the publication.[9]

DEMOGRAPHIC FACTORS

As I noted at the outset, the central issue in audience valuation involves advertisers' different valuations of different components of the media audience on the basis of their demographic characteristics. Analyses of the influence of demographic factors on audience valuation generally have taken either a market-level or an outlet-level approach. Market-level approaches involve examining the demographic composition of entire media markets (e.g., average age or income levels within geographically defined radio or television markets) and the effects of these demographic factors on what advertisers pay for audiences within these markets (e.g., Poltrack 1983; Webster and Phalen 1997).[10] Outlet-level approaches involve examining the demographic composition of the audiences for individual media outlets (e.g., the demographic composition of the audiences for individual radio stations) and the effects of these demographic factors on audience value (e.g., Koschat and Putsis 2000; Ofori 1999; Waterman and Yan 1999).

Whether at the market or outlet level, the three most basic demographic factors that affect audience value are age, gender, and income. These demographic characteristics are presumed to correlate with behavioral patterns pertaining to product-purchasing and media consumption habits. These product-purchasing and media consumption patterns are the true source of the variation in advertiser valuations. However, because most predominant systems of audience measurement do not link individual audience members' media consumption habits with their product-purchasing behaviors, demographics are the proxy used by both advertisers and content providers (see Monistere and Zimmerman 2001).

Looking first at the issue of age, younger audience members (e.g., those aged 18 to 49) generally are more highly valued than older audience members (e.g., those older than 50).[11] This is partly because consumers in the 18-to-49 age bracket are believed to spend the most on various consumer goods.[12] The media and advertising industries generally characterize younger consumers as spenders, whereas they characterize older consumers as savers. Thus younger consumers are believed to be more likely to act upon an advertisement. Although the 18-to-49 age bracket (and, more narrowly, the 18-to-34 age bracket) is generally the most highly valued by advertisers, teenagers are becoming an increasingly valuable segment of the media audience, mainly because of their increasing numbers in the population and their increasing purchasing power (Salamon 2001). This increase has been attributed in part to their greater purchasing autonomy, which has arisen from the increasing prominence of dual-career and single-parent households (Turow 1997).

Such changes within certain demographic categories can have a significant effect on advertisers' valuations of different audience segments. These valuations can change over time as the nature of the population changes or as advertisers' perceptions of different demographic segments change (see Bower 1985; Turow 1997). For instance, as the baby boom generation ages, elderly baby boomers are likely to be valued more highly than previous generations of seniors, because of their different spending habits, more active lifestyles, and different interests (see Vickery et al. 2001).

However, consumption patterns can only partially explain the high values placed on certain age brackets. Research suggests that the high valuations of these demographic groups may be far out of proportion to the extent to which their consumption patterns differ from the norm. For instance, Koschat and Putsis (2000) show that magazine readers aged 29 to 39 cost 7.5 times more than readers in other age brackets. However, consumers in this age category consume only 1.5 times as many goods and services as consumers in the least-valued age category (older than 53).

Thus other factors must be at work to explain the enormous differences in the values of these different audience segments. One of the most commonly cited factors is the presumption that older consumers already have established high levels of loyalty for specific brands of products, whereas younger audiences are not believed to have established such strong allegiances. Thus advertisements are believed to be less likely to sway older consumers (Turow 1997). In addition, capturing and retaining younger consumers, with their multiple decades of product purchasing ahead of them, represents a much more lucrative accomplishment than capturing older consumers who, even if they are persuaded to switch brands, will purchase that brand for a much shorter period of time (see Koschat and Putsis 2000). Finally, older audiences may be less valued than younger audiences because of their higher levels of media consumption. Older consumers' greater availability in the media audience means that they are easier to reach, which drives down their value to advertisers (Koschat and Putsis 2000).

Gender is another factor that can affect audience valuations, although the effects of gender are highly dependent upon the nature of product being advertised. Advertisers often value women highly because they typically make the majority of household purchasing decisions (Waterman and Yan 1999). However, women generally consume more media than men. The greater ease associated with reaching women exerts downward pressure on their value, while the greater scarcity of men raises their value to many advertisers (Reinholz 2000).

The other primary demographic factor that affects the valuations of media audiences is income. Advertisers typically value audiences with larger incomes more highly than they value audiences with smaller incomes (Berry and Waldfogel 1999; Bowman 1976; Fisher, McGowan, and Evans 1980; Kalita and Ducoffe 1995). Some products and services are likely to be purchased only by consumers of certain income levels, or higher-income consumers may be higher-volume purchasers of certain products. For this reason advertisers frequently will use income as a variable by which to screen out certain media outlets. If the average income of the audience for a particular media outlet or program is deemed too low to represent likely consumers, the advertiser is likely to advertise elsewhere.

However, as is the case with age, the extent to which purchasing habits alone drive the higher valuations of high-income audiences is questionable. Research examining the magazine industry shows that readers with incomes higher than $56,000 cost 6.2 times more than readers in other income brackets, whereas consumers in this income category consumed only 2.7 times as many goods and services as consumers in the lowest income category (less than $21,500). On the basis of these results the authors conclude that "consumption flows alone can explain only a small portion of the premium paid for these segments" (Koschat and Putsis 2000:228). Again, the issue of the greater scarcity of higher-income consumers in the media audience arises as a possible explanation.

An additional demographic factor that may affect audience value is ethnicity. Ethnicity may factor into audience valuations for several reasons. To a certain degree ethnicity correlates with income. The median family income for whites is almost $46,000, compared to approximately $30,000 for African Americans and $33,000 for Hispanics (U.S. Census Bureau 2001). However, research suggests that ethnicity has a downward effect on audience value that is independent of income (Ofori 1999; Webster and Phalen 1997). A number of factors may explain this phenomenon. Blacks and Hispanics consume significantly more television and radio on a weekly basis than whites (Nielsen Media Research 2000; Radio Advertising Bureau 2001). As is the case with the other demographic factors discussed thus far, the greater ease with which minority audiences can be reached by advertising messages may reduce their value to advertisers (Ofori 1999). Real or perceived differences in product-purchasing habits between whites and nonwhites may reduce further the value of minority audiences (Ofori 1999).

It is important to emphasize that these demographic variables affect the value of media audiences largely because they are presumed to serve as effective surrogate measures for product-purchasing intentions and behaviors (Stoddard 1986:RC14). That is, the advertiser values a certain demographic group on the assumption that members of that demographic group exhibit a certain type of product-purchasing behavior. Demographics therefore function as a presumably effective substitute for the data that advertisers truly require—data on product-purchasing habits and product-purchasing intentions (see Schroeder 1998). This indirect method of targeting consumers creates a situation in the audience marketplace where audiences are "continually looked at as Women 18–49 or Men 25–54 when specific consumption or intent to purchase targets are more appropriate" (Monistere and Zimmerman 2001:1). As this statement suggests, it is important to recognize that "in any age/sex demographic, there is a percentage of the audience that is in [a] product's true target and a percentage that is not. Conversely, there is a percentage of [a] product's true target that exists in a different age/sex demographic" (Monistere and Zimmerman 2001:1). The extent to which this is the case raises questions about the validity of demographic targeting as a means of reaching desired consumers.

A growing number of studies show that demographic data in fact do a poor job of predicting purchasing patterns, accounting for as little as 2 percent of the variance in consumers' purchasing behavior (D'Amico 1999; Schroeder 1998; Surowiecki 2002). As these numbers suggest, audience purchases based upon demographic data are not necessarily efficient in reaching the true target audiences for various products and services (D'Amico 1999; Monistere and Zimmerman 2001). As Assael and Poltrack note, "If demographics are not reliable surrogates of purchase behavior, then they cannot be regarded as reliable criteria for media selection" (1996:74). Thus just as the processes of audience forecasting and audience measurement are rife with uncertainty (see chapters 2 and 3), so too is the process of audience valuation. The valuations of audiences on the basis of demographic distinctions bear an uncertain relationship to the true value of these audiences to advertisers. And just as the audience marketplace often ignores questions surrounding the accuracy of the various systems of audience measurement, the marketplace often ignores questions about the value of demographic distinctions to the audience-purchasing process.

Research has demonstrated that media planning based upon product-purchasing data would be much more efficient and effective than planning based upon demographics (Assael and Poltrack 1991, 1993, 1999; J. Jones 1995), even when the planners use highly extensive demographic delineations (Assael and Poltrack 1994). However, the reliance on demographics as a proxy for purchasing patterns and intentions persists because most major audience measurement systems do not provide consumer behavior data;

or, if they do, such data generally are produced with less frequency than demographic data, or only for select markets, or the data only are available at significant additional expense. Measurement firms such as Nielsen and Arbitron experimented with offering such "single-source" data; however, they discontinued these programs (see Assael and Poltrack 1996).[13] The costs of gathering such data across the full range of desirable product-purchasing behaviors and intentions are enormous, which makes it difficult for such services to remain viable (D'Amico 1999; Surmanek 1996). Compiling representative samples of sufficient size to match content exposure with purchasing behavior—even for products for which purchase incidence is low— is particularly expensive and difficult (Assael and Poltrack 1996). Moreover, research suggests that imposing upon panel participants the responsibility of recording both their media consumption and their product purchases represents too high a burden. As a result participation levels decline to levels that undermine the validity and reliability of the data (Darkow 1996).

However, the fault for the absence of single-source data does not lie entirely with the measurement services. Some within the advertising industry contend that the industry has a low level of awareness of how poorly demographic classifications predict consumer behavior (D'Amico 1999). Moreover, the complexity that media buyers would face in coordinating media buys across a range of clients (each offering differing products and services and seeking their own unique "true target" audience) would increase dramatically. One study found that when media buyers had access to product-purchasing variables, they largely ignored the information in favor of traditional demographic variables, leading the authors to question the intensity of demand for such data (see Hulks and Santini 1994). Assael and Poltrack (1993) suggest that economies of scale may exist in demographic buys that outweigh the increased effectiveness of using purchasing behavior data in reaching target consumers (see also Stoddard 1986). During the participant observation research that I conducted for this study, media executives repeatedly stated that the majority of the research associated with media buying is handled by young, low-paid, inexperienced personnel who are not likely to engage in the type of sophisticated analyses such data would facilitate (and require)—and that even much of the available audience demographic data go unused.[14] This combination of factors may contribute to what David Poltrack of CBS describes as "a kind of ritualistic, inertial quality to the way ads get bought" (Surowiecki 2002:40). Consequently, advertiser demand for behavior-focused audience data probably has not reached a level that would motivate the research firms to supply such data.

From the standpoint of the media organizations that are selling audiences, any move toward audience measurement systems that focus on product-purchasing behaviors and intentions probably will cost them money. Under the current system advertisers value entire demographic groups. Under a behavior-based measurement system advertisers would probably be able to devalue a broader range of audience members, whereas whether the increased value of "true target" audience members (as identified by behavioral measures) would compensate media firms for the lost revenue is questionable. Imagine, for instance, McDonald's negotiating advertising rates on the basis of the number of viewers or listeners who have eaten at McDonald's in the past month, as opposed to on the basis of demographic categories. For media organizations such an economic model does not seem clearly preferable to the current system.

Moreover, the processes of developing, promoting, and distributing media content would have to change radically. These processes no longer could be guided by evidence and assumptions regarding the content preferences of various demographic groups (e.g., that men aged 18 to 49 like action movies). Instead, product-purchasing behaviors and intentions would serve as the basis for developing and presenting content. For example, instead of developing programs that appeal to men aged 18 to 49, television programmers would have to develop shows that appeal to fast food consumers or new car purchasers. Given the diversity of advertisers, and the diversity of consumer behaviors, it is unlikely that any comparatively systematic mechanisms of content development, promotion, and distribution could effectively be built upon an audience measurement and purchasing system that linked media consumption patterns with consumer behavior instead of demographics. Thus media organizations are unlikely to demand radical changes to the demographically focused systems now in place.

Finally, although this discussion has focused on demographic factors, it is important to note that the raw size of an audience may affect audience value on a per-audience-member basis (Fisher, McGowan, and Evans 1980; Harvey 1999), with larger audiences worth more on a per-audience-member basis than smaller audiences. In their analysis of the factors affecting the CPMs for cable television audiences, Waterman and Yan (1999) found that cable networks with smaller audiences tended to exhibit smaller CPMs, even when controlling for the demographic characteristics of these audiences. On the basis of these findings the authors concluded that "limitations on the TV household reach of cable networks have—so far—overwhelmed the narrowcasting advantages that cable networks appear to have in targeting more sharply segmented demographic or special interest groups" (654) (see also Kieschnik and McCullough 2000). A more recent study conducted by MTV Networks found that broadcast television's share of advertising revenues is 53 percent higher than its audience share, while cable's share of advertising revenues is 60 percent lower than its audience share (M. Larson 2002).

Such patterns may result from the efficiencies derived from engaging in fewer transactions in order to reach the desired number of consumers. This premium also may be derived from evidence that audience attentiveness and commercial recall are higher within higher-rated programs (Harvey 1999). Or, it may arise from the value that advertisers associate with the greater probable audience reach of a single ad placement (Fisher, McGowan, and Evans 1980; Higgins and Romano 2002). In the case of two ad placements some people may be in both audiences (unless the advertisements ran simultaneously on different channels), in which case the overall reach is lower than the single ad placement's. As a result the value of one million audience members reached by a single program or publication may be greater than that of one million audience members reached by a combination of two or more programs or publications. Finally, larger audiences maybe valued more highly because the measurement of large audiences has greater accuracy and reliability. As I discussed in chapter 3, most measurement systems provide more accurate and reliable data for larger audiences than they do for smaller audiences. Advertisers are willing to pay a premium for this greater accuracy and reliability (Webster and Phalen 1997).

MEDIA AUDIENCES ARE NOT COMMODITIES

Thus an extensive array of factors affects the value of media audiences. For this reason no two media audiences are perfect substitutes for each other. Despite this, researchers and professionals involved in the audience marketplace frequently have used the terminology *audience commodity* when discussing media audiences (e.g., Jhally 1982; Meehan 1984; Murdock 2000; Smythe 1981; Webster and Phalen 1997). Such terminology oversimplifies the complex nature of media audiences as economic products and the broad range of factors that affect their value. A commodity is, by strict definition, a product that is interchangeable with other products of the same type. As I have shown, the range of factors that affect audience value means that few (if any) audiences are likely to be of exactly the same type and are thus not likely to be perfectly interchangeable. Instead, audience products are highly differentiated across a broad range of factors

Moreover, even in the hypothetical instance in which two audiences are identical across all relevant market, media, and audience factors, they are still not likely to be perfectly interchangeable. From an advertiser's standpoint no two individual audience members—no matter how similar—are perfect substitutes for each other. As Wildman notes, "From an advertiser's perspective, two (or any number of) demographically identical viewers are not economic substitutes for each other because having access to one does not diminish the value to an advertiser of having access to the other" (1998:587). This is because each audience member represents an additional sales opportunity for the advertiser. Reaching audience member A should have no effect on an advertiser's desire to reach audience member B, as both represent potential purchasers of the advertiser's product.

Take, for example, UPN's strategy for selling the audience for its (now-canceled) *Star Trek: Voyager* program. The network emphasized to potential advertisers that the audience for the *Voyager* series was unique in that many of its viewers watched television only on Wednesday nights at 9 P.M., when *Voyager* aired (Consoli 1999). The thinking behind this sales tactic was that the *Voyager* audience had value regardless of the extent to which demographically similar audiences were available elsewhere, because none of those other audiences contained the individual consumers whom advertisers could reach by buying time during *Voyager*. In sum, to refer to media audiences as commodities neglects not only the wide range of factors that affect the value of aggregate audiences but also the perspective of the purchasers of audiences: that no two individual audience members are perfect substitutes for one another.

AUDIENCE VALUATION CASE STUDY:
MINORITY AUDIENCES AND COMMERCIAL RADIO

Policy concerns have driven the majority of research on the value of media audiences. A recent policy concern requiring audience valuation research involves the viability of minority-owned media outlets and media outlets that target minority audiences. A growing body of evidence suggests that advertisers place significantly less value on minority audiences than nonminority audiences (Ofori 1999; Rodriguez 2001; Webster and Phalen 1997). The implications for the viability of media outlets that target minority audiences are significant, because minority-targeted content faces a significant hurdle to remaining economically viable.

The general policy imperative behind the concern about the viability of these media outlets stems from policy makers' long-standing commitment to diversity in the sources of information and the content that these sources provide (Baynes 1999–2000; Napoli 1999a). The diversity principle extends, in part, from traditional democratic theory—that a democracy requires a well-functioning marketplace of ideas in which citizens' abilities to participate effectively are contingent upon their abilities to consider a wide array of ideas and viewpoints from a wide array of sources (Napoli 1999b; Sunstein 1993). Diversity concerns have economic motivations as well, because policy makers have sought to maximize the choices available to media consumers, thereby increasing their overall satisfaction (Entman and Wildman 1992; Napoli 1999b).

The pursuit of diversity objectives typically has taken the form of efforts to increase the diversity of sources, because policy makers generally have presumed that increasing the diversity of sources of information will lead to a greater diversity of content (Baynes 1999–2000; Napoli 1999a). This presumption has received empirical support (Mason, Bachen, and Craft 2001; R. Rogers and Woodbury 1996). Analysts have shown that minority-owned media outlets are significantly more likely to present minority-targeted content than are majority-owned outlets (Dubin and Spitzer 1995; Mason, Bachen, and Craft 2001; Ofori 1999).[15] Thus policy makers have considered the preservation and promotion of minority-owned media outlets to be an important means of pursuing diversity of both sources and content. As the Federal Communications Commission noted as far back as 1948, "It has long been an established policy of . . . the Commission that the American system of broadcasting must serve significant minorities among our population" (1948:15). Research has demonstrated that minority audiences focus much of their media consumption on minority-targeted programming and minority-owned outlets—and even increase their media consumption—when such services are available (Ofori 1999; R. Rogers and

Woodbury 1996; Waldfogel 2000), suggesting that the target audience values such content.[16]

Recent data, however, show that minorities own less than 4 percent of the full-power commercial radio and television stations in the United States, although they comprise roughly 29 percent of the population (National Telecommunications 2000). As a result of such disparities there is a fairly extensive history of policies designed to promote minority ownership of media outlets and the production of minority-targeted media content. Policies such as minority preferences in broadcast license allocation and tax certificates for the sale of broadcast outlets to minority-controlled organizations are just a few of the mechanisms that policy makers have pursued (see National Telecommunications 2000).

The Supreme Court has overturned some of these efforts (*Adarand Constructors, Inc., v. Pena* [1995]), and Congress has repealed others (Self-Employed Health Insurance Act of 1995), yet the promotion of minority-owned media outlets has remained a priority of both Congress (Communications Act of 1934, sec. 309(j), and subsequent revisions) and the Federal Communications Commission (1996).[17] The Telecommunications Act of 1996 directed the FCC to identify and remove market-entry barriers for small telecommunications firms and businesses owned by minorities and women.[18] In pursuing this mandate, the FCC commissioned a series of studies that addressed various dimensions of the potential barriers affecting the ability of minority-owned media and telecommunications firms to enter the market (e.g., Bachen et al. 1999; Ivy Planning Group 2000; KPMG 2000a, 2000b; Ofori 1999).

As the congressional directive suggests, policy makers increasingly are concerned that minorities face significant hurdles to having their ideas and viewpoints reflected in media content and to acquiring ownership of commercial media outlets (see National Telecommunications 2000). These concerns have received empirical support from the FCC's commissioned studies. Among the findings are that (a) discrimination limits minorities' access to the necessary capital to launch and maintain minority-owned media outlets (Ivy Planning Group 2000); (b) the FCC is more likely to hold comparative hearings on license allocations with minority applicants than it is for licenses allocations with no minority applicants (KPMG 2000a); and (c) minority applicants were less likely to win a license than nonminority applicants, even when controlling for other explanatory factors (KPMG 2000a).[19]

The FCC's research initiative also found that the lower values that advertisers place on minority audiences relative to majority audiences also may be a barrier to the viability of media outlets that target minority audiences (Ofori 1999). A survey of minority broadcast station owners found that selling advertising time was the most common difficulty that these broadcasters faced (National Telecommunications 2000). Evidence from an FCC-commissioned study suggests that advertisers value minority audiences at significantly lower levels than they value majority audiences (Ofori 1999). This means that the decisions of advertisers can undermine policy makers' objective to increase minority-targeted content.

METHODOLOGY

Policy research has demonstrated thus far only that media outlets providing minority-targeted *content* (i.e., formats that primarily appeal to minorities) are less able to monetize their audiences (Ofori 1999). So far, no research has directly examined the actual demographic composition of the audiences of these media outlets to determine whether a significant relationship exists between audience ethnicity and audience valuation.[20] The study I present here attempts to fill this gap by analyzing a sample of commercial radio stations.

Given the nature of the policy issue, this analysis uses a dependent variable—the power ratio—that provides an indication of the extent to which an individual station is capable of monetizing its audience. Power ratios are computed by dividing a radio station's share of total radio-advertising expenditures in its market by its share of the total radio-listening audience in that market. Thus a power ratio greater than 1 suggests that a station is able to capture a share of advertising dollars that exceeds its share of the total audience. Such a station is "overselling" its audience. A station with a power ratio of less than 1 is capturing a share of advertising dollars that is lower than its share of the listening audience. Such a station is "underselling" its audience. Because the power ratio controls for audience share, it provides a measure that is especially well suited to assessing the effect of audience composition on audience value. The power ratio data come from the 1999 Media Access Pro commercial database produced by BIA Research.[21]

I also have maintained an emphasis on audience composition for the independent variables. I regressed station power ratios for 1999 against Arbitron data from fall 1999 on the demographic composition of individual stations' audiences. Thus instead of incorporating each station's ratings or share points, or the raw number of listeners for the different demographic groups that are listening to each station, this analysis uses percent composition data (for similar approaches, see Koschat and Putsis 2000; Waterman and Yan 1999). Arbitron provides data on the percentage of each station's audience that is comprised of various demographic groups (according to age, gender, and ethnicity; see Arbitron 1996). Thus, for example, station A's audience may be 40 percent African American, while station B's audience may be 80 percent African American. Clearly, such figures provide no information about which station has the larger number of African American listeners. Station A may reach more African Americans than station B, if station A's total audience is much larger.

I decided that using pure composition figures was most appropriate, given the nature of the dependent variable (see Koschat and Putsis 2000). Using raw numbers or rating/share points would not address as effectively the issue of the viability of media outlets that target media audiences, given that these outlets are not defined in terms of audience size but in terms of the extent to which the composition of the outlets' audiences consist of minorities.

Arbitron breaks down each station's audience by gender within seven age categories.[22] Arbitron provides data on the average quarter-hour percentage of each station's (6 A.M. to midnight) audience that is comprised of each demographic group. For the purposes of this analysis I collapsed these demographic groups to produce two independent variables: the percentage of a station's audience comprised of men aged 18 to 54 (MEN1854) and the percentage of a station's audience comprised of women aged 18 to 54 (WOM1854). These two demographic categories roughly represent the audience groups with the highest demonstrated value to advertisers (see Hamilton 1998; Webster and Phalen 1997). Thus I expected to find a positive relationship between MEN1854 and WOM1854 and station power ratios.

I used broadcast band as a dummy variable (AM/FM; 0 = AM; 1 = FM) to account for the likelihood that FM stations are able to charge more for their audiences than AM stations, because of the better sound quality of FM signals (National Telecommunications 2000). Another independent variable that I used was the station's average quarter-hour share (6 A.M. to midnight) of the listening audience (SHARE) in order to account for the possibility that advertisers were paying a premium for larger audiences, independent of the composition of those audiences.[23] Although this analysis focuses on the issue of audience composition, as I noted earlier, research has suggested that advertisers will pay more on a per-audience-member basis for larger audiences (Fisher, McGowan, and Evans 1980; Waterman and Yan 1999).

To capture the ethnic composition of each station's audience, I used the two composition-based ethnicity variables provided by Arbitron. The first of these is the percentage of a station's average quarter-hour audience that is African American (AQBLACK). The second is the percentage of a station's average quarter-hour audience that is Hispanic (AQHISP). It is important to note that Arbitron does not report ethnic composition for stations in all the markets that it measures, only in those markets where the minority population is significant; nor do the company's syndicated reports provide data about other ethnic groups in any of its markets.

I included a number of market-level variables as control variables, to account for the possibility that station power ratios vary in accordance with market size and demographic fluctuations. I used two ethnicity variables (the percentage of Hispanics in the station's market [HISPANIC] and the percentage of African Americans in the station's market [BLACK]) as well as the per-capita income in the station's market (PERCAP). I controlled for market size by using total radio advertising revenues in the market (MARKREV). This variable was highly correlated with other potential measures of market size, such as total population and number of radio stations in the market. Using a market-size variable that most directly reflected market value was most appropriate, given the nature of the issues being addressed.

The inclusion of these market-level independent variables addresses the possibility that variations in market size and demographics affect audience share and revenue share (the two components of the power ratio) disproportionately, independent of a station's audience composition. Perhaps a more likely relationship involves interaction effects between audience ethnicity and market conditions. Thus, for instance, the extent to which African American–Hispanic audience composition affects audience value may be different in markets with higher African American–Hispanic compositions than in markets with lower African American–Hispanic compositions, given the different supply-and-demand dynamics for African American–Hispanic audiences in markets that are heavily African American–Hispanic versus those that are not. Similarly, in larger or wealthier markets, advertiser demand for

African American–Hispanic audiences may be different than in smaller or less wealthy markets. For these reasons I created six interaction terms. I created two interaction terms for interactions between audience ethnic composition and market ethnic composition (AQHISP*HISPANIC; AQBLACK*BLACK), to address the possibility that the effect of audience ethnicity on audience value varies in accordance with a market's ethnic composition. I also created two interaction terms for interactions between audience ethnic composition and market size (AQHISP*MARKREV; AQBLACK*MARKREV), to account for the possibility that the effect of an audience's ethnic composition on audience value varies in accordance with market size. Finally, I created two interaction terms for interactions between audience ethnic composition and the market's per-capita income (AQHISP*PERCAP; AQBLACK*PERCAP), to account for the possibility that the effect of audience ethnic composition on audience value varies in accordance with per-capita income in a station's market.

Using interaction terms typically raises problems of multicollinearity between the main effect independent variables and their associated interaction terms (Jaccard, Turrisi, and Wan 1990). To reduce such multicollinearity problems, I centered each main effect independent variable.[24] I used these centered independent variables to compute the interaction terms (see Cronbach 1987). Then I used these centered versions of the independent variables in the multivariate analysis.[25] Table 4.1 summarizes all the variables used in the study.

Although also incorporating data on the average income levels of the audience members for each station would have been desirable, such data were not available from the data sources used for this analysis. As I noted earlier, income data for the station audiences are not part Arbitron's syndicated reports (the reports obtained for this study) and are available only to Arbitron clients for an additional fee. This limited availability of audience income data, even to advertisers, probably limits the extent to which advertisers use such data in their audience-purchasing decisions. Regardless, such data would have made it possible to separate the effects of income from the effects of ethnicity. Given, as I have noted, that ethnicity is correlated with income, advertisers could be using ethnicity solely as a proxy for income. Although previous research has provided evidence that contradicts this assumption (Ofori 1999; Webster and Phalen 1997), my analysis cannot address this issue directly. However, as I have noted, even if lower valuations of minority audiences largely are a function of lower income levels, such

TABLE 4.1 Variable Labels and Descriptions

VARIABLE	DESCRIPTION
MARKET-LEVEL	
MARKREV	Total radio advertising revenues in market.
PERCAP	Per capita income in market.
BLACK	Percentage of market population that is African American.
HISP	Percentage of market population that is Hispanic.
STATION-LEVEL	
AMFM	Does a station broadcast on an AM or FM modulation? (0 = AM; 1 = FM).
MEN1854	Percentage of a station's average quarter-hour audience composed of men, aged 18 to 54.
WOM1854	Percentage of a station's average quarter-hour audience composed of women, aged 18 to 54.
SHARE	Station's average quarter-hour audience share in its market.
AQBLACK	Percentage of a station's average quarter-hour audience composed of African Americans.
AQHISP	Percentage of a station's average quarter-hour audience composed of Hispanics.
INTERACTION TERMS	

AQBLACK*BLACK; AQBLACK*MARKREV; AQBLACK*PERCAP; AQHISP*HISPANIC; AQHISP*MARKREV; AQHISP*PERCAP.

DEPENDENT VARIABLE	
LOGPR	Log of a station's power ratio (advertising revenue share/ audience share).

lower valuations still represent a threat to the principles of source and content diversity and to the provision of content that serves minority interests and concerns.

Finally, it is important to address a number of limitations in the scope of the database. First, Arbitron does not measure all radio stations in the United States. Of the roughly thirteen thousand radio stations in the United States, only about six thousand are in Arbitron-defined and -measured radio markets (National Telecommunications 2000). Moreover, Arbitron does not provide data about the ethnic composition of station audiences for all the radio markets that it measures. Generally, Arbitron provides such data only in markets that have a significant minority population. These factors limit the number of stations eligible for analysis and weight the stations included in this analysis toward those in markets with large African American and Hispanic populations.[26] The number of eligible stations was limited further because not all commercial radio stations report their revenues to BIA Research (BIA's reported response rate is roughly 80 percent). Where station revenues are not reported, it is impossible to compute the power ratio that serves as the dependent variable for this analysis. Because of these limitations, this data set contains 810 stations with Hispanic audience composition (and revenue) and 1,430 stations with African American audience composition (and revenue) data. The data set contains 461 commercial radio stations with reported revenues and with both African American and Hispanic audience composition data available. This latter set of stations is the focus of this analysis, as these stations represent the only context in which it is possible to investigate simultaneously the effects of both minority audience characteristics on audience value.

TABLE 4.2 Power Ratios of Minority-Targeting Versus Majority-Targeting Stations (N = 461).

STATION TYPE	MEAN POWER RATIO
Minority-targeting stations (121)	.82
Majority-targeting stations (340)	1.06

Note: $F = 27.41$ ($p < .01$).

TABLE 4.3 Correlation Matrix

	1	2	3	4	5	6	7	8	9	10	11	12	13	14	15	16	17
1. LOGPR	1.00																
2. MARKREV	.04	1.00															
3. PERCAP	-.001	.13**	1.00														
4. BLACK	.03	.38**	.46**	1.00													
5. HISP	.03	.15**	-.64**	-.21**	1.00												
6. AMFM	.18**	.01	-.06	-.03	.02	1.00											
7. MEN1854	.42**	.04	-.04	-.01	-.01	.25**	1.00										
8. WOM1854	.19**	.003	-.01	-.05	.04	.60**	-.07	1.00									
9. SHARE	.15**	-.13**	.01	-.03	-.07	.30**	-.06	.10*	1.00								
10. AQBLACK	-.18**	.11*	.16**	.30**	-.09*	-.05	-.15**	.20**	-.02	1.00							
11. AQHISP	-.06	.05	-.31**	-.11*	.46**	.04	.03	.14**	-.16	-.20**	1.00						
12. AQBLACK*BLACK	-.10*	.03	.13**	.20**	-.11*	-.07	-.08	.05	.01	.55**	-.12*	1.00					
13. AQBLACK*MARKREV	-.03	-.02	.01	.04	-.03	.05	-.04	.04	.06	.21**	-.08	.35**	1.00				
14. AQBLACK*PERCAP	-.02	.01	.04	.16**	-.01	-.10*	-.02	-.02	-.05	.33	**.02	.64**	.14**	1.00			
15. AQHISP*HISP	-.04	-.03	-.25**	-.08	.36**	.02	-.02	-.01	.06	-.13**	.48**	.03	-.02	.18**	1.00		
16. AQHISP*MARKREV	-.17**	.20**	.03	-.02	-.03	.07	.04	.02	.08	-.06	.06	-.07	-.25**	-.04	.05	1.00	
17. AQHISP*PERCAP	-.03	.03	.15**	.01	-.26**	-.01	.003	.04	.01	.02	-.31**	-.09	-.002	-.26**	-.70**	.15**	1.00

Note. * $p < .05$; ** $p < .01$.

RESULTS

Table 4.2 presents a mean power ratio comparison of stations that target minority audiences and stations that do not. For the purposes of this analysis I defined minority-targeted stations as those whose average quarter-hour audience is comprised of a majority of African American and/or Hispanic listeners (i.e., greater than 50 percent). As the table shows, those stations with a minority audience of greater than 50 percent have an average power ratio of .82, compared to an average power ratio of 1.06 for other stations (N = 461). This difference is statistically significant at the .01 level. As these results suggest, stations that target minority audiences tend to undersell their audiences, meaning that their share of the total radio audience is greater than their share of the total radio-advertising revenues in their markets.

Table 4.3 presents a correlation matrix for all the independent and dependent variables used in this study. Of particular importance is that correlations between the main effect variables and their associated interaction terms generally are modest. Before these variables were centered, some correlations between main effect and interaction terms were as high as .90, a level indicative of a potentially serious multicollinearity problem. There are, however, a few strong correlations between some interaction terms. The correlation between AQBLACK*BLACK and AQBLACK*PERCAP is .64 (p < .01). There is a similarly strong correlation (r = .70; p < .01) between the Hispanic versions of these interaction terms (AQHISP*HISP and AQHISP*PERCAP). However, tolerance statistics for all four of these independent variables are reasonably high (ranging from .39 to .52), alleviating concerns about multicollinearity in the multivariate analysis.

Table 4.4 presents the results of a hierarchical regression analysis for all stations for which both Hispanic and African American composition data were available.[27] I used hierarchical regression because I was including interaction terms (Jaccard, Turrisi, and Wan 1990) and in order to better examine the relative contribution of market-level versus station-level independent variables (given the nature of the dependent variable, I presumed that station-level independent variables would provide greater explanatory power than market-level independent variables).

The first set of independent variables that I entered into the model was the market-level control variables. As table 4.4 shows, these variables alone explain none of the variance in station power ratios. When station-level in-

TABLE 4.4 Hierarchical Regression for Natural Log of Station Power Ratio for Stations in Hispanic and African-American Measured Markets ($N = 461$)

	B	S.E.	ß
BLOCK 1: MARKET-LEVEL			
MARKREV	.00	.00	.02
PERCAP	.00	.00	.01
BLACK	.002	.01	.03
HISP	.002	.003	.04

Adjusted R^2 = .00

	B	S.E.	ß
BLOCK 2: STATION-LEVEL			
AMFM	-.29**	.06	-.26
MEN1854	.01**	.001	.49
WOM1854	.01**	.002	.44
SHARE	.05**	.01	.19
AQBLACK	-.01**	.001	-.27
AQHISP	-.003**	.001	-.20

Adjusted R^2 = .32**

	B	S.E.	ß
BLOCK 3: INTERACTION TERMS			
AQBLACK*BLACK	-.0002	.00	-.05
AQBLACK*MARKREV	.00	.00	-.03
AQBLACK*PERCAP	.00	.00	.09
AQHISP*HISP	-.0001	.00	-.09
AQHISP*MARKREV	-.00000001**	.00	-.20
AQHISP*PERCAP	-.000001	.00	-.09

Adjusted R^2 = .37**
R^2 Change = .05**

Note: $^*p < .05$; $^{**}p < .01$.

dependent variables are added (block 2), the adjusted R^2 increases from .00 to .32 ($p < .01$). As the table shows, all six station-level independent variables are significant in the expected direction. A negative relationship exists between modulation type and power ratios, with AM status having a negative effect on power ratios ($\beta = -.26$, $p < .01$). Both the MEN1854 and WOM1854 demographic composition variables are positively related to power ratios (MEN1854: $\beta = .49$; $p < .01$; WOM1854: $\beta = .44$; $p < .01$), indicating that the greater the extent to which a station's audience is composed of men and women aged 18 to 54, the larger the station's power ratio. A station's overall audience share (SHARE) also is positively related with a station's power ratio ($\beta = .19$; $p < .01$), providing evidence that sellers of audiences are able to charge a premium on a per-audience-member basis for larger audiences. Finally, in terms of ethnicity both the AQHISP ($\beta = -.20$; $p < .01$) and AQBLACK ($\beta = -.27$; $p < .01$) variables are negatively related to power ratios, suggesting that ethnic composition exerts a downward pressure on a radio station's ability to monetize its audience. The magnitude of the beta coefficients shows that the age/gender independent variables are the most important in terms of explanatory power, followed by the ethnicity variables. The AQBLACK and AQHISP coefficients are similar in size, although African American audience composition seems to exert a slightly stronger downward pressure on audience value than Hispanic audience composition (β of -.27 versus .20).

In block 3, I added the six interaction terms to the equation. As table 4.4 shows, adding the interaction terms explains only an additional 5 percent of the variance in the dependent variable (the adjusted R^2 increases from .32 to .37); however, this improvement in explanatory power is significant at the .01 level. Only one of the six interaction terms is statistically significant. The significant negative coefficient for the AQHISP*MARKREV interaction term ($\beta = -.20$; $p < .01$) indicates that the magnitude of the negative relationship between Hispanic audience composition and station power ratios decreases slightly as market size increases.

The analyses presented here represent the next step in determining the extent to which advertiser valuations of minority audiences affect the viability of stations that focus on serving minority audiences. Future research should seek to better separate any income effects from ethnicity effects. However, from a media policy standpoint, whether lower valuations of minority audiences are purely a function of income or also are a function of other factors, such as advertiser perceptions of minority spending and product usage patterns, the implications for diversity in the electronic media are the same—the viability of minority-targeted content suffers. This perspective suggests that policy makers generally seeking to preserve and promote diversity of sources and content in the electronic media and specifically to promote minority ownership of media outlets and the production of minority content need to investigate new strategies and tactics. Previous policy initiatives, such as minority preferences in the license allocation process and minority tax certificates, have focused on increasing the likelihood of minorities' becoming owners of media outlets. The results presented here suggest that if policy makers want to preserve and promote media outlets that target minorities, their efforts should address not only the barriers to establishing such media outlets but also the barriers to maintaining the financial viability of such outlets once they are established.

AUDIENCE VALUATION AND MEDIA CONTENT

The central underlying concern for the audience valuation analysis is that the content that media organizations produce reflects the differing valuations of different components of the media audience. That is, producers of audiences (i.e., media organizations) will produce more content designed to appeal to more highly valued audience segments (given their greater revenue potential) than content designed to appeal to less-valued audience segments (Owen and Wildman 1992; Rust and Donthu 1988; Turow 1997). As economists who have modeled the process of program choice have demonstrated, "when advertisers are willing to pay more for exposure to certain viewers, then the viewers who are worth more to advertisers will receive heavier weighting" in content production decisions (Owen and Wildman 1992:91).[28] Only when content providers engage in intense competition for highly valued audiences will they begin to offer content to less-valued audiences.

These principles are based on the fact that the decision regarding which audience to target essentially begins with the following equation:

$$R_i = (A_i/C_i) \times V_i$$

where R_i equals potential revenue for targeting audience segment i, A_i equals the size of audience segment i, C_i equals the number of competitors targeting audience segment i, and V_i equals the value to advertisers of one member of audience segment i. This equation shows that content providers will assess the proportion of a particular audience segment that they are likely to capture (given the level of competition), then multiply those raw numbers by the likely revenues per audience member. Whichever audience segment yields the largest results is likely to be the audience that the content provider targets (assuming production costs for reaching each audience segment are identical). It may be that the most highly valued audience segment already has attracted a large number of content providers, whereas a less-valued audience segment has not. In such a situation the less-valued audience segment represents the more lucrative opportunity for the content provider. But as this example suggests, content providers first will cluster around the most valuable audience segments, until competition reaches such a level that serving less valuable audience segments offers similar revenue possibilities. As a result highly valued audience segments are likely to have more content addressing their particular interests and preferences than are less-valued audience segments (Owen and Wildman 1992). In addition, any changes in the valuation of different segments of the media audience quickly will be reflected in the nature of the content that media organizations produce. In these ways the nature of the products available in the content market is deeply intertwined with the demands of consumers in the audience market (i.e., advertisers).

This process is intuitively obvious and clearly visible to any observer of the evolution of the media system. We can see, for instance, that the high value that advertisers place on males aged 18–34 is reflected in the abundance of cable channels that attempt to appeal to this demographic bracket (McAdams 2000b), primarily through an increasing amount of sports programming, as well as an increasing amount of programming with sexually suggestive or risqué content (Reinholz 2000). Advertisers' high valuations of professional women resulted in the rise of print publications that target this audience (Turow 1997). The CBS broadcast network continues to make programming decisions with an emphasis on attracting a much younger demographic (and thus higher CPMs) than the over-50 viewer that traditionally has characterized the network (Cohen 2001).[29]

These, however, represent only a few of the most obvious examples.[30] In other instances the relationship between audience valuation and media content is less apparent, yet the broader cultural and political implications are more profound. At the most basic level a number of analysts of the relationship between advertisers and media organizations have speculated that advertisers' increasing demand for narrower and more homogeneous audience segments, and the media system's increasing ability to satisfy such demand, are contributing to levels of social, cultural, and political fragmentation that undermine basic cultural cohesion and tolerance and threaten the functioning of the democratic process (e.g., Rogovin 1992; Sunstein 2001; Turow 1997). The premise of such arguments is that individual media consumers increasingly are able to consume media that cater exclusively to their specific interests and concerns, thereby limiting their exposure to the less familiar ideas and viewpoints that are essential to the development of culturally and politically well-rounded citizens (see Napoli 1999c) and thereby undermining any shared culture that binds citizens together (A. Shapiro 1999; Sunstein 2001).

In terms of more tangible effects perhaps one of the most important implications of the process by which content responds to advertiser demands for particular audience groups involves the issue of television violence. Television programmers frequently have been criticized for presenting excessive amounts of violent programming (Minow and LaMay 1996; *National Television Violence Study* 1996–98). The prevalence of violent programming long has been understood to be the result of high levels of audience demand for such programming. That is, programmers provide violent programming because viewers seem to find it appealing (as reflected in the ratings). However, when this issue is examined in greater detail, the specific dynamics of audience appreciation and content decision making illustrate the importance to this process of advertisers' differentiated valuations of different components of the television audience.

Specifically, research indicates that men and women aged 18 to 34 are the heaviest consumers of violent television programming, although they are the lightest viewers overall (Hamilton 1998). Indeed, being in this age bracket is the single most powerful predictor of whether an individual is a heavy consumer of violent programming (Hamilton 1998). As I discussed earlier, this age bracket generally is the most desirable to advertisers. That this age bracket also represents the most avid consumers of violent programming means that "for advertisers trying to reach younger adult viewers . . . , sponsoring different types of violent programming . . . may be one avenue to reach these viewers" (Hamilton 1998:55).

The relationship between highly valued audience segments (women and men aged 18 to 34) and their consumption of violent programming suggests that programmers seeking to attract and sell the most highly valued audience segment face a strong economic incentive to present violent programming. Thus it is not surprising that research has shown that the level of violence on television varies in accordance with the availability of television viewers in this age bracket (Hamilton 1998).

The broader social implications of this pattern raise obvious concerns, because the public and policy makers alike have been concerned for years about the effects on children of exposure to violent programming (C. Cooper 1996; Rowland 1983). Media effects research repeatedly has demonstrated that children are the most susceptible to media effects (see *National Television Violence Study* 1996–98; Surgeon General 1972). Thus children could exhibit both the strongest positive and negative effects of media content. Although advertisers do not value children especially highly, and programmers do not often directly target them with violent programming, children do represent a significant proportion of the audiences for violent programming because children watch so much television.[31] This means that advertiser valuations of one audience segment could be having a negative effect on another audience segment. That is, children—who are not the intended audience for violent programming and are not the intended target of advertisers—nonetheless find themselves in the position to consume large quantities of the violent programming produced in an effort to attract and sell a completely separate audience segment (Hamilton 1998). Thus content providers' efforts to reach a more highly valued audience segment are psychologically harming children, a less-valued audience segment. Given that children's susceptibility to media effects amplifies the potential positive effects that programming can have, a demographic group that could benefit the most from television actually may be harmed the most.

Another important content-based outgrowth of advertiser valuations of different audience segments involves the production of news content. The legal scholar C. Edwin Baker (1994), in a far-reaching analysis of the effects of advertising on newspaper content, provides compelling anecdotal evidence that advertisers' higher valuations of wealthier readers lead newspapers to skew editorial content in ways that attract high-income readers and actively repel lower-income readers. Baker cites a 1991 U.S. Commerce Department report on the newspaper industry that concluded that "to meet the changing needs of advertisers, some [American newspaper] publishers may take the route of several prominent papers and cut their circulation base to get rid of circulation that is not considered valuable to advertisers" (67). Shedding such unwanted readers, while retaining and attracting desired readers, typically involves shifts in content. For instance, some newspapers, in an effort to appeal to a wealthier demographic, have abandoned certain news categories, such as urban news, and expanded attention to other news categories, such as business news. These moves often have led to declines in circulation but an overall demographic composition that was more appealing to advertisers (Baker 1994). The disturbing irony of this situation is that one of the audience segments most in need of the informational and educational benefits of newspaper readership (i.e., lower-income citizens) is the one that newspapers are least interested in serving.

Baker's analysis also raises the issue of the viability of minority-targeted content in advertiser-supported media. Baker quotes a *Los Angeles Times* executive, who noted that providing greater coverage of minority issues would not make financial sense, because minority audiences were not believed to have the purchasing power to be responsive to the types of advertising that the *Los Angeles Times* carried (1994:68). This statement contributes to a growing body of research on media content decision making that suggests that advertiser-supported media are not likely to well serve minority tastes, both because of the small numbers of minority readers and their lower valuations by advertisers (Gandy 2000; Ofori 1999; Rodriguez 2001; Waterman 1986; Wildman and Karamanis 1998). As one recent analysis concluded, the emphasis on attracting valuable audience segments that has become increasingly prominent in the television news industry has meant that "every week—every day—stories about African-Americans, Hispanics, and Asians are kept off the air" (Westin 2001:83).

When we consider the issue purely in terms of raw numbers of audience members in different preference categories, it is perfectly understandable why minority-focused content is not likely to be widely available. To the extent that different audience groups have different content preferences, the greater the prominence of the "majority" audience relative to the minority audience, the lesser the extent to which minority-targeted content will be available (Waldfogel 2000). However, the negative effects of smaller raw numbers have an additional dimension. As I noted in the discussion of audience measurement in chapter 3, smaller audiences cannot be measured as

accurately or reliably as larger audiences. To the extent that niche audience–
or minority audience–targeted media content attracts smaller-than-average
audiences, it is likely to suffer an additional economic handicap as a result
of the lower valuations that advertisers are likely to place on lower-quality
audience data. This handicap is further exacerbated by the difficulties that
measurement firms traditionally have encountered in achieving levels of
participation and cooperation among minority audiences that are comparable to the levels achieved among majority audiences (see chapter 3). These
measurement handicaps can contribute further to the underprovision of
minority content. When we incorporate the additional factor of lower valuations for minority audiences that arise for reasons independent of audience
size—whether they are related to income, presumed purchasing patterns, or
the higher levels of media consumption of minority audiences—the proba-
bility of a dearth of minority content becomes even more pronounced.

All these factors affect not only what media outlets that target minorities
are able to earn from their audiences but what they are able to invest in programming. The lower revenues earned from minority audiences naturally
lead to lower levels of investment in content, which further undermines minority media outlets' ability to remain viable. The budget for any piece of
media content is a function of the size of the potential audience for that content (Owen and Wildman 1992). Thus, for example, television programs
with larger potential audiences (e.g., programs produced by a major broadcast network) generally have larger production budgets than programs with
smaller potential audiences (e.g., programs produced by niche cable channels).[32] Research also shows that audience members prefer media products
with higher production budgets to those with smaller production budgets
(Hamilton 1998; Owen and Wildman 1992). This tendency can be so powerful that audiences can be diverted from content that is meant to appeal to
them in favor of content for which they are not the primary intended audience. This pattern is perhaps best demonstrated by the performance of U.S.
films in foreign markets. Traditionally, foreign audiences have gravitated to
dubbed or subtitled U.S. films, often to the neglect of films produced do-
mestically that feature domestic actors and dialogue in their native lan-
guage. At the same time U.S. audiences largely ignore foreign-language
films, preferring Hollywood productions (Wildman 1994). These "one-way
flows," as they have been dubbed by economists (e.g., Wildman 1994), are
the result of the enormous difference in production budgets between most

Hollywood and foreign films. The greater this difference is for production budgets, the greater the relative appeal of Hollywood films. Thus audiences in countries where the production budgets for domestic films are small will demonstrate the greatest propensity for avoiding domestic films in favor of Hollywood films (Wildman 1994; Wildman and Siwek 1988).

This same logic has important implications for the availability of minority content in advertiser-supported media. Specifically, the smaller numbers and lower per-capita value of minority audiences exert downward pressures on the production budgets of minority content. These downward pressures create a situation in which minority content loses some of its appeal—*even to minority audiences*—relative to majority content. The difference in production budgets will be enough for some minority audiences to find the majority programming more appealing than the programming targeted at their particular interests and concerns. This greater relative appeal thus feeds the frequently heard observation that advertisers don't need to target minority audiences because they are sufficiently capturable by majority-targeted content (see Ofori 1999). To the extent that this phenomenon is true, it is probably partially attributable to the lower production values of minority-targeted content, which cause some minority audience members to "defect" to majority content in much greater proportions than majority audiences defect to minority-targeted content. This process represents another "one-way flow," one that in this case contributes to a cycle in which advertiser valuations of minority audiences affect minority content and vice versa. Obviously, this tendency reduces the potential audience for minority content, further undermining investment in the production of such content and the ability of such content to attract large enough audiences to remain financially viable.[33] Thus the lower valuations that advertisers place on minority audiences become part of a complex economic process that leads to lower levels of availability of such content (Wildman and Karamanis 1998).

However, advertiser valuations of minority audiences appear to be increasing, with tangible effects on content already evident. For example, in recent years advertisers have begun to place a higher value on reaching Hispanic audiences, primarily because Hispanics represent one of the fastest-growing segments of the population (Consoli 2000b; Turow 1997). In addition, the average income in Hispanic households has increased roughly 15 percent since 1990 (Porter and Nelson 2000). These developments mean that Hispanics represent a much higher level of product-purchasing power than they did in the past. Major advertisers, such as Procter and Gamble, General Motors, and AT&T, have increased their efforts to reach Hispanic consumers (Porter and Nelson 2000). As a result of this shift in advertiser valuations of Hispanic consumers, media organizations have begun to alter their content in an effort to attract Hispanic audiences. ABC recently became the first of the major broadcast networks to offer its nightly national newscast in Spanish (via the Secondary Audio Program channel). One advertising executive noted, "Any device that can make programming more inclusive, especially if it is the fastest growing demo group in America, will give that network an advantage" (Consoli 2000b:10).

THE SCARCITY PARADOX

The difficulty associated with reaching various demographic groups appears to have a positive effect on their value (Ahrens 2002; Surowiecki 2002). For instance, among the groups that television advertisers value most are men aged 18 to 34. In explaining the high value placed on this group, one advertising executive noted, "They're harder to reach. And the harder [they are to reach], the more valuable they are. Some advertisers are willing to pay a premium to reach that group, and they'll pay what it takes" (Reinholz 2000:74). It is important to recognize that the notion of scarcity in this context refers not to the overall availability of men aged 18 to 34 in the population but to their availability within media audiences.

This issue of the effect of the scarcity of different components of the media audience on their value—and its implications for the structure and behavior of media institutions—merits discussion. At the center of this logic is that the more media a particular demographic group consumes, the less valuable it is to advertisers, and, consequently, the less incentive media organizations have to produce content that specifically targets this group. This situation represents an economic arrangement that is, in many ways, exactly the reverse of how much of the economy operates. Consider, for instance, an unrelated product, such as fast food. Fast-food companies conduct substantial research that allows them to identify their most frequent customers (known as "heavy users") and their likes and dislikes. The companies then use this research to alter the menu and dining experience in ways that will appeal to these high-volume fast-food consumers, to keep them loyal and perhaps even increase their fast-food consumption (Ordonez 2000). Thus those who value fast food the most are likely to be best served by the typical fast-food establishment.

Or consider an example from nonadvertiser-supported media, such as the motion picture industry. Movie theater attendance data show that a disproportionate percentage of the audience is comprised of teenagers and young adults and that these demographic groups go to the movies much more frequently than other age categories (Litman 1998). Consequently, the motion picture studios devote the majority of their resources to producing films that appeal to these frequent moviegoers, with relatively few resources devoted to producing films that appeal to older adults. The general presumption here, which is a basic truism among marketers, is that, from a cost-benefit standpoint, it is wiser to target those with a positive predisposition toward a certain product than it is to target those with a negative predisposition toward a certain product. Thus frequent moviegoers (i.e., teenagers and young adults) find themselves well served by the productions of the motion picture studios.

Consider, in contrast, advertiser-supported media. In this case those audience members who consume the most media are in fact less likely to have content providers catering to their particular interests than those who consume less media (all other things being equal). Because advertisers place a value on scarcity, content providers have an incentive to develop media products that appeal to those who consume the least amount of media, rather than those who consume the most amount of media. Returning to the fast-food example, it would be as if fast-food establishments put all their resources into attracting customers who seldom eat fast food, to the neglect of the preferences of their loyal customers. Within the motion picture context, it would be as if the Hollywood studios focused on producing films that appealed to senior citizens. Such a strategy would be economic suicide for both industries, but it is a component of successful strategy in the audience marketplace.

Of course, the higher-than-average media consumption levels of these undervalued groups suggests that they are satisfied with the content options available to them. Such an argument neglects two key facts about media consumption. First, audience research repeatedly has demonstrated that media consumption is more a function of availability than it is a function of content preferences (see Webster and Phalen 1997). Thus, for example, the greater presence of older people and children in the television audience primarily is a function of lifestyles that offer more time for watching television. Second, given that the decision to consume media primarily is a function of availability, rather than a function of the particular content available, audience members generally will consume media even when their preferred contention option is not available. Individuals generally first make the decision to consume media, then decide what they will consume (Rust, Kamakura, and Alpert 1992; Webster and Wakshlag 1983). These tendencies are particularly pronounced in pure advertiser-supported media such as broadcast television and radio, where the content is free and therefore requires no monetary investment from the audience. Thus when typical audience members sit down to watch television, if they cannot find a program that they really like, they are more likely to watch a program that they find moderately appealing than they are to turn off the television. Similarly, if a radio listener's favorite station is playing a song that the listener does not like, that listener is more likely to change stations than turn off the radio.

These points illustrate that time spent consuming advertiser-supported media provides only the most superficial and rudimentary indicator of the level of satisfaction and benefit that audience members are receiving and no meaningful evidence that groups that consume high volumes of media content are more satisfied with the available content offerings than low-volume media consumers. High-volume media consumers could be much more satisfied with—and better served by—the media that they are consuming if content providers had a greater economic incentive to appeal to their most frequent customers. Instead, the unique economics of the audience marketplace dictate that low-volume media consumers are more likely to find highly satisfying content in those rare instances when they do consume media.

CHAPTER 5

NEW TECHNOLOGIES AND THE AUDIENCE PRODUCT

Historically, changes in audience measurement technologies have had profound effects on media technologies and vice versa. Indeed, the inherent dynamism of the audience marketplace largely is a function of frequent changes in both media and audience measurement technologies. Thus current and pending developments in both media and audience measurement technologies can affect the audience product.

Typically, analyses of the new media environment focus on the opportunities that it offers for both content providers and advertisers.[1] Thus, for instance, much has been made of the new media environment's ability to segment audiences into increasingly narrow niches, to provide increasingly interactive advertising platforms, and to facilitate additional windows for distributing media content, thereby distributing content costs across a larger audience base (e.g., "How to skin a potato" 2001; Hoang and Brechignac 2001; Howe 2001a; M. Larson 2001; Lewis 2000; Napoli 1998b; Negroponte 1995; Turow 1997).[2] Despite the prominence of such discourse, and the sense of optimism that it engenders, all is not well in the audience marketplace. The ongoing changes in the media environment contain a number of inherent threats. To provide a counterpoint to the more prominent opportunity-focused discourse, this chapter will focus on these threats to the quality of the audience product and the potential for increasing incongruities between each of the three components of the audience product (predicted audience, measured audience, actual audience).

NEW MEDIA TECHNOLOGIES, THE AUDIENCE
PRODUCT, AND THE AUDIENCE MARKETPLACE

As I showed in chapter 3, the development of new media technologies typically is accompanied by the development of new systems of audience measurement. Thus the arrival of television spurred methodological and technological advances in audience measurement that went well beyond print and radio audience measurement. The arrival of cable television similarly transformed the existing system of television audience measurement. And, most recently, the diffusion of the Internet has required the development of new technologies and systems of audience measurement (e.g., Porter 2001). The dynamic, then, is one of the audience measurement industry struggling to keep pace with the ever-changing media environment.

Today the media environment is in the midst of a particularly rapid and complex stage of evolution. A wide variety of new media technologies are available, such as digital video disc (DVD) players, personal video recorders (PVRs), handheld devices, direct broadcast satellite (DBS) systems, digital cable, and multiple means of Internet access, with additional technologies and services such as interactive television and video-on-demand just being introduced or in their trial stages. Two general attributes of the new media environment are of the greatest significance to the audience product. These are the increasing fragmentation of the media environment and the increasing audience autonomy that these new technologies provide. Both are defining characteristics of the new media environment that pose significant challenges to the processes of buying and selling audiences.

FRAGMENTATION

The question of the effects of fragmentation on media industries is not a new one (see Neuman 1991; Picard 1999). However, this question seldom has been addressed within the specific context of the processes of buying and selling audiences. First, however, it is important to establish the various dimensions of the process of fragmentation, as different aspects of it affect different aspects of the audience product. At the most basic level fragmentation refers to the process wherein traditional "mass audiences" (see Freidson 1953; Webster and Phalen 1997) are subdivided into smaller, more homogeneous segments, as a result of an increasingly segmented and complex media environment. As this description suggests, the fragmentation process has both a media component and an audience component. Audience fragmentation refers to the extent to which media audiences are more widely distributed across a variety of content options (see Neuman 1991; Webster 1986). Audience fragmentation perhaps is best represented by the decline of the Big Three (ABC, NBC, CBS) broadcast networks' share of the prime-time television audience, from more than 90 percent in the 1970s to less than 45 percent in 2001 (Media Dynamics 2001b) and the associated dispersal of television audiences across an ever-broadening array of cable channels. Today no single broadcast network regularly captures much more than 15 percent of the national audience (often less), and the majority of cable networks each typically content themselves with 1 percent or less of the national audience.[3] Audience fragmentation is facilitated by the increasing number of media options and their increasing capacity for carrying content that appeals to narrow audience segments—hence the term *media fragmentation*.

Media fragmentation takes two forms: intramedia fragmentation and intermedia fragmentation. *Intramedia fragmentation* refers to the expansion of a medium's ability to deliver multiple content options. Thus, for example, since the 1990s we have seen a dramatic increase in the average number of channels that a cable household receives. As of 2002 the average cable household received more than sixty channels (FCC 2002a), whereas the average in 1992 was only thirty-three (Crawford 2000). Households with digital cable systems can easily receive more than one hundred channels (in addition to music channels), plus dozens of pay-per-view options. The number of magazines published in this country increased from just over thirteen thousand in 1988 to almost eighteen thousand in 2000 (Magazine Publishers of America 2001), and the number of World Wide Web sites increased from roughly 1.5 million in 1997 to more than eight million in 2001 (Web Characterization Project 2001).

Intramedia fragmentation in broadcast television has been somewhat less pronounced, although the number of commercial VHF and UHF television stations in the United States increased from 734 in 1980 to 1,309 in 2001 (FCC 2002b). In addition, the number of broadcast networks has increased from three in the 1980s (ABC, NBC, CBS) to seven today (ABC, NBC, CBS,

Fox, WB, UPN, PAX), with the networks increasingly targeting fairly narrow audience segments (Yan 1999). We may be on the verge of an even more substantial degree of broadcast television fragmentation with the transition to digital broadcasting. Although digital television originally was designed to provide higher-quality television pictures (typically referred to as high definition television), many discussions of other ways to use the technology have focused on using the increased efficiency of digital signals to "multiplex" as many as six separate standard quality television signals in the space that would be occupied by a single high definition signal (FCC 1998). Thus if multiplexing becomes the dominant technological and economic model in broadcast television, the number of content options available over the air could increase sixfold.

The second form of media fragmentation taking place is *intermedia fragmentation*. This term refers to the addition of new media technologies to the media system, which expands the range of cross-media content options available to the typical media consumer. Thus, for instance, the advent of cable represented a significant historical example of intermedia fragmentation. The introduction and advancement of cable technology led to a dramatic increase in the number of available video programming options, well beyond what was provided by broadcast television alone. New technologies such as the Internet, direct broadcast satellite, and satellite-delivered radio further increase the enormous range of content options available across a growing array of distribution technologies.

As this discussion suggests, the dividing line between intermedia and intramedia fragmentation can be somewhat blurry. In many cases new media technologies do not represent an entirely new medium per se but rather a new means of delivering "old media" content. For example, the medium of television now is supplied by multiple delivery technologies, including analog and digital cable, microwave multipoint distribution services (MMDS), and direct broadcast satellite services (see Owen 1999). However, as will become clear, the distinction between intermedia and intramedia fragmentation remains useful, particularly within the context of understanding the implications for the audience marketplace.

One might question the relevance of any distinction between media fragmentation and audience fragmentation. The logic of this distinction is perhaps best illustrated by the fact that media audiences seldom are as fragmented as is possible technologically (see Webster and Lin 2002).[4] Looking at the audience erosion of the Big Three broadcast networks another way, although the average television household receives more than sixty channels, the Big Three broadcast networks still can, on occasion, command more than 40 percent of the prime-time audience (Media Dynamics 2001b), with each network's average prime-time audience still typically greatly exceeding that of even the most popular cable network. Similarly, as of March 2001, the top four on-line content providers (AOL, Microsoft, Yahoo! and Napster) accounted for more than 50 percent of the time that Americans spent on line (Jupiter Media Metrix 2001; see also Lake 2001), although millions of on-line content options are available to them.[5] These examples are meant to demonstrate that fragmentation is not simply about technology but also about how audiences choose to use these technologies (see Winston 1986).

Media fragmentation is technologically capable of supporting a much greater level of audience fragmentation than exists today. Audiences, however, are not becoming fragmented to such an extreme degree (see Picard 2001b). Thus increases in media fragmentation are not necessarily accompanied by comparable increases in audience fragmentation.[6] As will become clear, the nature of this relationship factors into how changes in the media environment are affecting the audience product.

As I noted earlier, much of the analysis devoted to the implications of fragmentation has focused on its benefits for the audience marketplace. The primary point of focus has been on the media system's increasing capacity to fulfill ever-narrower audience interests, which facilitates segmentation of the audience into increasingly homogeneous groupings (see Turow 1997). Such increasingly homogeneous audience segments are of value to advertisers, who seek to maximize the efficiency of their media buys by targeting only the most likely consumers of their products (see chapter 4). Because of this, the total value of the segmented parts is potentially greater than their value as an undifferentiated whole. In this scenario both advertisers and content providers benefit from the increasingly fragmented media environment. However, such fragmentation has important negative effects on the audience product as well (Napoli 2001a). These negative effects ultimately may outweigh the positive effects associated with the increased ability to target narrow audience segments.

THE PERILS OF FRAGMENTATION

At the most basic level increased fragmentation brings increased complexity to the audience-buying process. In an increasingly complex media environment, in which audiences increasingly are dispersed across a greater array of media and content options, the transaction costs associated with purchasing an audience naturally increase. The term *transaction costs* refers to the costs associated with purchasing a particular product or service that are not reflected in the price of the product or service (Williamson 1985). Representative examples of transaction costs would include the costs associated with gathering and analyzing the information necessary to make the best possible purchase and negotiating and contracting costs associated with each individual purchase. In the new media environment the advertiser must assess, evaluate, and perhaps purchase far more media options in order to reach the desired number and types of target consumers. Thus media fragmentation imposes increased analytical burdens, while the accompanying audience fragmentation imposes additional negotiating and contracting costs. All the costs associated with the analysis of these additional media options, and the negotiating and contracting of additional media buys, represent additional transaction costs in the process of buying audiences. As one audience researcher has noted, "It is now more complicated than ever to reach people, whether you're trying to sell a car or you're a plumber" (Tam 2002:B1).

The current situation in cable television provides a useful example of this phenomenon. The increasingly fragmented cable television industry has invested millions of dollars in software and processes to simplify the buying and selling of audiences. This system, called electronic data interchange (EDI), is intended to reduce the time and paperwork surrounding the massive quantity of transactions that take place within cable advertising. According to one cable executive, before the introduction of EDI, cable "was 10 times more labor-intensive to buy than broadcast" (Hall 2001:34). Obviously, more labor-intensive buys represent greater transaction costs to the purchaser, which affects the value of cable buys relative to other media options.

Some question whether such systems are effectively reducing the transaction costs associated with buying cable audiences. As one advertising executive noted recently: "We are getting absolutely killed on the labor side. You can do all the EDI . . . in the world, but [with] all those little ratings, we're getting absolutely smacked on labor and we're not getting paid for it by the clients" ("Fragmentation Face-Off" 2001:28). The analytical costs are particularly high. As Ephron and Peacock have noted, "Fragmentation offered the possibility of buying reach through dispersion, but the many combinations were more than the planners could handle" (2000:1). Research by Phalen (1998) on the audience-buying process suggests that "information overload" is an increasingly common affliction among media buyers and planners.[7] Information overload will be compounded as the number of media options to be assessed and evaluated increases. Thus increased media and audience fragmentation bring increased complexity to the process of analyzing and purchasing available media options and—most important— increased costs.

Analytical costs also are relevant to the increasing difficulty of predicting the behavior of media audiences in a fragmented media environment. Audience forecasting is a vital process in the audience marketplace, with accuracy in forecasting essential to the economic interests of both the buyers and sellers of audiences. However, in the new media environment audience forecasters face an increasingly difficult analytical challenge, because they must anticipate how audiences are going to navigate an increasingly complex media environment, and they must evaluate and predict the likely performance of a growing number of media products (see R. Cooper 1996; see also chapter 2). The data that I presented in chapter 2 supported the findings of earlier studies: Forecasters' ability to predict accurately the behavior of media audiences is in decline (Blumler 1996; Lin 1994; Wells 1997). According to Kirkham, within the television context fragmentation is leading to more "unpredictable fluctuation" in ratings (1996:221). Thus it appears that the media industry's ability to predict the behavior of media audiences has not been able to keep pace with the significant changes taking place within the media environment (Napoli 2001d).[8] As media fragmentation increases, the disparity between the predicted audience and the measured audience is likely to widen.

Intermedia fragmentation, which poses data-reporting challenges in regard to systems of audience measurement, brings greater uncertainty and analytical costs to the process of buying audiences. For example, a growing problem is measuring and reporting cable network audiences at the local level. In its syndicated market reports Nielsen Media Research reports the audience size and composition for individual cable networks for each market. Thus, for example, an advertiser wishing to reach viewers of the Lifetime cable network within a given market can examine the appropriate market report to determine Lifetime's audience reach there. However, the audience size and composition data reported by Nielsen are not likely to match the audience size and composition that the advertiser actually reached. First, the advertiser would have to purchase local spots on each of potentially dozens of individual cable systems within the market. More important to this discussion, however, is that within a given market, the audience for any single cable network can come from a variety of sources, including individual cable systems, direct broadcast satellite (which has exceeded 20 percent penetration levels in some markets), and other alternative delivery systems such as MMDS. Thus an advertiser considering placing an ad on multiple (or perhaps all) cable systems in a market cannot look to the reported Nielsen numbers for an accurate picture of how many viewers a local cable buy is likely to reach (Gold 2000; Higgins 2002).[9] Thus the infusion of multichannel video programming delivery services with a national reach, such as DBS, into the media mix is undermining existing systems for measuring and reporting cable network audiences at the local level and is thus bringing greater complexity, inaccuracy, and uncertainty to the process of buying and selling local cable audiences.

A similar problem is arising in regard to measuring radio audiences because listeners often are able to tune in to their favorite station either over the air or through the Internet. Internet radio audiences are not, as of this writing, incorporated into Arbitron's standard radio audience reports; thus these reports may, for some stations, significantly underrepresent their total listening audience.[10] However, effectively accounting for Internet audiences is a complex task (see Porter 2001; Twyman and Mundy 2001), as some listeners may be listening from within the station's market area, whereas others may be listening from another city, state, or even country. Given that local advertisers are the primary buyers of radio audiences, any effort to account for Internet listenership of radio stations will need to distinguish effectively between in-market and out-of-market listeners. Obviously, someone who lives in California and listens to a Chicago jazz station is of no value to a Chicago car dealership considering advertising on that station. Here again, then, intermedia fragmentation is introducing data-gathering and -

reporting challenges that undermine the accuracy of audience data and, consequently, the quality of the audience product (see Twyman and Mundy 2001). As both examples show, the greater the degree to which audiences can access the same content through multiple technologies, the greater the difficulty associated with accurately measuring and reporting the true audience size for that content. Cannon has described the current situation as one in which "media are proliferating faster than the sources of data needed to measure them" (Cannon 2001:3).

These examples lead into the broader issue of audience measurement and how fragmentation is, in many ways, crippling existing systems of audience measurement and thereby damaging the quality of the audience product. In chapter 3, I examined many shortcomings associated with existing systems of audience measurement. The key point here is that as the new media environment continues to evolve, these shortcomings are likely to become more pronounced, creating greater divergence between the measured audience and the actual audience.

A number of factors will contribute to this process. Perhaps the most basic involves intramedia fragmentation. As the number of content options that any one audience measurement service (recall that most audience measurement services still generally provide single-medium data) has to measure increases, the reliability of the data generated declines (Kirkham 1996; Webster, Phalen, and Lichty 2000). Thus as any individual medium becomes increasingly fragmented, fewer content providers will have audience generated estimates from a sample of consumers sufficiently large to meet the levels of reliability desired by advertisers. The greater the extent to which this intramedia fragmentation is accompanied by audience fragmentation, the more pronounced is the damage to the reliability of the audience data. That is, the more audiences distribute themselves across the variety of available content options, the smaller the audience is for any individual content option—and the less reliable are the measurement data.

For example, as the average number of cable channels continues to rise, audiences are being diverted not only from the broadcast networks but also from the "general interest" cable networks such as TNT, USA, and FX (Higgins 2001). However, each of the numerous new networks is attracting only a few viewers. One media buyer has gone so far as to describe the cable networks as "cannibalizing themselves" (M. Larson 2002:5). The end result is that the audiences for the new networks are not large enough to be measured with a high degree of reliability (particularly at the local level). At the same time the audiences for the larger networks are declining—which ultimately will undermine the reliability of these audience numbers as well. The possibility of "multiplexed" digital television signals promises to have a similar effect on broadcast ratings. Comparable intermedia effects are likely in the radio industry, as the introduction of low-power FM radio stations and satellite radio will contribute to greater fragmentation of radio audiences and consequently will undermine the reliability of radio audience estimates. Of course, increases in sample sizes might be able to counteract such effects; however, as I will discuss, sample size increases probably cannot keep pace with the rate of media and audience fragmentation.

Another measurement challenge posed by an increasingly fragmented media environment involves the effects of inter- and intramedia fragmentation on participants' ability to accurately recall and record their media consumption. Recall-based audience measurement systems, such as the paper diary used by Nielsen and Arbitron in the measurement of television and radio audiences, and the interviews used by MRI and Simmons in the measurement of magazine audiences, become increasingly unreliable as the number of available content options increases (Soong 1988). For most media consumers an increase in the variety of content options leads them to increase the number of content options that they consume (D. Ferguson and Perse 1993; Heeter and Greenberg 1988) (although not nearly to the degree that is possible). As viewers increase the number of different content options that they consume, they become less accurate in their recall of the content options to which they have been exposed in a given measurement period. Lower levels of recall of course mean greater levels of error in the audience estimates and, consequently, a greater disjunction in the measured audience and the actual audience and a decline in the quality of the audience product.

The increasing prominence of these shortcomings is reflected in the increasing frequency with which buyers and sellers of audiences are questioning whether existing systems of audience measurement will be able to cope effectively with the various challenges posed by an increasingly fragmented media environment (e.g., Ephron 2000; Ephron and Gray 2000; Gunter 1993; Hulks and Santini 1994; Menneer and Syfret 1994; Weiss 2001). A recent critique of diary measurement of television audiences illustrates the tension between incumbent measurement systems and the new media environment:

The television diary was developed when the environment for television viewing was much different than the present. In the early 60's, when the diary was widely implemented, there were few channel choices, and great stability in program lineups. The environmental simplicity was a positive mediator toward the ability of people to recall and record recent viewing. Over the past 30 years the number of channels has proliferated and program lineups are constantly changing. Increased environmental complexity places a substantial strain on the ability of people to recall their channel choices and the duration of tuning. *(Engel and Maiville 2000:1)*

Many of these criticisms also are applicable to the measurement of radio audiences, where the diary remains the primary approach and the number of radio stations in a given market has increased significantly since the 1970s. Underlying such critiques is the assumption that the situation is only going to get worse as the media environment becomes more fragmented. As one advertising researcher noted, "If we don't solve these issues sooner than later, it's going to get ugly" (Weiss 2001:3).

Even the people meter, which long has been considered the gold standard in audience measurement, is facing questions about its utility in the new media environment. As early as the mid-1990s analysts were raising questions about the people meter's ability to "cope with the requirements of the impending digital age" (Menneer and Syfret 1994:241), because of the growing problems with sample representativeness and shortcomings in effectively capturing out-of-home viewing, viewing via multiple technologies, and viewing of digitally compressed signals (see Menneer and Syfret 1994). According to the critics Hulks and Santini, "The current metered panels reflect an outdated model built around a mid-90s view of the nuclear family gathered around the television set. This 'classroom' effect may no longer reflect the true use of the television 'terminal'" (1994:276). More recently, a twenty-three-country survey found that U.S. customers of Nielsen Media Research are the least satisfied users of television people meter systems (Bachman 2002d).

A recent analysis of national people meter data provides a good illustration of the reasons for this dissatisfaction. According to Green (2002), Nielsen publishes ratings for approximately twenty-two hundred programs every week aired by seventy-nine national broadcast, cable, and syndication networks. Of these programs, only about 8 percent recorded household ratings greater than 2. In the current people meter sample a rating of 2 means that fewer than one hundred homes are watching. Thus the performance of more than 90 percent of the programs measured is based on a projection that uses fewer than one hundred homes, a number that raises serious questions about the reliability of audience estimates in an increasingly fragmented television environment.

One advertising executive recently articulated well the prognosis for the future, noting, "We do have pretty [poor] measurement, and it's going to be even worse as it gets more and more fragmented. . . . We don't know what we're buying to a certain degree and in the future it's going to get even worse" ("Fragmentation Face-Off" 2001:28). This statement, although made within the specific context of local broadcast television, is applicable (to varying degrees) to most advertising-supported media. This statement reflects the ongoing failure of existing systems of audience measurement to keep pace with changes in the media environment. As a result advertisers are experiencing growing uncertainty about the nature of the audiences that they are buying, and consequently they perceive the quality of the audience product as declining.

It is important to emphasize that many recent criticisms of existing systems of audience measurement are emanating from the advertising industry, whose perceptions are central to determining the value of the audience product. This is a particularly important point, as this criticism runs counter to the observation made in chapter 3, that participants in the audience marketplace traditionally have ignored the obvious shortcomings in the measurement systems and simply have treated the numbers provided as "the truth." The key assertion here, however, is that the enormous changes in the media environment may produce levels of inaccuracy and uncertainty that may overcome such behavioral tendencies—at least on the part of advertisers—and increasingly may factor into their media planning and buying decisions.

AUDIENCE AUTONOMY

A second key characteristic of the new media environment is that it is facilitating increasing levels of audience autonomy. In other contexts the term *audience autonomy* has referred to the extent to which audience members can form their own interpretations of the meaning of a media text (e.g., Fiske

1987, 1989). However, in the context that I am using the term here, its meaning is quite different. In this case the concept of audience autonomy refers to the degree to which audience members have control over the media products that they consume and are able to choose what, when, and how they consume them. Thus the new media environment is one in which audience members increasingly are able to seek out the content that interests them, when they are interested in consuming it, using the technology that they prefer, rather than being "programmed at" by media organizations and able to access certain content only at certain times and with certain technologies.

Developments such as personal video recorders (e.g., TiVo, ReplayTV, UltimateTV, and DISHplayer; see Lewis 2000), on-demand music and video clips available over the Internet, and the increasing availability and diversity of pay-per-view television programming all enhance the degree to which individual media consumers are able to control the media consumption process. These developments build upon older technologies, such as the VCR and the remote control device, which effectively ushered in the era of increased audience autonomy (see Eastman and Newton 1995; Bellamy 1993; Levy 1989). The remote control device increased the ease with which viewers could browse, mute the volume, or switch back and forth between channels, thereby giving them greater control of the viewing process (see Eastman and Newton 1995). The VCR allowed viewers to pause, stop, view in slow motion, fast forward, and rewind content, thereby bringing an unprecedented level of control to when and how they watched video programming. The VCR's "time-shifting" capability increased this control because it allowed viewers to record a program and view it at their convenience (see Lindstrom 1989). Of course, the VCR's potential to increase audience autonomy through time shifting never was fully realized, partly because of the complexity associated with programming the device (see Klopfenstein 1989).

The new media environment, however, is one in which viewers can use time shifting much more easily. Personal video recorders automatically record chosen programs, with minimal programming by the consumer (these devices actually "learn" viewer preferences and record programming accordingly), in addition to providing all the features characteristic of the VCR (e.g., slow motion, rewind, etc.). Personal video recorders go beyond VCRs, however, by allowing viewers to actually pause live television and to record two programs simultaneously, thereby further freeing viewers from the dictates of programming practices. The increased autonomy is reflected in an early TiVo advertisement, in which television viewers tossed a network programming executive out his office window.

Cable and satellite pay-per-view systems, which run movies on continuous loops (often starting every hour or half-hour), represent similar opportunities for audience autonomy, as viewers can watch a film roughly at their convenience. Developing video-on-demand systems, which allow viewers to order programming precisely when they wish to view it (some systems are offering pause and rewind features as well) represent the next advancement in audience autonomy that cable and satellite services can provide. AOL Time Warner has begun offering a subscription-based video-on-demand service, which gives subscribers access not only to a library of movies but also to previously aired episodes of original HBO programming such as *Sex in the City* and *The Sopranos* (Grotticelli 2001). Advanced cable and satellite systems also are increasingly offering sophisticated interactive program guides, which provide viewers with detailed information about available programming, channel searching without leaving the channel they are watching, and automatic reminders of when certain programs are starting. All these features further empower audience members in their interaction with content providers.

The Internet may represent the apex of audience autonomy, because users can download a wide range of content options, including text, video, and audio, at their convenience (see A. Shapiro 1999). Few pieces of on-line media content are "scheduled" in the traditional sense.[11] Even in these instances, the content typically is archived on line and made available for an extended period of time. Thus time shifting is seldom an issue within the context of a medium that is inherently asynchronous. In addition, the interactive capabilities of the Internet facilitate unprecedented levels of audience control in the selection of content. For instance, users can personalize their news pages so that they deliver only news on selected topics (A. Shapiro 1999; Sunstein 2001) or they can have this content delivered directly by e-mail each morning.[12] Similarly, a number of Web sites offer users the ability to program their own "radio station." Users assemble their own playlists, thereby freeing themselves from the dictates of radio station program directors and disc jockeys.

Even the fragmentation of the media environment is contributing to greater audience autonomy. At the general level the increased channel capacity of the current multichannel video environment makes it increasingly easy for viewers to consume the program type that they most prefer, rather than accepting second- or third-choice options, because of the greater likelihood that their preferred program type is available (Youn 1994).[13] Thus, for instance, premium cable channels such as HBO run popular programs or films many times during the week on their many separate channels (digital cable and satellite subscribers can receive up to eight different HBO channels [plus alternate time zone feeds] with their HBO subscription), so that viewers increasingly are able to view a program at their convenience. Similarly, the broadcast networks are increasingly rebroadcasting their prime-time programs on affiliated cable networks at different times during the week of the original airing (Flint and Orwall 2001).[14] Today, if radio listeners miss a broadcast of their favorite radio program, that program frequently is available on line for an extended period of time. In sum, both intermedia and intramedia fragmentation make it increasingly easy for audience members to consume the content that they prefer at a time and place that is convenient for them. This is the essence of audience autonomy.

THE PERILS OF AUDIENCE AUTONOMY

As this collection of examples demonstrates, the media environment quite obviously is evolving in such a way as to increase the autonomy of the typical media consumer. What is less obvious, however, is what this evolutionary shift means to the process of buying and selling audiences: Increased audience autonomy can have numerous harmful effects on the audience product.

First, the increases in audience autonomy make it increasingly difficult to anticipate effectively the behavior of media audiences. In a media environment of increased audience autonomy, media organizations' traditional strategies and tactics for managing "audience flow" and controlling the behavioral patterns of their audiences will become less effective (Adams 1993; Eastman 1998; Youn 1994). Thus, for instance, the strategy of using established lead-in and lead-out programs to attract and retain audiences has grown less effective over time, in part because audiences have a range of technologies and services at their disposal that make it easier for them to find an alternative program, rather than accept the program on the channel that they have been watching (Davis and Walker 1990; Eastman 1998). Increased channel options make it less likely that a viewer simply will stick with a single channel throughout the course of a viewing session, while technologies such as the remote control and interactive program guides make it increasingly easy for viewers to navigate the multichannel programming environment and be informed about the content options available to them. While the notion that media audiences could become completely "liberated" from the dictates of media programmers oversimplifies the nature of the relationship between audience member and content provider (see Neuman 1991; Sunstein 2001), it is safe to say that the increasing autonomy is working against traditional means of controlling media audiences—and therefore is making their behaviors less predictable.

The increased audience autonomy of the new media environment also is making it easier for audiences to avoid the advertisements that provide the economic foundation of advertiser-supported media. Such concerns are not new. The introduction of car radios with preprogrammed station buttons facilitated channel switching and avoidance of commercials. The television remote control device was widely feared because it too facilitated channel switching and volume muting and, as a result, the avoidance of commercials (Abernethy 1990; Yorke and Kitchen 1985). The arrival of the VCR, with its capacity for fast-forwarding through commercials, represented additional opportunities for avoiding commercials and created similar apprehension within the media industry (Napoli 1997b; Sapolsky and Forrest 1989). Some estimates of television ad exposure have placed commercial avoidance at more than 30 percent of the measured audience for a given program (Abernethy 1992).

History has shown that none of these developments led to the collapse of any audience markets; however, it is important to recognize that these technologies did contribute to significant changes in programming and advertising strategies and tactics. For instance, a variety of "seamless" programming strategies developed in the early 1990s (Eastman, Neal-Lunsford, and Riggs 1995). Most of these strategies, including moving directly from one program to the next without commercial interruptions ("hot switching"); shortening or eliminating opening title sequences; and running end credits alongside programs' final scenes, were designed to minimize viewers' inclination to switch channels between programs (with modest effect; see Eastman et al. 1997). Some analysts argue that the advertising industry had to become increasingly creative in an effort to develop advertisements that are entertaining enough that viewers opt to watch or listen to the ads rather than change channels or use the mute or fast-forward functions (Bellamy 1993), while others point to the increased prominence of product placement within content as an outgrowth of audiences' increasing ability to avoid traditional advertisements (Lewis 2000; Stanley 2002). Research also suggests that program producers have altered their content in an effort to combat the increased "grazing" by remote control. Specific shifts include a greater emphasis on making the first few minutes of a program extremely dramatic or compelling, an emphasis on faster-paced programming, and programming structured in terms of shorter, independent segments (Eastman and Neal-Lunsford 1993).

New media technologies, however, may offer even greater opportunities for avoiding advertising. Higher-end televisions increasingly offer "picture-in-picture" features that allow viewers to watch two channels simultaneously, with one channel minimized in the corner of the screen. Obviously, such a feature makes it easier for viewers to switch channels during a commercial and switch back when the commercial break ends. More significant is the advent of personal video recorders, which bring unprecedented ease to commercial avoidance. TiVo devices have the traditional fast-forward functions of a VCR.[15] ReplayTV devices, however, originally came with a "QuickSkip" function that allowed viewers to move ahead in increments of thirty seconds (the standard commercial length). New versions of the ReplayTV device instead allow viewers to automatically delete commercials (Wingfield 2001).[16] Early indications are that almost 90 percent of users of TiVo and ReplayTV devices use these features to avoid commercials (Lewis 2000), providing an idea of the potential such devices have for radically empowering television viewers against advertising intrusions. One recent study found that of all the features provided by a personal video recorder, the ability to fast-forward through commercials was the feature that PVR owners used most frequently (D. Ferguson and Perse 2001). Although the (at this point) sluggish diffusion of PVRs may raise questions about the ultimate effect of this device on audiences' exposure to commercials, the integration of such devices into services such as direct broadcast satellite (for example, the DISHplayer device that Echostar makes available to its subscribers) and digital cable systems suggests that PVR services (if not free-standing devices) are likely to become a prominent (and permanent) component of the new media environment (see Abramson and Lefton 2001). In a media environment of increased complexity, devices such as PVRs that help consumers manage their media consumption are likely to become increasingly desirable and increasingly necessary. Forrester Research estimates that fifty million households will own a personal video recorder by 2007 (Harmon 2002).

The more an audience for an individual media product can avoid the advertisements embedded in that product, the lower is the value of that audience to advertisers, particularly when measurement systems are oriented toward measuring content audiences, not advertisement audiences. In such situations the measurement system is unlikely to be able to capture effectively the extent to which audience members are avoiding advertisements. As a result the gulf between the content audience—as reported by the measurement system—and the advertisement audience widens and the value of the audience product declines.

PVR owners need not even avoid advertisements for the audience product to suffer as a result of PVR diffusion. Audience members who watch a program—and its advertisements—may receive lower valuations from advertisers because their viewing is time shifted. A recent memo from an advertising industry researcher asked: "If an advertiser buys *NYPD Blue* on Tuesday night and 10 percent of its audience watches it on Friday after midnight, should that audience be given equal value as the 'live' prime-time audience?" (Harmon 2002:A1).

COMBATING THE NEW MEDIA ENVIRONMENT

As it should be clear by now, the new media environment poses numerous challenges to the quality of the audience product. Much is being done to combat these challenges, with a flurry of new or improved measurement systems being tested and deployed, along with new techniques for capturing and maintaining audience attention. Inherent in all these efforts is the need to counteract the fragmentation and audience autonomy that increasingly characterize the contemporary media environment and that will become increasingly prominent in the media environment of the future.

In terms of responding to the increasing unpredictability of media audiences, participants in the audience marketplace are devoting more resources to audience research and increasing the degree to which such research findings dictate content production decisions. According to Kirkham, television "stations and advertising agencies are now devoting an increasing amount of effort and resources to attempting to predict future ratings levels" (1996:221). Today impressive numbers with test audiences can get a prime-time program on the air even when the consensus among programming and advertising executives is that the program lacks the attributes necessary for success (Schlosser 2001).[17] More evidence of the increased reliance on pretesting data can be seen in CBS/Viacom's recent decision to commit millions of dollars to a permanent, state-of-the-art audience research facility in the MGM Grand Hotel in Las Vegas (Consoli 2001a). The facility represents the first effort by a broadcast network to establish a permanent off-site facility devoted to measuring audience reactions to programming. Originally developed for testing CBS broadcast network programming, the facility has expanded to serve other units under the CBS/Viacom umbrella, including MTV, VH1, Nickelodeon, and Blockbuster Video (Consoli 2001a). The newspaper industry increasingly is using market research to guide content and format decisions, adding or removing entire sections on the basis of readership surveys (Berger 2001; McManus 1994; Underwood 1993). Even motion pictures are being test-marketed with an unprecedented level of rigor and intensity, with test results factored prominently into the editing and marketing of the final product (Lerner 1999; Puig 2000; Tasca 1998). However, little evidence exists that efforts such as these ever have been effective at predicting media audiences (Bielby and Bielby 1994; Gardini 2001); consequently, it seems highly unlikely that their utility will improve in an environment of increased fragmentation and increased audience autonomy.

In terms of counteracting the increased avoidance of advertising that is a function of increased audience autonomy, advertisers and media organizations are making efforts on several technological and strategic fronts. By many accounts, product placement within media products is becoming even more widespread and overt than in the past, and advertisers are pursuing more aggressively the integration of advertising and entertainment content (labeled "advertainment"; see Rich 2001). A good example of this process is BMW's recent advertising initiative; the auto maker's ad agency hired high-profile film directors such as Ang Lee and John Frankenheimer to direct short films that prominently featured BMW automobiles. Segments of the films air as television advertisements; however, to see the entire film one must visit the BMW Web site (Howe 2001b). Other companies, such as Ford, Volkswagen, and Coca Cola, are duplicating BMW's strategy in an effort to "keep their brands in front of consumers—even as traditional ads are increasingly muted, channel-surfed and TiVo-ed into oblivion" (Rich 2001:60).

A related integration strategy is UPN's recent announcement that it was considering allowing advertisers to place small symbols or logos (commonly called "ad bugs") in the corner of the screen (Elliott 2001). Assuming viewers do not react negatively to such an initiative, the strategy has the potential to minimize ad avoidance and, perhaps most important, create a situation in which advertisers can assume a high correlation between the audience for the program and the audience for the advertisement. Programs such as *Survivor,* and *Who Wants to Be a Millionaire?* have pursued a more traditional integration approach by integrating sponsors' products into the program content to an unprecedented degree. Contestants on *Survivor,* for example, win sponsors' products for successfully meeting various challenges.[18]

Such strategies have become even more pronounced in the motion picture industry, where corporations and products are receiving unprecedented levels of exposure and integration into story lines. Perhaps the most high-profile example in recent years is the Tom Hanks film *Castaway,* which prominently featured and favorably depicted Federal Express. The managing director of global brand management for Federal Express worked with the *Castaway* screenwriter for two years, creating what has been described as "the most advanced form of product placement ever seen" (D. Rogers 2001). Even book publishing has begun to follow this trend. In 2001 Bulgari paid the British author Fay Weldon to write a novel that prominently features the Italian jewelry firm (M. J. Rose 2001). All these efforts are a clear manifestation of the philosophy that "either the ads will need to become as entertaining as the programs or the programs will need to contain the ads, so they cannot be stripped out" (Lewis 2000:11).

In other cases advertisers are essentially using technology to force their ads upon audience members, with little effort at integrating advertising and entertainment. On the Internet "pop-up" ads, which often appear unsolicited on users' screens, are becoming increasingly prominent (Media Dynamics 2001a; Thompson 2001). Some DVDs have been programmed so that they begin with an advertisement that viewers cannot skip or fast-forward through.

Despite such efforts, the history of the effects of technologies such as the VCR and the remote control device tells us that, while advertisers can reduce the magnitude of advertisement avoidance, they cannot eliminate it. The levels of advertisement avoidance that exist in the current media environment will become more pronounced as opportunities for audience autonomy increase.

Finally, turning to the issue of audience measurement, the measurement firms are working hard to surmount the measurement challenges posed by an increasingly fragmented media environment. Historically, measurement firms have explored a variety of (sometimes outlandish) alternative systems of audience measurement. Typically, these efforts have focused on developing passive measurement systems that eliminate any need for audience input (Lu and Kiewit 1987; McKenna 1988), thereby minimizing the recall error that is exacerbated by increased media fragmentation. For instance, radio researchers have explored the possibility of placing sensors at various roadside locations. These sensors would pick up a signal from participating motorists that would allow the measurement firm to determine to which station the car radio is tuned. Nielsen Media Research has, at various times, considered sonar, infrared, facial recognition, and retinal scanning systems for measuring television audiences (Lu and Kiewit 1987; Purdye and Harvey 1994). Nielsen explored these systems in the hope that they would allow it to count the number of viewers in front of the television set and even to distinguish among them, without requiring the viewers to engage in any activities such as filling out diaries or pushing buttons.[19] However, issues of cost, practicality, and, in the case of the infrared system, privacy have prevented any of these systems from moving beyond the experimental stage.[20]

The current efforts at improving systems of audience measurement are somewhat less imaginative, if more practical. For instance, Nielsen Media Research is planning to double to ten thousand the number of households in its national people meter sample, a move that the *Wall Street Journal* described as underscoring "how increasing audience fragmentation is complicating the task of measuring who is watching what on television" (Beatty 2001a:B6). Of course, substantially higher costs to Nielsen subscribers will accompany such an increase in sample size, raising questions of whether subscriber resistance will delay or halt the effort (Beatty 2001a). Nielsen also is developing and testing an "active-passive" meter system that will be able to handle "digital and convergent television technologies" (Nielsen Media Research 2001a:1), in which multiple programs and commercials run simultaneously.

Perhaps Nielsen's most significant methodological advancement is the introduction of "local people meters" (see Lotoski 2000, 2001). Nielsen hopes to eventually replace (at least in large markets) the existing audimeter–paper diary hybrid system used to measure local television audiences with the people meter system now used to measure national television audiences. The company is using local people meters in Boston and plans to gradually extend the system to other large markets (Lotoski 2000). Such a shift in the techniques and technology for measuring local television audiences would bring greater detail, accuracy, and timeliness to local television audience data, because people meters can report audience demographic data every day, whereas the current system makes only household data available immediately—and only in those markets in which the company uses audimeters. The current system provides demographic data only quarterly (more frequently in larger markets), during sweeps periods when it distributes paper diaries to all local markets (see chapter 3). Local people meters also would reduce the substantial recall error typically associated with the use of paper diaries. Of course, local people meters also represent a substantially more expensive method than paper diaries for measuring local television audiences. In Boston, Nielsen has instituted a 30 percent fee increase to subscribers to cover the increased costs of the local people meter (Bachman 2002b). Thus Nielsen is likely to introduce local people meters only in those markets where subscriber revenues are sufficient to cover the costs (which is why local people meters probably will not find their way to small markets in the foreseeable future).

Given how the introduction of people meters at the national level affected the competitive dynamics within the television industry (specifically in terms of helping the cable industry better compete with broadcasters; see chapter 3), it is not surprising that AT&T (now Comcast), the largest cable operator in the Boston market, partially underwrote the Boston trial of local people meters and that the broadcast industry is intensely critical of the local people meter initiative (see Bachman 2001a; Lotoski 2000; 2001), refusing to provide financial support to the new system (Bachman 2002a; Hudson 2001).[21] By refusing to subscribe to the new system, broadcasters place themselves in the difficult position of not having Nielsen audience data in their possession when dealing with advertisers (Bachman 2002b), not having access to data to analyze program performance, and not being able to use Nielsen data in their promotional materials (Trigoboff 2002a). In fact, the widespread use of local people meters could do for local cable systems trying to compete with local broadcast stations what the original people meter initiative did for national cable networks that were competing with national broadcast networks for advertising dollars.

In Boston the local people meter is producing HUT levels that are 5 to 15 percent lower than diary-measured HUT levels, depending upon the time of day.[22] In addition, the data show higher viewership levels for children, teens, and young adults and slightly lower viewership levels for older adults (Hudson 2001). Such shifts in overall HUT levels and the demographic composition of the television audience can have a significant effect on the audience marketplace. Obviously, lower overall HUT levels could reduce the amount that advertisers are willing to spend on television advertising, given the lower audience reach that they are achieving. At the same time, however, demographic shifts produced by the change in measurement system may have a positive economic effect. Specifically, increases in the number of young adults in the audience (a highly valued demographic; see chapter 4) could result in higher overall CPMs.

From the standpoint of intermedia competition, local people meter data show declines in viewing levels of broadcast television across nearly all demographic groups, whereas cable viewing has increased across some demographic groups and shown only small declines in other demographic groups. Perhaps most important, prime-time broadcast viewership shows significant declines in the 18-to-34 and 18-to-49 age brackets, while prime-time cable viewership shows significant increases in the 18-to-34 age bracket and only slight declines in the 18-to-49 age bracket. This pattern suggests that broadcaster resistance to the local people meter is likely to remain intense. However, should the local people meter generate the necessary financial support to become a viable and widespread system of local television audience measurement, these results suggest that it may significantly alter the competitive dynamics between the cable and broadcast television industries at the local level.

The diffusion of local people meters may affect not only intermedia competition but content decision making as well. For instance, Lotoski (2000) speculates that the minute-by-minute ratings data from local people meters could lead to radical changes in the construction of local news broadcasts. Lotoski speculates that news directors may find it necessary "to program each newscast on a minute-to-minute basis to a different demographic target according to the day of the week" (2000:11). Consequently, "the specter of newscasts packed with one sensational story after another is a valid and frightening fear. Rating wars, typically fought on a monthly basis, would be reduced to an endless string of minute skirmishes" (11). Similarly, the quarterly ratings wars that take place during sweeps, when programmers unleash their biggest and best programming, could become a thing of the past, as continuous measurement undermines the logic of lumping such programming together during certain times of the year. Lotoski speculates that "the hyping, 'watch-to-win' sweepstakes and powerhouse programming during these months may become a phenomenon of the past, with special events distributed throughout the entire year" (2000:12).

It also seems plausible that the availability of up-to-the-minute ratings data could facilitate much higher levels of volatility in the scheduling practices of local television programmers. Underperforming programs probably would be pulled from the lineup much faster because the greater availability of data would facilitate more rapid decision making.[23] Similarly, stations may be more likely to experiment with and adjust schedules, because they would have more information immediately about the effectiveness of their scheduling decisions. The behavior of cable systems might be affected as well. The availability of more up-to-date and better-quality data on the demographics of the audience will provide cable systems with greater analytical resources in determining their ideal programming mix. Individual cable networks whose relatively poor demographic performance at the local level comes into sharper relief as a result of local people meter data may find it more difficult to obtain carriage on local cable systems, or they may find themselves moved further up the dial. As these speculative examples suggest, the processes of producing and scheduling local television programming could undergo massive change if Nielsen elects to install people meters throughout a large number of local television markets.

Perhaps more significant than Nielsen's local people meter initiative is Arbitron's development of the personal portable meter (PPM; also referred to as the portable people meter) (see Moss 2002; Patchen and Kolessar 1999). Arbitron has already tested this device in the United Kingdom and now is testing it in the United States (Patchen and Harris-Kojetin 2001).[24] It is roughly the size and shape of a pager and in fact is meant to be carried like one. Participants in the measurement process are expected to carry their PPM with them from the moment they wake up in the morning until the moment they go to sleep at night. The device records and time-stamps an inaudible signal embedded in all participating audio broadcasts (i.e., radio, television, and Internet broadcasts). Thus the device can record what stations/sites/programs the participants were exposed to, when this happened, and for how long. As this description suggests, the PPM requires not only the participation and cooperation of consumers but the participation and cooperation of media organizations. To have their content measured by the PPM, media organizations must install a VCR-sized deck that produces the necessary audio signal. At the end of the day participants return the PPM to a docking station, which sends the day's media exposure data to Arbitron overnight. The PPM is motion sensitive. Thus if it detects no motion for an extended period of time, the device shuts down and does not record audio signals (Patchen and Harris-Kojetin 2001).

One significant aspect of this device is that it represents a countermeasure to not only the increasing intramedia fragmentation that I have outlined but also to intermedia fragmentation. The passive dimension of the personal portable meter might be able to overcome many inaccuracies that arise because radio listeners must record their listening habits in a radio environment of greater channel abundance. Thus the PPM will record the fifteen minutes during which a listener switched away from her favorite Top 40 radio station to a news radio station in order to obtain traffic and weather information, a move that she might well have forgotten to record in a paper diary. The PPM also will record when a listener is in an office or a health club and a radio station is playing in the background. People are unlikely to record such listening under the diary system. (Whether such exposure should be included in audience estimates is another important issue.)

The personal portable meter also makes it easier to measure audience attention across three different media platforms: television, radio, and the Internet (McConochie and Uyenco 2002). Thus the PPM may counter effectively the problem of intermedia fragmentation that makes measuring an entire audience for a media product increasingly difficult (Menneer 2001). Indeed, Nielsen Media Research has entered into a development agreement with Arbitron (Bachman 2000a), suggesting that the personal portable meter may represent not only the future of radio audience measurement but the future of television audience measurement as well. As one advertising researcher notes, "This potentially would offer a way of looking at all electronic media on the same platform" (Bachman 2000a:6).

Unfortunately, the PPM does not address problems such as low levels of participation and generating sufficiently large and representative samples for an increasingly fragmented media environment, which suggests that it is not a complete solution to the declining quality of the audience product. In fact, the PPM system represents a substantially more expensive approach than the diary systems now used to measure radio and local television audiences (Twyman and Mundy 2001). It also is likely to be more expensive than any software-based systems for measuring exposure to audio and video on the Internet. Thus there is a question of whether sample sizes might actually decrease (out of economic necessity) when Arbitron deploys the PPM nationally. In measuring radio audiences (probably the primary application for this technology for the immediate future), smaller sample sizes might be offset by the greater accuracy afforded by the PPM technology. However, if the PPM is ever to become a true cross-media audience measurement platform, sample sizes must expand substantially to account for the effects of both intramedia and intermedia fragmentation. Whether competing media (radio, television, Internet) would be willing to pool the resources necessary to make such a system financially viable is what ultimately will determine whether the PPM becomes the basis for the first true cross-media measurement system.

Early indications are that, like earlier shifts in measurement technologies, a transition to the personal portable meter would result in a significantly different portrait of the media audience and, consequently, could cause changes in the competitive dynamics and content decision making within the relevant sectors of the media industry. Preliminary data from tests of the PPM show an overall increase in the size of the television audiences; however, average broadcast station ratings are a full point lower than current measures and average cable ratings that are more than double (from 1.0 to 2.1) current measures (Bachman 2001b; Patchen and Webb 2002). On the basis of these results it would appear that the PPM has the potential to continue the effects of the people meter by improving the cable industry's competitive position relative to the broadcast industry and by providing greater economic support for programmers who are providing content that targets narrow demographic niches.

The PPM also presents a different demographic portrait of the overall television audience. Specifically, the PPM measurement system produces dramatic increases in the number of men older than 18 in the television audience and in the number of people aged 6 to 17 in the television audience. The PPM also produces moderate increases in the number of 18- to 34-year-olds in the television audience (Patchen and Webb 2002).

The PPM's preliminary portrait of the radio audience offered less dramatic shifts. Overall radio listening was relatively consistent between the PPM and diary measurement systems; however, the PPM showed that more people listen to radio daily but for shorter periods of time and to a greater variety of stations than the diary method reflects (Patchen and Webb 2002). The PPM also produced significant shifts in when people listen to radio—showing that they do more listening on weekends and late at night and less during morning drive time (rating of 10.2 with the PPM versus 11.7 with the diaries; see Bachman 2001b). Such results may increase the value of the weekend and late-night dayparts for advertisers, thereby promoting greater investment in the content presented during these times. When demographic data are made public (no demographic data had been released as of this writing), we may find substantial demographic shifts in the composition of radio and television audiences; this may produce further shifts in the competitive dynamics between media industry segments and in the content production decisions of radio and television programmers.

The increased detail and immediacy of the personal portable meter data probably would also have a significant effect on radio content. The PPM would, for the first time, provide radio stations with the type of minute-by-minute "overnight" data that some segments of the television industry have received for years. Currently, audience data are available only quarterly and in fifteen-minute increments. According to one industry executive, the more immediate and detailed feedback provided by the PPM "would change the way programmers think about everything they do" (Bachman 2001c:6). Possible effects include much greater volatility in programming lineups (because instantaneous feedback would facilitate more rapid decision making); greater selectivity in the airing of individual songs (because stations would know almost immediately which songs led listeners to switch stations); and format reorganizations for individual radio programs (because stations could eliminate individual segments that repel audiences).

A number of other new audience measurement systems are in the works. Local cable television audiences, which remain poorly measured under the existing Nielsen system, now are being measured in some markets with a new set-top meter system that combines set-top meter data with recall data from telephone surveys (Weiss 2001).[25] ADcom, the company that provides the service, intends to supplement the generally poor quality of local cable audience data provided by Nielsen. Because the ADcom system uses audimeters, it allows for the reporting of household ratings on a daily basis. In addition, participants in metered households occasionally receive a viewing log that lists which programs the various television sets in the household were tuned to the previous day. Participants then are expected to identify who was watching which shows. ADcom then uses these aided recall reports to construct the demographic composition of the audience for individual programs (see Baniel and Ephron 2001). In addition, the company is seeking to provide single-source data by also gathering product-purchasing behavior data from its panel members (Baniel, Monistere, and Smyth 2001).

Another emerging system, called Target TV, relies on the data gathered by means of digital cable set-top boxes. This system, a joint venture of the QVC shopping network and the cable system operator Comcast, captures channel-tuning data every five seconds; however, this system obviously is limited to the measurement of digital cable subscribers and is not inherently capable of capturing demographic data. To the extent to which these new measurement systems are able to increase the value of local cable audiences, they may improve local cable systems' ability to compete with local broadcasters for advertising dollars. These increased revenues may in turn contribute to the increased availability of locally produced cable programming (something that today occurs to a significant degree only in a few large television markets).

Despite this array of new developments in the field of audience measurement, audience measurement systems are unlikely to keep pace with the rate of media and audience fragmentation. One reason involves the costs associated with making the necessary improvements. These costs must be covered by the purchasers of audience data (media organizations and advertisers). For them to be willing to spend the money, these improvements must clearly be in their best financial interests—that is, they must increase the value of the audience product that they are buying or selling.

Advertisers are, of course, likely to value any improvements that bring greater accuracy and reliability to the audience product. However, advertisers generally make a much smaller contribution to bottom line of audience measurement firms than do media organizations. Thus the extent to which advertisers can drive improvements in systems of audience measurement is limited.

The situation for media organizations is more complex. For a media organization to support increases in sample size or improvements in a measurement technology, the changes must increase that organization's revenue prospects in the audience marketplace. Presumably, any improvements in the accuracy and reliability of a measurement system will do just that, because advertisers generally will pay more for audience data that they deem to be more accurate and reliable (Webster and Phalen 1997). However, as I have already discussed, increases in sample size or improvements in measurement systems may in fact benefit some categories of content providers to the detriment of others. For instance, increased sample sizes or more advanced measurement systems may benefit niche content providers more than they benefit mass-appeal content providers and may in fact increase niche providers' ability to draw advertising dollars away from mass-appeal content providers (see chapter 3). In such a situation the mass-appeal content providers (who are inevitably larger and contributing more heavily to the measurement firm's bottom line) are likely to resist paying for larger sample sizes or improvements in measurement techniques or technologies. Or, as the discussion of the preliminary results of the personal portable meter and local people meter demonstrated, new measurement technologies can produce new portraits of audience behavior that improve the audience size and/or composition (in terms of valuable demographics) of some content providers while diminishing the audience size and/or composition of other content providers. Obviously, any media organization whose ability to compete in the audience marketplace is undermined by a new measurement system is unlikely to be willing to help support the launch of such a system—even if the new system unquestionably is more accurate than the existing system. Thus within the media industry, support for improvements in audience measurement is unlikely to be unanimous. Without widespread support the costs of drastically improving an audience measurement system are not likely to be covered, and any improvements probably will be small, gradual, and incremental rather than substantial, rapid, and far reaching. Unfortunately, according to one media researcher whom I consulted during the participant observation component of this study, the single greatest challenge facing audience measurement is convincing the media industry to pay for the research that could improve audience measurement methodologies. As this researcher noted, many participants in the audience marketplace "have an enormous investment in the status quo" and thus are resistant to funding changes.

This perspective raises important questions about the future of nascent improvements in existing audience measurement systems. Recently, Clear Channel Communications, one of the nation's largest radio station chains, briefly threatened to stop subscribing to Arbitron's data services during a contractual dispute with the company. At the time Clear Channel alone represented nearly $28 million in annual revenue for Arbitron (22 percent of Arbitron's annual revenue). As industry analysts noted, the loss of the Clear Channel account probably would hamper—and perhaps even halt—the development of the personal portable meter (Ordonez 2001a). More important, if a large radio group such as Clear Channel finds that the audience data produced by the PPM differ from previous data in ways that hurt the company's ability to compete for radio advertising dollars (e.g., by showing lower listenership levels or less valuable demographic compositions across stations), the company probably could prevent, alter, or delay any transition to the new measurement system. When a group of radio industry executives recently met with the Radio Advertising Bureau to discuss their concerns about the PPM, of particular concern were early PPM data showing increases in television viewing relative to radio listening; radio executives worry that "with the PPM their medium will get less of the ad pie" (Bachman 2002c:6).

Industry consensus at this point is that, even if the PPM initiative can gain the funding necessary to begin replacing radio diaries, PPM's future in the area of television audience measurement is dependent upon Arbitron's receiving a substantial investment from Nielsen (Moss 2002). Whether Nielsen is willing to enter a joint venture with a competitor is so far uncertain, particularly given Nielsen's ongoing local people meter experiments (Trigoboff 2002c). As this example illustrates, while the techniques and technologies of audience measurement may be able to sustain a certain level of quality in the audience product, the audience product is not a function of technology alone. The economics of the audience marketplace can significantly affect the means of producing the audience product.

The impending transition to the local people meter in television audience measurement provides another useful case in point. As I have already noted, the local people meter initiative is facing intense resistance from the broadcast television industry (see "Stations Resist" 2001). Broadcasters recall how, at the national level, people meters enhanced the cable industry's ability to compete for national advertising dollars and fear comparable effects at the local level. Data from Boston show that this is exactly what is likely to happen. Moreover, preliminary data show across-the-board declines in HUT levels under the local people meter system, which could weaken support for the local people meter even from within the cable industry. Should local people meter data continue to project smaller audiences, the television industry is unlikely to underwrite a national rollout of the local people meter service.

The key question that this situation raises is whether the greater accuracy and reliability generally attributed to local people meter data will increase the value of local television audiences to advertisers sufficiently to compensate for the smaller audiences. This is a vitally important empirical question that has not yet been effectively investigated. However, the relevance of the answer is limited because risk-averse television stations are not likely to pay for a system that may reduce their audiences, given that they cannot be certain that the greater accuracy will bring sufficient revenue increases to compensate for the audience loss. Thus from a long-term perspective, it may make sense for a particular segment of the media industry to embrace a new measurement system that genuinely is capable of providing greater accuracy, because such actions may protect the long-term value of the audience product. However, the short-term damage from such shifts in measurement systems is more likely to guide the decision making.

MODELING AUDIENCE BEHAVIOR

Perhaps the best evidence that existing systems of audience measurement will not be able to keep pace with the new media environment lies in the ongoing efforts at developing systems of "modeling" audience behavior. Modeling initiatives are under way in both television and Internet audience research. These initiatives generally involve less direct measurement of audience behavior and rely on probabilities to determine who is consuming what media product. It is important to emphasize that the impetus for modeling initiatives stems from the increasing ineffectiveness and perceived inaccuracy of existing systems and from the costs associated with using more sophisticated measurement technologies across the larger samples that the increasingly fragmented media environment requires (see Engel and Maiville 2000; Ephron and Baniel 2000; Ephron and Gray 2000).

Looking first at television, researchers are testing the viability of a system of modeling the demographic composition of television audiences based primarily upon data derived from basic audimeters (see Ephron and Gray 2000). Viewer modeling uses the demographic data obtained when a household becomes part of an audimeter panel to develop probabilities for which household audience members watch which individual programs. Thus at the most basic level, if the participant is a single-person household, the audimeter can easily determine the demographic composition of the household viewers. Further demographic determinations can be made by determining which set is tuned to a particular program. Thus, according to Ephron, "You know that if the set in the kitchen is tuned to Oprah, it's probably a woman who's watching. If it's football in the den, it's probably the man" (Weiss 2001:4). For those remaining households whose individual viewers cannot be determined by such methods, demographic probabilities obtained from national people meter samples or occasional surveys would be used to make audience demographic determinations (Engel and Maiville 2000; Ephron and Gray 2000). Thus while at some point a company still needs to measure audience demographic data under this system, it needs to do so only occasionally or only at the national level (thereby eliminating local sweeps or the need to install local people meters).

Similarly, a Cambridge, Massachusetts, firm is developing artificial intelligence software that can tell which family member is surfing the Internet or television channels based on the person's mouse clicks or remote control patterns (Stoughton 2001). Such software, if effective, could bring greater efficiency and accuracy to the system of Internet audience measurement by eliminating the need for different family members to log in each time they go on line. This log-in process, and its associated inconvenience, may discourage participation among some selected participants and may contribute to inaccuracy if a family member fails to log out before another family member gets on line or if users intentionally or unintentionally log in as other family members. Eliminating these sources of inaccuracy and nonparticipation may significantly increase the quality of the Internet audience product.

Modeling systems such as those being developed in the television and Internet contexts also may be able to combat the effects of intermedia fragmentation on the quality of the audience product by facilitating the measurement of cross-media consumption. Thus, for example, relying on passive audimeters instead of people meters or diaries can reduce the burden on participants enough to facilitate measuring other areas of media consumption, such as magazine reading or Internet use within the same household (Ephron and

Gray 2000). In an environment of increased intermedia fragmentation, such cross-media measurement data would be increasingly valuable, particularly in light of the growing body of evidence that media consumers increasingly "multitask" (i.e., consume multiple media simultaneously or switch rapidly back and forth between media) (*MTV Networks/Viacom Study* 2000). Existing measurement systems are poorly equipped to determine how media consumers are using different media in concert with one another and how content delivered by one medium might interact with that of another medium. Understanding such behavioral patterns is likely to become central to maximizing the value of the audience product in the new media environment. However, any single-medium measurement system that imposes significant burdens on the participants essentially rules out imposing additional media measurement systems or obligations on these same participants (Ephron and Gray 2000), thereby limiting the extent to which multimedia consumption patterns can be incorporated into the dynamics of the audience marketplace.[26]

Developments such as television viewer modeling and intelligent Internet monitoring software suggest that measuring audiences in the future may not require direct monitoring of individuals' media consumption in order to produce acceptable aggregate data on audience behavior patterns. Developments of this sort represent a response to the strains that fragmentation is placing upon existing systems of audience measurement and the unique audience research needs that arise from an increasingly fragmented media environment. It remains to be seen, however, whether such developments represent more accurate and/or cost-effective alternatives to traditional approaches and whether all stakeholders in the audience marketplace would embrace such developments. It seems particularly likely that advertisers would not highly value any audience product derived from modeling audience behavior because such a product would represent even more of a statistical abstraction than existing audience products.

MEDIA-BASED AUDIENCE MEASUREMENT SYSTEMS

Another means of coping with the difficulties associated with measuring an increasingly fragmented and autonomous media audience might involve moving away from audience-based systems of audience measurement and toward media-based systems of audience measurement. Such an evolution would take advantage of the increasingly interactive nature of new media technologies (see Foley, Magnani, and Terry 2001). Most interactive media technologies (those in which the content provider and the audience member share information) have the capacity for "built-in" audience measurement systems. Cable television represents a prime example, because the more advanced cable systems and set-top boxes increasingly have the ability to monitor the viewing habits of cable subscribers (Sprenger 1999). As cable systems upgrade from analog to digital, the interactive capabilities of these networks increase, thereby increasing the extent to which these networks can monitor and record subscribers' media consumption behaviors (Harvey, Jarvis, and Booth 2002). Nielsen Media Research recently entered into a strategic partnership with Gemstar–TV Guide, the company that provides interactive program guides to cable systems. The partnership is intended to "provide for collaboration between the two parties to develop state-of-the-art research information products from the proprietary data captured by Gemstar–TV Guide International's Interactive Program Guides" ("Gemstar–TV Guide" 2001:1). In addition, the American Association of Advertising Agencies and the Advertising Research Foundation recently announced a plan to create a massive television ratings database from the growing universe of digital set-top boxes, including cable and satellite converters and other digital devices (Mandese 2002).

Congress has, however, imposed limits upon the use of such data. Specifically, the Cable Act of 1992 prevents cable systems from selling subscribers' viewing data to third parties. However, the act does not restrict cable systems from using such data internally (i.e., in making programming decisions).[27] It also is important to note that the restrictions imposed by the Cable Act do not directly address video services delivered through telephone networks or satellite, which may mean that they have more freedom to exploit any audience behavior data that they gather.

The development of "built-in" audience measurement systems also is taking place in the Internet environment. The inherently interactive nature of the Internet means that a Web site automatically logs the visitors to that site. In chapter 3, I discussed how this process has led to the development of server log analysis to determine the characteristics of the Internet audience. However, as I also noted in that chapter, such systems cannot effectively gather the demographic data required by advertisers, although the planting of "cookies" on hard drives and the various means by which these cookies can be used to derive user demographic data (Hemphill 2000) suggest that it is possible to use some form of server log analysis to obtain the necessary demographic data. Regardless of the specific means used or its ultimate effectiveness, the key point here is that interactive media technologies such as cable television and the Internet have the built-in capacity to monitor audiences' media consumption.

Other new media developments, including personal video recording devices such as TiVo and ReplayTV, represent similar opportunities for taking advantage of interactive media technologies to automatically monitor media consumption behaviors. Personal video recorders operate as interactive, subscription-based systems: The device downloads program schedules and uploads diagnostic information and viewing behavior data (Martin 2001). Inherent in this system is the ability to link subscriber information (including demographic data) with media consumption patterns, to aggregate such data, and to subject it to analysis—although PVR providers insist that they are doing no such thing (see TiVo 2001).

The key difference that all these examples represent over the older systems of audience measurement is that all users of these media technologies become potential subjects for analysis. In this regard these systems have the capacity to overcome the sample-size problems that are becoming increasingly acute in an ever-fragmenting media environment. Essentially, these technologies and services represent the opportunity to be freed from the limitations imposed by constructing and maintaining representative samples. In the most extreme scenario measurement firms would no longer use samples to project audience estimates for individual television programs or Web sites and instead would derive them from a census of all television or Internet users. Of course, for this scenario to become reality for television, digital set-top box and/or PVR penetration would have to become nearly universal, neither of which seems likely to happen. Even projecting from all users of these technologies to the population as a whole would be problematic, given the likelihood that users of these technologies would not (at least in the short term) accurately represent the population as a whole. However, the distortions associated with projecting from such an unrepresentative sample may be less significant than the distortions associated with traditional sample-based measurement systems, which are becoming increasingly incapable of accurately and reliably capturing audience behavior in the new media environment.

It also is important to emphasize that such "built-in" audience measurement systems could be truly passive—audience members would have to do nothing to have their consumption behaviors recorded. They do not necessarily even need to agree to take part in the measurement process. This, however, is where legal and ethical issues have begun to arise. In the wake of continuing high levels of concern about privacy invasions within the context of Internet use (Federal Trade Commission 2000; Hemphill 2000), a flurry of concern has arisen about potential privacy invasions in the interactive television environment. Reports showing the potential for interactive television systems to gather extremely detailed viewing information without necessarily receiving the consent of the consumer (e.g., Burke 2000; Center for Digital Democracy 2001; Martin 2001) have generated a substantial amount of attention in the news media (e.g., Chunovic 2001; Koerner 2001; Stoughton 2001) and have led to congressional hearings and an FTC investigation into the privacy policies of interactive television service providers (Dingell, Towns, and Markey 2001).[28] Given the extent to which privacy concerns are becoming an increasingly prominent aspect of the new media environment, it seems unlikely that media-based systems of audience measurement ever will be able to replace completely the existing audience-based audience measurement systems.

Media-based measurement systems also would have to overcome decades of tradition in audience measurement. As Ivie and Terlizzi (2001) note, the auditing and accrediting experience of the Media Rating Council has been limited to measurement systems using sample-based approaches (until 2000, when a publisher applied for accreditation for a Web site–based measurement process). Consequently, at this point no established, institutionalized standards exist in regard to what comprises a high-quality media-centered measurement system. This situation will further slow any possibility of migration from audience-centered to media-centered measurement systems.

In the end, although media institutions will use a variety of strategies and tactics to maintain the quality of the audience product, these efforts are not likely to overcome the negative effects that the new media environment has created. Figure 5.1 illustrates this dynamic by revisiting the audience product as originally depicted in figure 1.1. Figure 5.1 depicts the various mechanisms discussed throughout this book for improving the congruence between the predicted audience and the measured audience, and between the measured audience and the actual audience, as forces pushing toward the center of the model. Thus media organizations' increasing reliance upon pretesting of media products is intended to work in conjunction with content-selection strategies involving a reliance on past successes (in terms of genre, format, personnel, etc.; see chapter 2) and the variety of "seamless"

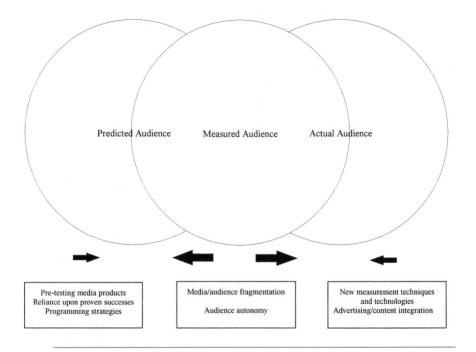

FIGURE 5.1 The Audience Product Revisited

programming strategies to bring greater control and predictability to audience behavior and improve the congruence between the predicted audience and the measured audience. At the same time audience measurement firms are improving their techniques and technologies for measuring audiences, and content providers are exploring new means of integrating media content and advertising content in an effort to bring greater congruence to the measured audience–actual audience relationship.

However, as figure 5.1 shows, the more powerful forces (represented by the larger arrows) are the increasing fragmentation of the media environment and the increasing audience autonomy that the media environment facilitates. These forces are working against both predicted audience–measured audience congruence and measured audience–actual audience congruence. The strength of these forces is such that the quality of the audience product is likely to decline as the media environment continues to evolve.

CHAPTER 6

THE FUTURE OF THE AUDIENCE MARKETPLACE

What might the decline in the quality of the audience product mean for the future of advertiser-supported media? The effects could be wide ranging, affecting, for example, where and how advertisers spend their marketing dollars; the content production decisions of media organizations; and the pursuit of new revenue streams or business models by content providers.

THE DYNAMICS OF BUYING AND SELLING AUDIENCES

Continued declines in the quality of the audience product probably would affect the structure of audience transactions and where marketing dollars are spent, with advertisers increasingly avoiding traditional advertising-supported media and/or resisting traditional pricing structures. The most common transactional form in the audience marketplace currently involves exposure-based pricing, typically on a cost-per-thousand (CPM) basis. However, as the quality of the audience product declines and the reliability of any exposure-based transaction suffers, exposure-based pricing is likely to increasingly lose ground to alternative pricing structures. The most obvious alternative involves cost-per-action (CPA) forms of pricing, which base pricing not on the number of audience members exposed to a message but on the number of audience members who exhibit some sort of measurable response to the advertising message.

Cost-per-action models already have become quite prominent in the Internet environment. Typically, these CPA models are based either upon "click-through" rates for an on-line advertisement or upon the number of purchases that are generated by the advertisement (with the content provider typically receiving a percentage of the revenue derived from such purchases). Such pricing models have achieved prominence in the Internet environment largely because of its unique interactive and behavioral monitoring capabilities. However, such pricing models have begun to infiltrate other media as well. For instance, direct response advertising has become increasingly prominent in broadcast and cable television. Such advertising often uses "per-inquiry" pricing models, whereby programmers receive compensation based on the number of consumers who make a purchase by calling a telephone number displayed on screen (Waterman 2001). As more people sign up for interactive television services, the technological capabilities for developing additional means of structuring such cost-per-action pricing models will develop. Of course, as I noted in chapter 2, media organizations may have good reason to resist such pricing models, because the result could be lower overall revenues. However, the key point here is that in an environment in which the traditional audience product (i.e., one based upon exposure to advertising messages) is in decline, media organizations may be forced to embrace such alternative pricing models out of economic necessity.

Pressure from advertisers may force media organizations to adopt CPA pricing models, in part because the new media environment offers advertisers an increasing number of alternatives for reaching potential consumers. In the face of declines in the quality of the audience product delivered by media organizations, advertisers can, on the one hand, turn to traditional alternative sources of message delivery, such as billboards (for which a more advanced audience measuring system is in development), direct mail, and event sponsorship. Although these marketing venues have their own weaknesses, they probably will have greater appeal relative to mass-media advertising if the quality of the audience product delivered by media organizations is declining. Moreover, Internet-based services such as e-mail and the Web are facilitating new one-to-one electronic marketing techniques (C. Larson 2001; Rust and Oliver 1994), giving advertisers additional alternatives to the audience product delivered by media organizations. In these alternative marketing contexts, predicting and measuring audiences are less central to the transaction, and thus the new techniques may become increasingly appealing to advertisers frustrated by the growing uncertainty and risk associated with the traditional advertising-supported media. One study has estimated that personal video recorders alone will cost the television industry an estimated $12 billion in advertising revenue by 2006 (M. Larson 2001) as advertisers reduce what they are willing to pay for television audiences and/or move some of their advertising dollars to other media. In a recent criticism of local television audience data, one advertising executive expressed advertisers' growing frustration with traditional media: "It is so bad I would be surprised if anybody continued to spend money based upon that information" ("Fragmentation Face-off" 2001:28). Procter and Gamble recently announced its intention to cut back on its use of spot television as a result of the weak measurement system (Harvey, Jarvis, and Booth 2002). Statements and actions such as these reflect increased displeasure with the quality of the audience product delivered by advertiser-supported media and an increased likelihood that advertisers will look elsewhere in their efforts to reach consumers with advertising messages.

THE EVOLVING AUDIENCE MARKETPLACE AND MEDIA CONTENT

Given the interdependency of the audience market and the content market, any declines in the quality of the audience product are likely have a significant effect on media content. At the most basic level any declines in the quality of the audience product will, as I have suggested, diminish its value to advertisers and probably will mean lower overall revenues for content providers. As I noted in chapter 4, the budget for any piece of media content is a function of the size and value of the potential audience for it (Owen and Wildman 1992). Because the new media environment is likely to be one in which it is increasingly difficult to monetize audiences, it also is likely to be one in which investment in content—at least on a per-media-product basis—is likely to decline as well.

This phenomenon will not manifest itself simply in the form of lower production budgets for individual content options. Indeed, a general decline in production budgets for individual media products may not occur at all. Instead, we are likely to see an increase in the extent to which content is "windowed," "repurposed," or "syndicated" across media platforms or channels, as well as reused within individual platforms or channels. This is a way of distributing content production costs across a larger audience base and using individual pieces of media content to fill up greater proportions of the "content hole" (i.e., the total amount of time or space to be filled with media content).

Such strategies certainly are not new. Windowing and syndicating media content are core strategies designed to take advantage of the public good nature of media content (see Owen and Wildman 1992; Werbach 2000). In addition, most new media technologies must, at least in their early stages, function primarily as distribution platforms for content first produced for other media, because providing such content generally is less expensive than producing original content (see Waterman and Grant 1991; Werbach 2000); these new technologies do not, in their early stages, have a sufficient audience base—or sufficiently reliable measurement systems—to attract the advertising dollars necessary to pay for original content. Digital cable provides perhaps the most recent example of this phenomenon, with one analyst describing that environment as one in which "there's very little new to watch; mostly just a lot more of the same old, same old content" (Beatty 2002:B1). However, once these new technologies have established a substantial audience base, as well as a reasonably accurate and reliable system of audience measurement, they are able to capture sufficient revenues to fund the production of original content. Cable's evolution from a dumping ground for Hollywood movies and old network television series to a significant source of original programming provides a useful case in point. Broadcast television similarly relied much more heavily on Hollywood films in the past than it does today.

The key point here, however, is that as the quality of the audience product declines, the pressure to reuse, recycle, and repackage media content will become more intense. In an increasingly fragmented, increasingly autonomous media environment, in which it will become increasingly difficult to monetize audiences, the extent to which both old and new media technologies and services will be able to support the production of original content will drop. As a result the media environment of the future is likely to be one in which content increasingly is repeated, repackaged, and recycled within and across delivery platforms. Recent developments, such as the broadcast networks' increasing use of basic cable networks for re-airing recent episodes of current prime-time series (Flint and Orwall 2001; McClellan and Schlosser 2001) and the extent to which cable networks repeat their original programming multiple times within the same week or month (even running original programs two or three times within the same day—sometimes back to back) provide an indication of the difficulties associated with monetizing audiences sufficiently to support the production of original content across a full broadcast schedule. Indeed, an existing technology such as cable television may in fact have already passed its peak in terms of its ability to provide original content. While it may appear that cable networks' reliance on old broadcast network reruns and Hollywood films has declined (although researchers should empirically assess whether this is indeed the case), it is important to remember that when cable programmers do produce original content, they typically repeat it so frequently that the production costs on a per-hour or per-audience-member basis probably drop to levels approximating the costs for acquiring content originally produced for other media. This increased repetition needs to be taken into account when considering the extent to which cable programmers truly are providing "original" programming throughout the day. As the quality of the audience product declines, the difficulties associated with covering production costs will become more pronounced, and such repetition, repackaging, and recycling strategies will become even more prominent.

Applying this same logic to new media technologies, it may, for example, be a long time before the Internet functions as any sort of meaningful source of original content. The highly fragmented and autonomous nature of the Internet environment undermines the process of establishing an accurately and reliably measured audience that can be monetized sufficiently to support the production of original content. Consequently, the long-term future of the Internet as a media content provider probably will be as a secondary distribution channel for content produced for other media (see also Napoli 1998b). Given that, to a certain degree, the rate at which consumers embrace a new media technology is a function of the perceived quantity and quality of the content available, declines in the quality of the audience product could undermine content production for new media technologies, thereby also undermining the rate at which new technologies diffuse through the population. Certainly, a technology such as the Internet has, to this point, diffused at a remarkable rate, but the recent slowdown in Internet diffusion may be attributable in part to perceptions among more hesitant adopters that it offers little content of interest or value. Were the on-line audience marketplace a more lucrative one, perhaps more appealing content would be available and even more people would be on line.

The declining quality of the audience product also may affect some types of content more dramatically than others. Consider, for instance, content that targets a narrow audience segment. As I showed in chapter 5, a main force driving a decline in the quality of the audience product is the inability of audience measurement firms to keep pace with an environment of increasingly fragmented media technologies and the associated increasing fragmentation of media audiences. As the media environment becomes increasingly fragmented, audience estimates for all content providers are drawn from a decreasing number of actual audience members. This process will undermine the quality of the audience product for all content providers but will disproportionately harm those content providers that target smaller niche audiences, because smaller audiences cannot be measured as accurately or reliably as larger audiences (see chapter 3). To the extent that niche media outlets attract smaller-than-average audiences, they are likely to suffer an economic handicap as a result of the lower valuations that advertisers are likely to place on lower-quality audience data. Thus even if these small niche audiences are demographically desirable, their value to advertisers will diminish. A demographic is valuable only if it is measured in a way that advertisers consider reliable.

Certainly, niche content providers always have suffered from this handicap. However, as the media environment grows increasingly fragmented (and, it is assumed, measurement systems do not keep pace), the magnitude of this handicap will become more pronounced. In an environment in which shortcomings of audience measurement systems increasingly undermine the economic value of niche audiences, content providers will be able to earn less from the audiences that they do attract and thus will be able to invest less in their programming, which will undermine further their ability to compete in the audience marketplace (Picard 1999). One recent analysis describes the gap between cable networks' share of the television audience and their share of advertising dollars as ever expanding (M. Larson 2002:5) and says that in the most recent "up-front" buying period (2002) broadcast networks experienced significant gains in terms of overall revenues and CPMs, while most cable networks experienced only modest gains or, in many instances, declines, although the cable audience continues to grow while the broadcast audience continues to shrink (McClellan and Romano 2002). Such patterns suggest that the economic challenges associated with serving small niche audiences are growing more intense. The potential irony here is is that even in an increasingly fragmented media environment, the strategy of targeting a narrow homogeneous audience segment may in fact become less appealing.

Current developments in the cable television industry help illustrate this point. Cable channels such as Court TV, the History Channel, Oxygen, and ESPN, which target fairly narrow audiences and originated with the intention of producing original content that appeals to narrow audience groups, have altered their programming in similar ways. Thus, for instance, Oxygen airs reruns of the syndicated first-run action-adventure series *Xena: Warrior Princess;* Court TV airs reruns of canceled broadcast network series such as the NBC series *Homicide: Life on the Streets;* and the History Channel frequently airs old Hollywood films with historical subject matter. Recently, the cable sports network ESPN launched a sports-themed talk-variety show in an effort to move beyond the network's traditional audience (male sports enthusiasts) and attract "casual sports fans and more women" (Romano 2002b:22). The key commonality among these examples is that these niche programmers are supplementing their niche content with content produced to appeal to broader audiences. Similar efforts are apparent in cable news as well, where the conservative-leaning Fox News channel hired Geraldo Rivera (an outspoken defender of former President Bill Clinton), whereas the more liberal CNN hired the conservative commentator Jonah Goldberg. Industry analysts have described these moves as efforts by both networks to broaden their appeal to viewers across the political spectrum (Carter 2002). Blumler has described such processes as a tendency to "expand outward from a homogeneous audience base toward a more heterogeneous appeal" (1996:105).

Previous analyses of the media environment emphasize that, even in an era of increased media and audience fragmentation, economic incentives to attract traditional "mass audiences" remain (Blumler 1996; Neuman 1991). These analyses, however, generally do not include the declining quality of the audience product as a force behind the continued pursuit of mass audiences. Indeed, the key point here is that niche content providers must pursue such audiences in order to combat the lower-quality data associated with attracting a true niche audience and that such tactics will, by necessity, become more pronounced in the media environment of the future. Consequently, the media environment of the future may offer a greater number of content options, more of which actually seek to attract a fairly broad demographic. At the very least, the media environment will be one in which the production budgets for niche-oriented products lag even further behind those designed to appeal to heterogeneous audiences.

In the end, all these processes lead down the same general path—one in which the media system's increasing technological capacity for providing content that serves a wide range of audience segments and audience interests is being undermined, from an economic standpoint, by this same capacity. As a result, instead of thriving, the traditional audience marketplace may find itself staggering under the weight of an increasingly fragmented media environment in which audiences possess an increasing amount of autonomy. Ultimately, while the technological capacity for a media system of truly diverse content offerings serving a true diversity of audience interests is enormous, the economic capacity to do so is limited. As a result the extent to which genuine increases in diversity of content offerings accompany increases in content delivery capacity may diminish.

A SHIFTING ECONOMIC FOUNDATION

If, as I have suggested thus far, the media environment of the future is one in which the traditional mechanisms of monetizing audiences are likely to prove less lucrative (see also Picard 2001a), we should expect to see shifts in the underlying business models that media organizations use. Specifically, media organizations are likely to move away from traditional advertising-supported models of content provision and increasingly seek to cultivate and exploit alternative revenue streams. This is not to say, however, that media audiences will not remain important sources of value. Indeed, perhaps one of the most important revenue sources in the media environment of the future will be the personal demographic and behavioral data of media consumers. The way the media environment is evolving will make it increasingly easy to gather certain types of data about media consumers (see chapter 5). Thus while effective measuring of audience exposure to media content is becoming increasingly difficult, on the other hand, obtaining personal information about media consumers—such as age, gender, and some product-purchasing and -usage behaviors—is becoming easier. Marketers place a high value on such data. For instance, it is widely believed that Blockbuster Video's most valuable asset is not its facilities or video and DVD library but its database of customer demographic data and video rental histories. Such data have become increasingly vital in the Internet context, where many content providers have found both the advertising- and subscription-based models to be largely untenable thus far. As a result the media environment of the future probably will be one in which media organizations increasingly will seek ways to gather and charge for the personal data of the audiences that they attract. Media organizations also are likely to increasingly focus on other potential revenue streams, such as commerce and research services. In the magazine industry, for example, publishers are not only marketing their subscriber databases more aggressively and more creatively but also are providing additional services to advertisers such as event marketing, primary research, and supplying speakers for advertiser-sponsored functions (M. Rose 2001).

Significant institutional shifts are also likely to occur as the traditional means of reaching consumers decline in value and effectiveness. Consider, for instance, the discussion in chapter 5 of the increased emphasis on product placement in response to the declining quality of the traditional audience product. This trend already has begun prompting unique collaborations by the advertising and creative industries. For instance, the Interpublic Group, one of the world's largest advertising holding companies, recently initiated efforts to purchase literary agencies and Hollywood talent agencies in a step toward streamlining the process of integrating consumer products into entertainment content. According to one Interpublic executive, "Clients want brands integrated into plots" (Vranica 2002: B1). However, the consensus in the advertising industry is that advertisers get involved in the creative process much too late. Moves such as Interpublic's would allow the integration of product-marketing much earlier in the creative process. Such an institutional convergence between the advertising and creative industries is likely to become more prominent in the future and ultimately may represent the predominant institutional arrangement in a media environment in which fragmentation and audience autonomy compel an ever-tighter integration of content and advertising.

The issue here is bigger than the simple notion that movies, television programs, books, and magazine articles will increasingly incorporate commercial messages. The larger issue involves the changing institutional identities of the organizations that produce these cultural products and the associated changes in the nature of the process by which these products are produced. Issues of artistic or journalistic integrity may become increasingly prominent. More likely, such issues will become increasingly moot, as the institutional integration of advertising and content production becomes the norm rather than the exception. In any case the set of assumptions and expectations that audience members bring to the consumption of cultural products will need to change if the institutional dynamics surrounding the production of these products changes dramatically.

In an environment of declining quality of the audience product, we also may enter a period of media evolution in which all media increasingly shift toward more audience-payment forms of media content. As I noted in chapter 1, different media differ in the extent to which they rely upon advertising revenues to fund the production of content. Moreover, many segments of the media industry have evolved over time in terms of the extent to which they rely upon advertising revenue. Thus, for instance, the newspaper industry once received the bulk of its revenues from readers, rather than advertisers. Over time, however, the newspaper industry relied more heavily on advertising revenues than subscriber revenues (Baker 1994).

As the media environment continues to develop in ways that undermine the quality of the audience product, an evolutionary pattern away from advertising revenues is likely to accelerate. Such a trend already appears to be well underway in the Internet context. Many sites that once provided visitors with free content now are charging fees on either a monthly, yearly, or à la carte basis (T. Jones 2001; Mangalindan 2002; Zeitchik 2001). Although this shift has multiple causes (the declining economy; the lack of evidence of Internet advertising effectiveness), the generally low quality of the audience product in the Internet environment, because of the difficulties associated with accurately and reliably measuring Internet audiences, must be among the factors.

Looking beyond the Internet, emerging media technologies such as satellite radio, interactive television, digital cable, and digital television broadcasting are likely to focus on audience payment for content rather than advertising support (Albiniak 2001; Alleyne 2001), suggesting that the traditional advertiser-support model is a less viable business strategy for new media technologies. The idea that the media environment of the future increasingly will emphasize direct pricing and not advertising-supported models is not a new one (e.g., Waterman 2001). The investment-banking firm of Veronis, Suhler, and Associates (2001) predicts that the percentage of media consumption time that audiences spend with advertiser-supported media will decline from 61 percent in 1999 (down from 69 percent in 1995) to 55 percent in 2004, while the percentage of time that audiences spend with direct-payment forms of media will increase from 39 percent in 1999 to 45 percent in 2004 (up from 31 percent in 1995). The key point here is that declines in the quality of the audience product will be an important driving force behind any such transition.

If such a transition takes place, the media environment of the future will be one in which the audience and content markets increasingly are divorced from one another. As a result media content will become less a reflection of advertisers' audience preferences and more a reflection of the preferences of those audience segments with the greatest willingness to pay. Such a shift in the economic underpinnings of media content could have a significant effect on the nature of the content that media organizations produce. As I discussed in chapter 4, advertisers tend to value some segments of the media audience more than others. They value audiences within the 18-to-49 age bracket more highly than audiences in other age brackets. They value audiences with higher incomes more highly than audiences with lower incomes. The data from my analysis even suggest that advertisers value white audiences more highly than African American or Hispanic audiences. These valuations are, naturally, reflected in the nature of the content offerings that advertiser-supported media organizations make available. Should media organizations migrate away from advertising support and rely more heavily on audience payments for content, those audience segments with the greatest willingness to pay for content will find the greatest amount of content offerings targeting their particular interests—and these audience segments may turn out to be very different from those that advertisers traditionally have valued most highly. Future research should devote greater attention to the question of how the willingness to pay for media content varies in accordance with demographic factors and how such willingness to pay perhaps also varies across media technologies. Such research would provide a clearer picture of how the media content in a more heavily audience-supported media environment would differ from the content available in the current media environment. Perhaps many of the same inequities present in the current media environment would be replicated. Or perhaps different inequities would arise.

THE ELUSIVE, INTANGIBLE, UNPREDICTABLE AUDIENCE PRODUCT

It is important to emphasize that none of these speculations is meant to suggest the impending demise of advertising-supported media, only a decline in the viability of such an approach to financing the delivery of media content. However, given the nature of the audience product, perhaps such a shift is inevitable. The audience product is perhaps one of the most difficult to produce, most poorly manufactured, and most difficult to purchase products available in our economy. Consequently, it remains a high-risk, highly uncertain product market.

Advertisers purchase audiences, and media organizations produce and distribute content on the basis of what are—at best—educated guesses about the size and composition of the audience to be produced. Efforts to rationalize and bring greater certainty to this process rely upon strategies and tactics that are of questionable utility. As a result the ability to precisely control the parameters of the product being produced is limited to an extent not found in many other segments of the economy.

In addition, even when an audience is produced and delivered, significant questions remain regarding whether the audience product that has been produced and paid for is a reasonably accurate representation of the audience that actually consumed the media product. Ironically, certain participants in the audience marketplace have a vested interest in maintaining such discrepancies and systematically undermine efforts to alleviate this problem. That purchasers of audiences never are able to determine with absolute certainty the exact nature of the product they have purchased means that they face a level of uncertainty in their transaction that few—if any—other consumers in our economy must face.

Finally, the very process by which advertisers determine which segments of the media audience are most worth pursuing is based upon assumptions that are—at best—of questionable validity and reliability and—at worst—may bring no significant increases in efficiency to the audience transaction. Economic and analytical limitations among all participants in the audience marketplace have, however, allowed such imperfect criteria for determining the value of media audiences to persist, and they probably will persist into the foreseeable future. As a result purchasers of audiences seldom can say with any degree of certainty that the audience that they are in fact attempting to purchase is in fact the audience that it is in their best interests to reach.

In an environment of such high uncertainty and consequently such high risk, instability is to be expected. Shifts in the techniques and technologies of audience measurement, in the technologies for the delivery of media content, or in the demographic makeup of the media audience or its economic or behavioral characteristics all can drastically affect the dynamics of the audience marketplace. That we achieve a deeper understanding of these processes is of the utmost importance, because the nature of some of our most significant, widely consumed, and influential cultural and political products is a reflection of this highly unpredictable, largely intangible, and ultimately unstable audience marketplace.

NOTES

INTRODUCTION

1. Exceptions to the rule that media firms operate in dual-product and simultaneous markets would be those media organizations that sell their content to audiences free of advertising. Subscription cable networks such as HBO and Showtime fall into this category, as do most books, recorded music, and motion pictures (for both theaters and home viewing [e.g., DVD, VHS]). In these instances, the media firms operate solely in the content market, attempting to sell content to audiences. They do not participate in the audience market, given that they do not attempt to sell their audiences to advertisers.
2. Owen and Wildman (1992) extensively discuss the offering of different tiers and bundles of service options.
3. Many more cable networks are available today than most cable systems have the capacity to offer. Consequently, cable systems have a wide range of choices when constructing their lineups and are likely to drop networks that do not produce satisfactory audience numbers.
4. As I discuss in chapter 3, the Internet has facilitated some means of monitoring audience behavior that do not require the explicit permission and cooperation of the audience member (e.g., cookies, web bugs, and server logs). However, as I also discuss in chapter 3, these methods generally provide data that are considered inferior to those methods requiring audience permission and cooperation.
5. For a thorough review of the various approaches to audience research, see McQuail (1997).
6. For a recent exception see Berry and Waldfogel's 1999 analysis of the market for radio audiences.
7. For a thorough review of the program choice literature, see chapter 4 of Owen and Wildman (1992).

8. For analyses of the means by which audience members become more aware of available content options, see Gantz and Eastman (1983) and Heeter and Greenberg (1988). These analyses show that while most audience members actively seek information about available content options, their information seeking is not so thorough that they become fully informed about the entire range of options.

9. For instance, television channel repertoires generally reach a maximum of about thirteen channels (Heeter 1985; Media Dynamics 2001b; Nielsen Media Research 1999), although the average household receives more than sixty channels (Media Dynamics 2001b). Similarly, the average Internet user's repertoire of regularly visited Web sites is about twelve (Nielsen Media Research 1999). The important point here is that these repertoires represent filtering mechanisms that effectively restrict audience members' knowledge of the full range of available content options.

10. An examination of the work cited in the program choice literature clearly shows virtually no consultation with—or integration of—the large and growing body of audience behavior theory and research.

11. For early examples of this administrative research, see Lazarsfeld and Field (1946) and Gary Steiner (1963). Paul Lazarsfeld frequently is identified as the founder of this administrative tradition of audience research (E. Rogers 1994) because of his frequent interaction with, and service to, the media industries (Sills 1996).

12. Similar terminology and concepts are used across media even when such usage would not seem appropriate. For instance, media buyers often convert magazine audience data into "ratings" to facilitate comparisons with television programs. They regard the cumulative readership of an issue as the magazine's "rating" and use that number in comparison with a traditional television rating, which is the average quarter-hour audience for a program. Such an approach involves comparing apples to oranges, as a television program's total audience (e.g., cumulative audience) is likely to be significantly larger than its average quarter-hour audience. Despite such discrepancies, such comparisons are commonplace in media buying (see Mandese 2001).

    As Leckenby and Hong (1998) note, "History is on the side of the usage of the 'old tools' in the 'new media.' When radio and television came along as new media available to advertisers, many of the techniques in reach/frequency estimation as well as the terminology of magazines and newspapers were applied to these new media. . . . History points toward an interactive relationship between media planning applications in the 'old' and 'new' media" (8). Similarly, the terms *reach, frequency,* and *gross rating points* are now being used in regard to the Internet (see Collins and Bhatia 2001; Chandler-Pepelnjak 2002).

13. For an overview of the participant observation methodology, see Jorgensen (1989).

1. THE AUDIENCE MARKETPLACE

1. Consumer magazines include general interest magazines, such as *People* and *Newsweek,* as well as more specialized magazines, such as *Cat Fancy,* that also are directed at the consumer market, as opposed to industry professionals (trade magazines).
2. Silk and Berndt (1993, 1994) reached similar conclusions in their analysis of advertising agencies in the United States. They found strong incentives for advertising agencies to exploit economies of scope in audience markets, which the authors defined in terms of an agency's ability to provide clients with services across a broad range of media types (e.g., television, newspapers, magazines, etc.).
3. For analyses of the issue of ownership concentration in the media industries, see Bagdikian (1997) and Compaine and Gomery (2000).
4. CBS programming executives used this "cradle-to-grave" description during a presentation that I attended of the fall 2001 CBS prime-time schedule.
5. However, within some markets a fairly limited number of firms control the bulk of media buying. For instance, eight media-buying firms control more than 90 percent of the roughly $30 billion spent on national television advertising ("TV Ad Buyers" 2001).
6. See Shoemaker and Reese (1996) for discussions of numerous other anecdotal examples of advertisers' influence on content, as well as for a discussion of a variety of research studies showing that such influence is widespread and consistent.
7. For instance, Mediamark Research, Inc., a leading provider of magazine audience data, recently added thirty-five questions to its national survey that seek to "place people into psychographic categories" in order to "help ad agencies and publishers identify consumer groups that have the greatest affinity with their products so they can design, target and distribute the products more effectively" ("Mediamark Probes Consumer Psyche" 2001:48).

2. THE PREDICTED AUDIENCE–
MEASURED AUDIENCE RELATIONSHIP

1. See chapter 5 for a discussion of the probable evolution from CPM to CPA models in the audience marketplace.
2. In the belief that Las Vegas represents the single best place in the country to recruit a demographically diverse audience, CBS/Viacom recently completed construction of a permanent audience research facility within the MGM Grand hotel-casino there (Consoli 2001a).
3. For instance, the broadcast networks often schedule blocks of youth-targeted programs on Friday and Saturday evenings, as well as programs that appeal primarily to viewers older than 50.

188 2. THE PREDICTED AUDIENCE

4. Webster and Phalen (1997) developed their model primarily from research on television audience behavior. However, the authors emphasize that the model has applicability to other media contexts, and researchers have begun to apply it to other media, notably, the Internet (Napoli 2000; Webster and Lin 2002).

5. The "UHF handicap" figures prominently in early television industry research, given that UHF signals generally are more difficult to receive with over-the-air antennae than are VHF signals. However, given the prevalence of cable television today, and the equalizing power that it exerts in regard to signal quality, the magnitude of the UHF handicap has diminished substantially.

6. A program's "lead-in" is the program that precedes it in the channel's lineup. A program's "lead-out" is the program that follows it in the channel's lineup.

7. For a more detailed discussion of the implications of such findings, see Napoli (1997c, 1999a).

8. Mitgang (2000) describes the brief existence (from the late 1970s to the mid-1980s) of Television Audience Assessment, a service launched by the Markle Foundation in an effort to provide systematic data on audience assessment of television content that would supplement traditional audience exposure data. The underlying premise of the service (supported by research) was that audiences pay more attention (and leave the room at commercial breaks less often) to programs rated higher in quality. Consequently, higher-quality programs will generate higher levels of attention to—and recall of—advertisements. However, the service failed to catch on with advertisers, and Television Audience Assessment ceased operations in 1986.

9. A complete review of the theory and research on audience behavior is beyond the scope of this book. I encourage readers to consult Webster and Phalen (1997) for an excellent treatment of this subject.

10. In this case those instances in which the predicted household share matched the actual household share over the first seven weeks of the season were defined as accurate predictions (Wells 1997).

11. Note that, despite the decline in the magnitude of lead-in and lead-out effects, programming strategies that attempt to capitalize on lead-in and lead-out effects have remained prominent in the television industry. Programming executives whom I studied during the participant observation component of this study consistently based program scheduling decisions on presumed lead-in and lead-out effects. Thus while the magnitude of these effects has declined, their persistence means that they remain a significant element of contemporary television programming strategy.

12. In the face of increased broadcast network competition, and increased competition from cable networks, the broadcast networks no longer are as patient with struggling programs. Such programs are now more likely to get canceled quickly, rather than be granted time to develop an audience. During the participant observation research that I conducted for this book, programming ex-

ecutives repeatedly stated that they could not be as patient with struggling programs as they could in the past. One study has shown that the mortality rate for new prime-time network programs (i.e., the percentage of new programs that do not return for a second season) increased from 60 percent in the early 1960s to more than 70 percent in 1999–2000 (see Media Dynamics 2001b).

13. The participant observation data that I gathered for this study repeatedly demonstrated that broadcasters focus only on their broadcast competition when presenting their shows to advertisers, developing their broadcast schedules, and assessing the probable performance of their programs.

14. The magnitude of forecasting error for each network that I studied in fact increased in accordance with the median age for each network's audience. NBC traditionally has had the second-youngest audience among the networks that I studied (see McClellan 2001), and it exhibited the second-lowest level of forecasting error. ABC traditionally has had the third-youngest audience (although its average audience age recently dipped slightly below NBC's) among the networks studied (McClellan 2001), and it ranked third in terms of magnitude of forecasting error. These results suggest a relationship between audience age and predictability that future research should investigate more thoroughly.

15. For a thorough discussion/critique of spinoffs and their underlying logic, see Gitlin (1983:64–69). Bielby and Bielby (1994) demonstrate that the single greatest predictor of a television pilot's being added to the prime-time schedule of a Big Four broadcast network is whether the program originated with a producer with a hit program to his or her credit.

16. This statement was made during a sales meeting that I attended during the participant observation component of this study.

3. THE MEASURED AUDIENCE–
ACTUAL AUDIENCE RELATIONSHIP

1. For extended discussions of sampling techniques in audience research, see Buzzard (1992) and Webster, Phalen, and Lichty (2000).

2. Webster, Phalen, and Lichty extensively discuss this form of error, called "sampling error" (2000:104–109).

3. Bolton Radio Research, for instance, found that individuals who participate in the process of radio audience measurement tend to be very interested in radio and music; thus their radio consumption patterns are likely to deviate from the norm (see Bolton 1999a).

4. For much more extensive reviews of the history and techniques of audience measurement, see Buzzard (1990) and Beville (1988).

5. It is important to note, however, that RADAR (Radio's All Dimension Audience Report), the Arbitron measurement service that focuses on national radio network audiences, still uses telephone recall surveys (see note 6).

6. Arbitron also measures national radio network audiences via its RADAR report. The RADAR service, which recently was acquired from the audience measurement firm Statistical Research, Inc., conducts phone interviews almost year-round and produces detailed reports four times a year regarding audience size and composition for national radio networks such as ABC, Westwood One, and AMFM.

7. It is important to note that Arbitron, like most commercial audience measurement firms, does not divulge all the methodological details of its measurement process. Thus the descriptions of the various measurement processes discussed here are lacking in some important methodological details.

8. For a defense of the paper diary system, and an argument for its continued utility in the new media environment, see Arbitron (2001a).

9. One media executive has described local television audience measurement, which relies heavily upon diaries, as "the worst measurement of television audience viewing in the country" (Saltzman 2001:28). Research has found that people meter data generally are more statistically reliable than diary data (see Soong 1988).

10. In addition, concepts such as reach, frequency, and shares are being transferred from broadcast audience measurement to the Internet (see the introduction).

11. According to Kalyanam and MacEvoy (1999), geographic determinations cannot be made for about 15 percent of all users.

12. Cookies are unique identifiers placed by file servers on a personal computer's hard drive. Cookies allow a Web site to track the browsing behavior of individual terminals. It is important to note, however, that users can delete cookies and that they can configure their browser to refuse cookies, thereby limiting their effectiveness as a tool for monitoring Web traffic.

13. ISPs generally assign different IP addresses to users each time they log in.

14. For an extensive study of the error levels of server log data, see Dreze and Zufryden (1998). For a detailed review of the various challenges associated with establishing standards of accuracy and reliability in server log measurement systems, see Ivie and Terlizzi (2001).

15. The "late-night" daypart (11:30 P.M.–1 A.M.) generally sees the largest HUT-level increases as a result of introducing the audimeter to a local television market. Prime-time HUT levels increase only about 13 percent, while HUT levels in mornings and afternoons increase as much as 37 percent (*Introducing Meters* 2000). These variations are a reflection of those time periods when participants in the measurement process are more likely to remember to record their television viewing. Thus, for instance, the large HUT-level increases for the late-night daypart suggest that many viewers fail to record when they are watching television right before going to sleep (perhaps they are viewing in bed; perhaps they have already fallen asleep, with the television still on).

16. Danaher and Beed (1993) conducted this study by performing a "telephone coincidental" survey, in which the respondents were asked what they were doing when the phone rang. The authors compared the responses to the data generated by the people meters for that date and time.

17. Moreover, household willingness to participate in the measurement process declined with the introduction of the people meter, most likely because this device requires more work by participants than does the audimeter (Milavsky 1992).

18. Nielsen has rules barring station employees from taking part in their surveys, although the violation initially was not caught in this case.

19. Within the television industry, advertisement exposure data are available only as a premium service, one that only the largest agencies can afford (Consoli 2001b). One critic has described obtaining commercial ratings from Nielsen as a "complex procedure seemingly designed to discourage the practice" (Green 2002:74).

20. A number of sales personnel articulated this perspective during the participant observation component of this study.

21. Analysis of the many research and promotional documents that I obtained while conducting the participant observation component of this study showed a continued tendency toward treating minute differences in ratings as legitimate shifts in program and/or station performance, although such differences typically were smaller than the sampling error. Thus Gitlin's 1983 conclusions appear to remain relevant today.

22. A similar pattern exists today within the context of emerging cable networks, which must meet minimum audience size thresholds for Nielsen to report their audience data. Becoming part of the Nielsen ratings reports is central to establishing the legitimacy of a young cable network as a viable advertising option (see Romano 2002a).

23. It is important to note that these studies were conducted at the peak of the dotcom boom and that the importance of traffic figures in the valuation of Internet firms has declined (Miles 2001) along with the valuations of most of these firms.

24. This strategy was discussed during station scheduling meetings that I attended during the participant observation component of this study. Of course, this strategy is useful only in large local markets where audimeters are recording set-tuning activity, not in markets where diaries are the only source of measurement.

25. In one meeting of broadcast networks and their affiliates that I attended as part of the participant observation component of this study, an exemplar affiliate gave a presentation that focused on the effectiveness of an automobile giveaway contest conducted during the May 2001 sweeps period.

26. A massive pop-up ad campaign made the Web site for the X10 camera the fourth most-visited Web site in the country in June 2001, according to Jupiter

Media Metrix. During this same period the site was ranked 116th by Nielsen NetRatings (Thompson 2001).

27. Station call letters also are announced frequently in the form of a short musical jingle in an effort to increase the likelihood that they will be remembered by listeners in the Arbitron sample (MacFarland 1997).

28. It is important to note that rating distortion is different from "hypoing," which involves station activities designed to prompt more listenership during measurement periods (see Arbitron 2001b:6). As the definition suggests, hypoing does not involve specifically targeting diary keepers.

29. Nielsen Media Research has changed its national Television Index methodology for one such niche audience "to reverse the undercounting of Hispanics in its sampling" (Consoli 2002a:6), a move that will likely lead to higher ratings for Hispanic television programming and higher advertising rates for Hispanic-targeted television networks (see also Tam 2002).

30. Although measurement systems typically favor content providers that attract larger audiences, it is important to emphasize that this is not *always* the case. McGlathery (1993), for instance, demonstrates that magazines with smaller circulations may benefit from the common procedure in magazine audience measurement of asking participants a screening question that seeks to eliminate nonreaders of specific titles. The concern in this process comes from the probable confusion or inaccurate recall among those categorized as casual readers (those who have read at least two of the last four issues of a magazine). According to McGlathery, "A smaller circulation title will almost always benefit from the confusion since half of the confused readers will be applied to a small base. This will be to the relative advantage of the smaller title increasing their screen-in levels disproportionately higher, particularly among infrequent readers" (1993:34).

31. An analysis of the new Bookscan system, which tracks book sales, reached similar conclusions: The established system by which bestseller lists are compiled is skewed toward independent bookstores, and the new system—which is not skewed in this manner—may produce bestseller lists that are far less literary or intellectual in their orientation and thus may produce a stronger emphasis on lowest-common-denominator content in the book-publishing industry (see Shandler 2001). Again, the logic here depends upon altered content decisions by the affiliated media that make content decisions based upon bestseller lists (radio and television talk shows, magazines, etc.), thereby feeding into a cycle that makes certain genres or authors more financially appealing to publishers than in the past.

4. AUDIENCE VALUATION

1. Note that many studies of the value of media audiences refer to themselves in terms of studying the pricing of "time," in the case of electronic media (e.g.,

Besen 1976; Peterman 1979; Takada and Henry 1993) or "space" in the case of print media (e.g., Reimer 1992). It is important to re-emphasize that such terminology mischaracterizes the nature of the actual product (audiences) being sold.

2. Not all research on the subject of audience substitutability has found substitutability across media. Seldon and Jung (1993) found negative cross-price elasticities between print and broadcast media, suggesting a complementary relationship between them, while Busterna (1987) found no cross-elasticity of demand between daily newspaper advertising and eight other media.

3. The UHF handicap not only hindered the growth in the number of broadcast stations in individual markets but it also impeded any expansion in the number of national broadcast networks (Noll, Peck, and McGowan 1973). Because few television markets in the United States contained more than three VHF stations, a fourth network would be required to affiliate primarily with UHF stations. Given the lower audience reach of UHF stations and lower valuations of UHF audiences, such a broadcast network never would have the revenue potential of the traditional Big Three (see Besen et al. 1984). Consequently, programming investments for this fourth network would always lag behind the Big Three, and its long-term ability to compete for national television audiences and national advertising dollars would be undermined.

4. Consequently, the economic health of UHF stations has improved tremendously, with the number of commercial UHF stations on the air increasing from 88 in 1965 to 650 in 2000 (Media Dynamics 2001b). In addition, the number of national broadcast networks has increased from three in 1985 to seven in 2002. These emerging networks rely primarily upon networks of UHF stations, a strategy that would not have been viable without the diffusion of cable television (see Thomas and Litman 1991). However, given that approximately 15 percent of households still receive their television programming exclusively through over-the-air antennae, the UHF handicap persists as a factor that affects what television broadcast stations are able to charge for their audiences, although the magnitude of this effect has diminished substantially.

5. For somewhat contradictory findings, see Reimer (1992).

6. This hesitancy to advertise during news broadcasts became particularly acute in the wake of the September 11 terrorist attacks, as advertisers grew concerned that their ads would follow unsettling or disturbing news stories (Beatty 2001b).

7. The other viewer categories were "Silver Sliders" (those who watch some of a show but tune in often); "Occasionally Committeds" (those who watch most of a show but tune in less often); and "Viewers Lite" (those who only watch some of a show and tune in less often) (see Weissman 1999).

8. For instance, as one cable executive argued, it may be possible that Gold Card viewers represent traditional "couch potatoes" and thus may be less selective and less attentive in their viewing (see Weissman 1999).

9. Within this context media buyers saw the price paid for the publication as a measure of its "wantedness" (see "ABC's New Order" 2001:SR18).

10. Typically, analyses of this sort examine average levels of audience value within a market, using measures such as the average CPM within a market (see Poltrack 1983; Webster and Phalen 1997).

11. During the up-front presentations for five of the major broadcast networks (ABC, CBS, Fox, WB, and UPN) that I attended as part of the participant observation component of this study, every one of the networks emphasized its objective of either reducing the average age of its audience or (in the case of the WB, which hoped to maintain an average audience age younger than 30) maintaining the current average age of its audience. The WB network demonstrated what was perhaps the most extreme example of an emphasis on young audiences. The WB's slogan for its presentation was "The Night Is Young." The theme song for the presentation was The Who's "My Generation," with its famous line, "Hope I die before I get old."

12. The value of younger audiences was at the heart of the highly publicized effort by ABC to lure David Letterman away from CBS to replace Ted Koppel's *Nightline* program. The average age of Letterman's *Late Show* audience is 47, whereas the average *Nightline* viewer is 52, a small difference in age that amounts to a $5,000 difference in the cost of a thirty-second commercial (Ahrens 2002).

13. Nielsen does gather consumer data from households when they stop participating in the people meter sample but does not attempt to gather such data while the households are participating in the measurement process.

14. As one television programming executive noted during the participant observation component of this study, "some twenty-three-year-old kid analyzing data tends to keep things simple."

15. According to Ofori (1999), 75 percent of all radio stations owned by minorities program a minority format. In contrast, only 8 percent of majority-owned stations program a minority format.

16. Some policy scholars have argued that diversifying content by increasing the availability of minority-targeted content benefits both minority and majority audiences (Rogovin 1992). Behind this argument is the basic assumption that much of the benefit of a diverse marketplace of ideas derives from citizens' exposing themselves to a diversity of sources and ideas (see Napoli 1999a).

17. Adarand Constructors, Inc., v. Pena, 515 U.S. 200 (1995); Self-Employed Health Insurance Act of 1995, Pub. L. No. 104–7, sec. 2, 109 Stat. 93 (1995); Communications Act of 1934, Pub. L. No. 416, 48 Stat. 1064 (1934). Section 309(j) of the Communications Act of 1934 requires the FCC to advance opportunities for minorities, women, and small businesses to participate in allocations for spectrum-based services. The Self-Employed Health Insurance Act of 1995 contained a rider that repealed the FCC's minority tax certificate program, which was intended to increase minority ownership of broadcast outlets.

18. Telecommunications Act of 1996, Pub. L. No. 104–104, 110 Stat. 56 (1996), codified in scattered sections of 47 U.S.C. 257 (1996).

19. The FCC uses the comparative hearing process to decide which applicants receive a license.

20. The Webster and Phalen (1997) study focused on market-level valuations, as opposed to station-level valuations.

21. BIA Research gets the audience share data directly from Arbitron. BIA's own primary research on station revenues produces the revenue share data. Both radio industry investors and the FCC use BIA's data in their analyses and decision making.

22. The age categories are teens; 18–24; 25–24; 35–44; 45–54; 55–64; and people older than 65.

23. I used share data instead of ratings data because shares provide a more direct indication of how a station is performing relative to other stations in its market. In contrast, a rating of 15 could represent a very different level of relative performance across markets of different sizes and different numbers of stations.

24. For each centered independent variable, I subtracted the independent variable mean from the independent variable value for each case (see Cronbach 1987).

25. I also conducted the multivariate analysis by using the noncentered independent variables, with no significant difference in explanatory power or substantial differences in the independent variable–dependent variable relationships. However, tolerance statistics were low for a number of the interaction terms, signaling a multicollinearity problem.

26. It is important to recognize that stations in markets for which minority composition is not measured still could have a large proportion of minority listeners in their audience.

27. For the regression analysis I used the natural log of the power ratio as the dependent variable. Residuals were normally distributed with constant variance. In addition, tolerance statistics indicated no significant multicollinearity among the independent variables.

28. An obvious exception to this situation would be if the less-valued audience segments were, in terms of raw numbers, much larger than the higher-valued audience segments, and there were sufficiently few competitors for the less-valued audiences that a programmer could anticipate an audience size that, when multiplied by the value per audience member, would produce revenues exceeding the size-times-value calculation for the higher-valued audience segment.

29. It should be noted that all Big Four broadcast networks have experienced increases in the median age of their audience, and all are making efforts to reverse this trend (McClellan 2001).

30. For an extensive analysis of the relationship between advertiser valuations of different audience segments and media content, see Turow (1997).

31. A good example of this point occurred during the participant observation component of this study, when one television programming executive described children's programming as "a dead business."

32. All cable networks have smaller potential audiences than most broadcast networks, given that roughly 15 percent of homes still do not subscribe to either cable or direct broadcast satellite service. In addition, not all cable systems carry all cable networks, so individual cable networks differ significantly in the percentage of cable subscribers to which they actually have access.

33. See Picard (1999) for a discussion of the "spiral effect" in the audience—content relationship. Specifically, Picard illustrates that as the audience for a particular media channel declines, its content budget will decline as well. This, in turn, will drive additional audience members away, which will reduce further its content expenditures—thus the downward spiral.

5. NEW TECHNOLOGIES AND THE AUDIENCE PRODUCT

1. "The new media environment" refers not only to the Internet but also to such new technologies such as personal video recorders, digital cable, direct broadcast satellite, satellite radio—the entire array of new media technologies that tend to fragment audiences into narrower segments.

2. Media economists use the term *window* to refer to the new opportunity for distributing content that a new technology presents. Thus the introduction of the VCR meant a new window for movies after the theatrical window. In book publishing the hardback is window 1, and the paperback is window 2; this process allows one piece of content to keep earning revenues by gradually moving down through different price points (i.e., if you wait for the paperback, you pay less).

3. Comparable fragmentation in the television audience can be found at the local level as well.

4. Webster and Lin (2002) demonstrate that for many media, including the Internet, audience distribution tends to follow a Pareto distribution, in which a small proportion of the available media content options account for a very large proportion of the media audience.

5. Lake (2001) reports on a Nielsen NetRatings study that shows that 45 percent of the top five Web sites in twenty-six countries are affiliated with Microsoft.

6. For his well-known discussion of the issue of fragmented versus mass audiences and the social and economic forces at work to preserve mass audiences, see Neuman (1991).

7. In Phalen's (1998) study one research director notes that information overload is "probably the biggest problem we have in this industry" (22).

8. Even nonadvertiser-supported media such as the motion picture and music industries are finding it more difficult to anticipate audience behavior in the new media environment (see Ordonez 2001b; Hayes 2000).

9. One media buyer has described the process of sifting through audience data to make a reasonably accurate determination of the measured audience delivered by a local cable buy as requiring "lessons in numerology" (Higgins 2002:20). Neilsen has initiated an effort to correct this flaw in its measurement system (Albiniak, 2002).

10. Arbitron has launched a service detailing radio audience listening on the Internet. Arbitron faces competition in this arena from another new firm, Measurecast, which focuses on providing audience estimates for streaming audio sites (Measurecast 2001; Porter 2001).

11. The few examples of scheduled on-line content include live chats with celebrities and events such as the Victoria's Secret Fashion Show.

12. The media futurist Nicholas Negroponte (1995) famously referred to audiences' impending ability to easily create the Daily Me—their personalized daily newspaper.

13. Youn's 1994 study shows, for instance, that viewers in cable households spend 50 percent of their viewing time watching their favorite program type, whereas viewers in noncable households spend only 25 percent of their viewing time watching their favorite program type. Thus increased channel capacity results in an increased ability to watch the type of program that one prefers.

14. *Repurposing* is the term that the networks have adopted for re-airing their first-run programming on cable networks (see Flint and Orwall 2001; McClellan and Schlosser 2001).

15. The designers of TiVo deliberately avoided providing a complete commercial-skipping function in order to avoid an adversarial relationship with programmers. See Lewis (2000).

16. The introduction of this function, along with a function allowing ReplayTV users to e-mail recorded programs to other ReplayTV subscribers, led to a lawsuit from entertainment companies such as Viacom, Disney, and NBC's parent company, General Electric (Wingfield 2001).

17. NBC's situation comedy *Emeril* made the fall 2001 prime-time schedule despite the nearly unanimous opinion of programmers and advertisers that the show was of poor quality. However, because the program tested well among certain audience groups, NBC put the program on its fall schedule (Schlosser 2001). The program performed poorly when broadcast and was canceled in its first season.

18. The London-based media company Shine Entertainment (a joint venture of the media-buying firms MindShare and the Media Edge) focuses specifically on developing television programming that includes products in the content before a network ever considers it (Consoli 2001c).

19. The infrared system was designed to detect and identify the different patterns of body heat emitted by different members of the participating household.

20. The major privacy concern at issue was that an infrared system that relied

upon body heat patterns to distinguish viewers also could detect any romantic activities taking place in front of the television set.

21. I frequently heard such criticisms and threats during the participant observation component of this study. It is worth noting that as I am writing this, only four Boston-area broadcast stations (WNDS-TV in Derry, New Hampshire; two PBS stations; and the Univision affiliate in Boston, WUNI-TV) had subscribed to the local people meter service ("Nielsen Signs WUNI-TV" 2002). All these stations have small and/or niche audiences and actually may benefit from the improved data reliability and demographic reporting that the local people meter would provide (Trigoboff 2002b).

22. I obtained this information during the participant observation research that I conducted at a broadcast industry rep firm. During the research period Nielsen Media Research provided these preliminary results to its subscribers.

23. Some industry analysts have argued that the increasing difficulty of establishing a new hit television program in syndication is a function of the rise in the number of markets measured by audimeters. The greater availability of up-to-the-minute data on program performance means that "local stations are pulling out of shows faster than ever" (Frutkin 2002a:11).

24. As of this writing, Arbitron was testing the personal portable meter in the Philadelphia radio market (see Bachman 2001d).

25. As of this writing, ADcom was providing local cable audience data in the San Francisco, Dallas, and Jacksonville, Florida, markets, with plans to begin service in Sacramento and Cleveland (Trugman 2002).

26. However, experiments now under way "fuse" data from different audience measurement systems in an effort to estimate the cross-media consumption patterns of the typical media consumer.

27. See the Cable Television Consumer Protection and Competition Act, Pub. L. No. 102–385, 106 Stat. 1460 (1992), codified as amended at 47 U.S.C. 521–609 (1992).

28. In their letter requesting the FTC investigation, House members John Dingell (D-Mich.), Edolphus Towns (D-N.Y.), and Edward Markey (D-Mass.) raised concerns that "TiVo, Inc. . . . violates its own privacy policy by collecting information about its customers' program viewing selections. The charges against TiVo are serious and certainly raise questions as to whether they violate the prohibition in section 5 of the Federal Trade Commission Act against 'unfair or deceptive practices'" (2001).

REFERENCES

ABC's new order: Will changing subscription rules bring about a circulation "renaissance"? 2001. *Mediaweek,* October 22, p. SR18.

Abernathy, Avery M. 1990. Television exposure: Programs versus advertising. *Current Issues and Research in Advertising* 13(1–2): 61–77.

Abramson, Ronna and Terry Lefton. 2001. The fight for the top of the TV. *Industry Standard,* May 28, pp. 42–44.

Adams, William J. 1993. TV program-scheduling strategies and their relationship to new program renewal rates and rating changes. *Journal of Broadcasting and Electronic Media* 37(4): 465–74.

———. 1994. Changes in ratings patterns for prime time before, during, and after the introduction of the people meter. *Journal of Media Economics* 7(2): 15–28.

———. 2000. How people watch television, as investigated using focus group techniques. *Journal of Broadcasting and Electronic Media* 44(1): 78–93.

———. 2001. Focus group analysis: Can it help explain present audience discontent with broadcast network television? Paper presented at the annual meeting of the Association for Education in Journalism and Mass Communication, Washington, D.C., August.

Adams, William J., Susan T. Eastman, Larry J. Horney, and Mark N. Popovich. 1983. The cancellation and manipulation of network television prime-time programs. *Journal of Communication* 33(1): 10–27.

Ahrens, Frank. 2002. In TV's numbers game, youth trumps ratings; but some question the marketing profiles behind the Letterman tug of war. *Washington Post,* March 13, p. A1.

Albarran, Alan B. 1996. *Media economics: Understanding markets, industries, and concepts.* Ames: Iowa State University Press.

Albert, Steven. 1998. Movie stars and the distribution of financially successful films in the motion picture industry. *Journal of Cultural Economics* 22:249–70.

Albiniak, Page. 2001. XM satellite radio set to fly. *Broadcasting and Cable,* September 3, pp. 26–28.

————. 2002. Local-ratings overhaul. *Broadcasting and Cable*, October 21, p. 16.

Alexander, Allison, James Owers, and Rodney Carveth, eds. 1998. *Media economics: Theory and practice.* 2d ed. Mahwah, N.J.: Lawrence Erlbaum.

Alleyne, P. Llanor. 2001. Now it's AM/FM/XM. *Broadcasting and Cable*, July 30, p. 8.

Ang, Ien. 1991. *Desperately seeking the audience.* New York: Routledge.

Appel, Marion. 2001. Raising diary response among young people: E-diaries, phone motivation, and incentives. In *Proceedings of the ESOMAR/ARF World-wide Radio Conference and Exhibition,* 103–13. New York: European Society for Opinion and Marketing Research/Advertising Research Foundation.

Arbitron. 1996. *A guide to understanding and using radio audience estimates.* New York: Arbitron. .

————. 2001a. *The Arbitron radio listening diary: Why the diary is an effective research tool in the digital age.* New York: Arbitron.

————. 2001b. *Rating distortion and rating bias: A handbook on Arbitron Radio's special station activities policy.* New York: Arbitron.

Assael, Henry and David F. Poltrack. 1991. Using single-source data to select TV programs based on purchasing behavior. *Journal of Advertising Research* 31(4): 9–17.

————. 1993. Using single-source data to select TV programs: Part 2. *Journal of Advertising Research* 33(1): 48–56.

————. 1994. Can demographic profiles of heavy users serve as a surrogate for purchase behavior in selecting TV programs? *Journal of Advertising Research* 34(1): 11–17.

————. 1996. Single- versus double-source data for TV program selection. *Journal of Advertising Research* 36(6): 73–81.

————. 1999. Relating products to TV program clusters. *Journal of Advertising Research* 39(2): 41–52.

Atkin, David and Barry Litman. 1986. Network TV programming: Economics, audiences, and the ratings game, 1971–1986. *Journal of Communication* 36(3): 32–50.

Bachen, Christine, Allen Hammond, Laurie Mason, and Stephanie Craft. 1999. *Diversity of programming in the broadcast spectrum: Is there a link between owner race or ethnicity and news and public affairs programming?* Report submitted to the Office of Communications Business Opportunities, Federal Communications Commission, Washington, D.C.

Bachman, Katy. 2000a. Nielsen, Arbitron agree to agree. *Mediaweek*, June 5, pp. 6–7.

————. 2000b. Signing up satellite: SIR and Arbitron move to measure satellite radio. *Mediaweek,* November 13, p. 10.

————. 2001a. Nielsen, stations face off on meters. *Mediaweek,* April 30, pp. 6–7.

————. 2001b. PPMs count more eyes, ears. *Mediaweek,* July 30, pp. 8, 10.

————. 2001c. Arbitron faces tough talk. *Mediaweek,* August 13, pp. 6–7.

————. 2001d. Arbitron test yields spikes. *Mediaweek,* September 24, p. 6.

————. 2002a. Boston balks at Nielsen. *Mediaweek,* February 4, p. 8.

————. 2002b. A sweeps without ratings. *Mediaweek,* April 22, p. 8.

————. 2002c. Arbitron hits snag on PPM. *Mediaweek,* June 24, p. 6.

————. 2002d. Nielsen earns low grades in new international survey. *Mediaweek,* June 24, p. 6.

Bagdikian, Ben H. 1997. *The media monopoly.* 5th ed. Boston: Beacon.

Baker, C. Edwin. 1994. *Advertising and a democratic press.* Princeton, N.J.: Princeton University Press.

Baldwin, Thomas F., D. Stevens McVoy, and Charles Steinfeld. 1996. *Convergence: Integrating media, information, and communication.* Thousand Oaks, Calif.: Sage.

Baniel, Linda and Erwin Ephron. 2001. Using set-tuning data as a recall aid to obtain viewing data. *ADcom Information Services.* http://www.adcoms.com/press/articles/Using%20Set%20Tuning%20Data.htm (June 18, 2001).

Baniel, Linda, Daniel Monistere, and Ernest P. Smyth. 2001. Single-source data—qualitative and ratings data combined: A wealth of information available from ADcom cable panel households. Paper presented at the Advertising Research Foundation Week of Workshops: Improving Television Measurement—New Approaches to Measurement, Chicago, October.

Barnes, Beth E. and Lynne M. Thomson. 1988. The impact of audience information sources on media evolution. *Journal of Advertising Research* 28(5): RC9–14.

————. 1994. Power to the people (meter): Audience measurement technology and media specialization. In Ettema and Whitney, *Audiencemaking,* 75–94.

Barnett, George A., Hsiu-Jung Chang, Edward L. Fink, and William D. Richards Jr. 1991. Seasonality in television viewing: A mathematical model of cultural processes. *Communication Research* 18(6): 755–72.

Barwise, Patrick and Andrew Ehrenberg. 1988. *Television and its audience.* Beverly Hills, Calif.: Sage.

Bates, Benjamin J. 1983. Determining television advertising rates. *Communication Yearbook* 7:462–75.

————. 1991. Models, methods, and assumptions: The usefulness of a multimethod approach to the examination of influence in TV pricing. *Journal of Media Economics* 4(1): 49–66.

Baughman, James L. 1997. *The republic of mass culture: Journalism, filmmaking, and broadcasting in America since 1941.* 2d ed. Baltimore, Md.: Johns Hopkins University Press.

Baynes, Leonard M. 1999–2000. Life after *Adarand:* What happened to the Metro Broadcasting diversity rationale for affirmative action in telecommunications ownership? *University of Michigan Journal of Law Reform* 33:87–132.

Beatty, Sally. 2001a. Nielsen plans new pricing as part of bid to double "people meters." *Wall Street Journal,* June 29, p. B6.

————. 2001b. NBC says viewers aren't put off by ads during disaster coverage. *Wall Street Journal,* November 13, p. B4.

————. 2002. Who's watching this stuff? Digital TV channels struggle to take root as many run old content, are hard to find. *Wall Street Journal*, April 24, pp. B1, B3.

Becker, Lee B. and Klaus Schoenbach, eds. 1989. *Audience responses to media diversification: Coping with plenty.* Hillsdale, N.J.: Lawrence Erlbaum.

Becker, Lee B., Sharon Dunwoody, and Sheizaf Rafaeli. 1983. Cable's impact on use of other news media. *Journal of Broadcasting* 27(2): 127–40.

Beebe, Jack H. 1977. The institutional structure and program choices in television markets. *Quarterly Journal of Economics* 91:15–37.

Bellamy, Robert V. Jr. 1993. Remote control devices and the political economy of a changing television industry. In J. R. Walker and R. V. Bellamy Jr., eds., *The remote control in the new age of television*, 211–19. Westport, Conn.: Praeger.

Benvenuto, Angela. 1987. More clients will use cable TV when cable fills its data vacuum. *TV/Radio Age*, February 16, p. 72.

Berger, Kevin. 2001. The incredible vanishing book review. *Salon.com*. July 19. http://www.salon.com/books/feature/2001/07/19/book_reviews/index.html (October 3, 2002).

Berry, Steven T. and Joel Waldfogel. 1999. Free entry and social inefficiency in radio broadcasting. *RAND Journal of Economics*, 30(3): 397–420.

Besen, Stanley M. 1976. The value of television time. *Southern Economic Journal* 42(2): 435–41.

Besen, Stanley M., Thomas G. Krattenmaker, A. Richard Metzger, and John R. Woodbury. 1984. *Misregulating television: Network dominance and the FCC.* Chicago: University of Chicago Press.

Beville, Hugh M. Jr. 1988. *Audience ratings: Radio, television, cable.* Hillsdale, N.J.: Lawrence Erlbaum.

Biddle, Jeff. 1991. A bandwagon effect in personalized license plates? *Economic Inquiry* 29(2): 375–88.

Bielby, William T. and Denise D. Bielby. 1994. "All hits are flukes": Institutionalized decision making and the rhetoric of network prime-time program development. *American Journal of Sociology* 99(5): 1287–313.

Biocca, Frank A. 1988. Opposing conceptions of the audience. *Communication Yearbook* 11:51–80.

Blumler, Jay G. 1996. Recasting the audience in the new television marketplace? In Hay, Grossberg, and Wartella, *The audience and its landscape*, 97–111.

Blumler, Jay G. and Elihu Katz, eds. 1974. *The uses of mass communications: Current perspectives on gratifications research.* Beverly Hills, Calif.: Sage.

Bogart, Leo. 2000. Buying services and the media marketplace. *Journal of Advertising Research* 40(5):37–41.

Bolton, Ted. 1999a. Hypertargeting: How to find diarykeepers. *Bolton Radio Research Corporation.* http://www.boltonresearch.com/2.0/ARTICLES/HYPER.HTM (October 3, 2002).

————. 1999b. Reaching the people who count versus counting the people you reach. *Bolton Radio Research Corporation.* http://www.boltonresearch.com/2.0/ARTICLE/REACH.HTM (October 3, 2002).

Boivin, Yvan and Francois Coderre. 2000. Fewer is better. *Journal of Advertising Research* 40(4): 45–53.

Bower, Robert T. 1985. *The changing television audience in America.* New York: Columbia University Press.

Bowman, Gary W. 1976. Demand and supply of network television advertising. *Bell Journal of Economics* 7(1): 258–67.

Burgi, Michelle. 1997. Is it SMART to fight Nielsen? *Mediaweek,* October 6, p. 26.

Burke, David, ed. 2000. *Spy TV: Just who is the digital TV revolution overthrowing?* Hove, England: Slab-O-Concrete Publications.

Busterna, John C. 1987. The cross-elasticity of demand for national newspaper advertising. *Journalism Quarterly* 64(2–3): 346–51.

———. 1988a. National advertising pricing: Chain versus independent newspapers. *Journalism Quarterly* 65(2): 307–12.

———. 1988b. Television station ownership effects on programming and idea diversity: Baseline data. *Journal of Media Economics* 1(2): 63–74.

Butsch, Richard. 2000. *The making of American audiences: From stage to television, 1750–1990.* New York: Cambridge University Press.

Buzzard, Karen S. 1990. *Chains of gold: Marketing the ratings and rating the markets.* Metuchen, N.J.: Scarecrow.

———. 1992. *Electronic media ratings: Turning audiences into dollars and sense.* Boston: Focal Press.

Cable Television Advertising Bureau. 1999. Pumping up the quads. http://www.cabletvadbureau.com/Info%20Center/Quad%20Study%20Response.htm (October 3, 2002).

Cable Television Advertising Bureau and A. C. Nielsen Company. 1983. *Cable audience methodology study.* New York: Cable Television Advertising Bureau and A. C. Nielsen.

Cannon, Hugh M. 2001. Addressing new media with conventional media planning. *Journal of Interactive Advertising* 8(2). http://jiad.org/vol1/no2/cannon/ (October 3, 2002).

Cantor, Muriel G. and Joanne M. Cantor. 1986. Audience composition and television content: The mass audience revisited. In S. J. Ball-Rokeach and M. G. Cantor, eds., *Media, audience, and social structure,* 214–25. Newbury Park, Calif.: Sage.

Carter, Bill. 2002. Moves by Fox and CNN signal a new push for new audiences. *New York Times,* January 4, p. C1.

Center for Digital Democracy. 2001. *TV that watches you: The prying eyes of interactive television.* Washington, D.C.: Center for Digital Democracy.

Chandler-Pepelnjak, John. 2002. Forecasting reach, frequency, and GRPs on the Internet. In *Proceedings of the ESOMAR/ARF Week of Audience Measurement Conference: Online,* 163–80. New York: European Society for Opinion and Marketing Research/Advertising Research Foundation.

Chang, Briankle G. 1987. Deconstructing the audience: Who are they and what do we know about them? *Communication Yearbook* 10:649–64.

Chan-Olmsted, Sylvia. 1991. Structural analysis of market competition in the U.S. TV syndication industry, 1981–1990. *Journal of Media Economics* 4(3): 9–28.

Chunovic, Louis. 2001. New TV technologies raise privacy red flag. *Electronic Media,* July 9, p. 10.

Clancey, Maura. 1994. The television audience examined. *Journal of Advertising Research* 34(4): S1–10.

Clarkin, Greg. 1990. Sex, lies, and cable. *Marketing and Media Decisions,* April, pp. 46–52.

Coffey, Steve and Horst Stipp. 1997. The interactions between computer and television usage. *Journal of Advertising Research* 37(2): 61–67.

Cohen, Warren. 2001. CBS's new reality: Out with the old. *Inside.com.* www.inside.com/jcs/Story?article_id=31057&pod_id=11 (May 18, 2001).

Collins, Jim H. and Manish Bhatia. 2001. Integrating Internet site audience measurement into media planning and buying. In D. S. Fellows, ed., *Proceedings of the ESOMAR/ARF Worldwide Audience Measurement Conference and Exhibition,* 21–44. New York: European Society for Opinion and Marketing Research/Advertising Research Foundation.

Compaine, Benjamin M. and Douglas Gomery. 2000. *Who owns the media? Competition and concentration in the mass media industry.* Mahwah, N.J.: Lawrence Erlbaum.

Comstock, George, Steve Chaffee, Natan Katzman, Maxwell McCombs, and Donald Roberts. 1978. *Television and human behavior.* New York: Columbia University Press.

Consoli, John. 1999. Exploiting *Voyager:* UPN is trying to sell uniqueness of "Star Trek" spinoff's audience. *Mediaweek,* October 18, p. 12.

———. 2000a. Broadcast's demo dilemma. *Mediaweek,* March 6, pp. 4–5.

———. 2000b. Nets speaking Spanish. *Mediaweek,* October 9, p. 10.

———. 2000c. Turning hits into dollars: Early-season successes could lead to a strong scatter market. *Mediaweek,* October 16, pp. 9–10.

———. 2000d. For prime time, reality sets in. *Mediaweek,* October 30, pp. 6–7.

———. 2001a. Viacom to up its bet in Vegas. *Mediaweek,* June 11, p. 8.

———. 2001b. AAs call for wide use of commercial ratings data. *Mediaweek,* September 3, pp. 5–6.

———. 2001c. For advertisers, it's showtime. *Mediaweek,* November 5, pp. 4–5.

———. 2002a. Hispanic nets hike profile. *Mediaweek,* May 20, p. 6.

———. 2002b. Out-of-home moving ahead. *Mediaweek,* September 2, p. 5.

Cooper, Cynthia A. 1996. *Violence on television: Congressional inquiry, public criticism, and industry response: A policy analysis.* Lanham, Md.: University Press of America.

Cooper, Roger. 1993. An expanded, integrated model for determining audience exposure to television. *Journal of Broadcasting and Electronic Media* 37(4): 401–18.

———. 1996. The status and future of audience duplication research: An assessment of ratings-based theories of audience behavior. *Journal of Broadcasting and Electronic Media* 40(1): 96–111.

Crawford, Gregory S. 2000. The impact of the 1992 Cable Act on household demand and welfare. *RAND Journal of Economics* 31(3): 422–49.

Cronbach, Lee. 1987. Statistical tests for moderator variables: Flaws in analysis recently proposed. *Psychological Bulletin* 102:414–17.

D'Amico, Theodore F. 1999. Magazines' secret weapon: Media selection on the basis of behavior, as opposed to demography. *Journal of Advertising Research* 39(6): 53–60.

Danaher, Peter J. and Jennifer M. Lawrie. 1998. Behavioral measures of television audience appreciation. *Journal of Advertising Research* 38(1): 54–65.

Danaher, Peter J. and Terence W. Beed. 1993. A coincidental survey of people meter panelists: Comparing what people say with what they do. *Journal of Advertising Research* 33(1): 86–92.

Darkow, Michael. 1996. Compatible or not? Results of a single-source field experiment within a TV audience research panel. *Marketing and Research Today* 24(3): 150–61.

Darmon, Rene Y. 1976. Determinants of TV viewing. *Journal of Advertising Research* 16(6): 17–20.

Davis, Donald M. and James R. Walker. 1990. Countering the new media: The resurgence of share maintenance in primetime network television. *Journal of Broadcasting and Electronic Media* 34(4): 487–93.

DeCoursey, Jennifer. 1995. Buyers peg new-season winners and losers. *Advertising Age,* June 12, pp. S14–15.

Demers, Elizabeth and Baruch Lev. 2000. A rude awakening: Internet shakeout in 2000. Working paper, University of Rochester.

den Boon, Arie K. 1994. The reliability of television audience ratings. *Marketing and Research Today* 22(4): 255–68.

Dimmick, John and Eric W. Rothenbuhler. 1984. Competitive displacement in the communication industries: New media in old environments. In Ronald E. Rice and Associates, eds., *The new media: Communication, research, and technology,* 207–304. Beverly Hills, Calif.: Sage.

Dingell, John D., Edolphus Towns, and Edward J. Markey. 2001. Letter to FTC Chairman Robert Pitofsky. March 28. http://www.house.gov/commerce_democrats/press/107ltr30.htm (April 8, 2001).

Dizard, Wilson Jr. 1997. *Meganet: How the global communications network will connect everyone on Earth.* Boulder, Colo.: Westview.

Donato, Paul J. 1996. Research in a world of expanding media options. Chicken or egg? *Journal of Advertising Research* 36(1): 35–42.

Donthu, Naveen. 1994. Double jeopardy in television program choice. *Journal of the Academy of Marketing Science* 22(2): 180–85.

Downey, Kevin. 2001. Nielsen sweetens diary system: Cash incentives work to boost response rates. *Media Life Magazine.* September 4. http://www.medialifemagazine.com/news2001/sept01/sep03/2_tues/news2tuesday.html (October 3, 2002).

Dreze, Xaxier and Fred Zufryden. 1998. Is Internet advertising ready for prime time? *Journal of Advertising Research* 38(3): 7–18.

Dubin, Jeffrey and Matthew L. Spitzer. 1995. Testing minority preferences in broadcasting. *Southern California Law Review* 68(4): 841–84.

Dupagne, Michel. 1997. A theoretical and methodological critique of the principal of relative constancy. *Communication Theory* 7(1): 53–76.

Eastman, Susan T. 1998. Programming theory under stress: The active industry and the active audience. *Communication Yearbook* 21:323–78.

Eastman, Susan T. and Jeffrey Neal-Lunsford. 1993. The RCD's impact on television programming and promotion. In J. R. Walker and R. V. Bellamy Jr., eds., *The remote control in the new age of television,* 189–209. Westport, Conn.: Praeger.

Eastman, Susan T. and Gregory D. Newton. 1995. Delineating grazing: Observations of remote control use. *Journal of Communication* 45(1): 77–95.

Eastman, Susan T., Jeffrey Neal-Lunsford, and Karen E. Riggs. 1995. Coping with grazing: Prime-time strategies for accelerated program transitions. *Journal of Broadcasting and Electronic Media* 39(1): 92–108.

Eastman, Susan T., Gregory D. Newton, Karen E. Riggs, and Jeffrey Neal-Lunsford. 1997. Accelerating the flow: A transition effect in programming theory? *Journal of Broadcasting and Electronic Media* 41(2): 265–83.

Edmondson, Brad. 1997. TV execs to Nielsen: Get SMART; Can the Nielsen ratings survive 500 channels, the Internet, and a new competitor? *American Demographics,* October, pp. 10–15.

Ehrenberg, Andrew S. C. 1968. The factor analytic search for program types. *Journal of Advertising Research* 8(1): 55–63.

Ehrlich, Isaac and Lawrence Fisher. 1982. The derived demand for advertising: A theoretical and empirical investigation. *American Economic Review* 72(3): 366–88.

Ehrlich, Matthew C. 1995. The ethical dilemma of television news sweeps. *Journal of Mass Media Ethics* 10(1): 37–47.

Elber, Lynn. 1999. Teen shows rule; adult fare rare. *Washington Times,* September 11, p. D1.

Elliott, Stuart. 2001. UPN weighs ad logos in prime time. *New York Times,* August 23, p. C1.

Endicott, R. Craig. 2001. One hundred leading national advertisers. *Advertising Age,* September 24, pp. S1–26.

Engel, Bill and Mark Maiville. 2000. Estimating audience demographics with the aid of multiple measures. Paper presented at the Advertising Research Foundation/European Society for Opinion and Marketing Research Worldwide Electronic and Broadcast Audience Research Conference, Bal Harbour, Fla., May.

Entman, Robert M. and Steven S. Wildman. 1992. Reconciling economic and noneconomic perspectives on media policy: Transcending the "marketplace of ideas." *Journal of Communication* 42(1): 5–19.

Ephron, Erwin. 2000. Nielsen's secret passive meter. *Mediaweek,* September 18, p. 32.

Ephron, Erwin and Linda Baniel. 2000. Can set meters save money? A comparison of set meter and peoplemeter panel costs. Paper presented at the Advertising Research Foundation Week of Workshops, Surviving the Internet—Television: Today and Tomorrow, New York, October.

Ephron, Erwin and Stuart Gray. 2000. Why we can't afford to measure viewers. Paper presented at the Advertising Research Foundation/European Society for Opinion and Marketing Research Worldwide Electronic and Broadcast Audience Research Conference, Bal Harbour, Fla., May.

Ephron, Erwin and James Peacock. 2000. MRI and media mix: The weakness of the critical television data in the MRI single-source database limits its value for media-mix optimizations. Manuscript.

Ephron, Erwin, Bill Harvey, Denman Maroney, Bill Moran, and Jim Spaeth. 2001. Making better media decisions: Update of the classic ARF media model. In D. S. Fellows, ed., *Proceedings of the ESOMAR/ARF Worldwide Audience Measurement Conference and Exhibition,* 197–215. New York: European Society for Opinion and Marketing Research/Advertising Research Foundation.

Ettema, James S. and D. Charles Whitney, eds. 1994. *Audiencemaking: How the media create the audience.* Thousand Oaks, Calif.: Sage.

Fattah, Hassan. 2000. The metrics system: Advertisers and e-businesses alike are questioning the effectiveness of on-line ad traffic measurement. But is there a better way? *Mediaweek,* November 13, pp. 66–70.

Federal Communications Commission. 1948. *Public service responsibility of broadcast licensees.* Washington, D.C.: GPO.

———. 1996. Section 257 proceeding to identify and eliminate market entry barriers for small business, *Federal Communications Commission Record* 11:6280.

———. 1998. Digital television consumer information bulletin. November. www.fcc.gov/Bureaus/Engineering_Technology/Factsheets/dtv9811.html (December 5, 2001).

———. 2002a. Annual assessment of the status of competition in the market for the delivery of video programming. January. http://hraunfoss.fcc.gov/edocs_public/attachmatch/FCC-01–389A1.txt (October 3, 2002).

———. 2002b. Broadcast station totals as of September 30, 2001. http://www.fcc.gov/Bureaus/Mass_Media/News_Releases/2001/nrmm0112.txt (June 14, 2002).

Federal Trade Commission. 2000. *Privacy on line: Fair information practices in the electronic marketplace.* Washington, D.C.: GPO.

Ferguson, Douglas A. 1992. Channel repertoire in the presence of remote control devices, VCRs, and cable television. *Journal of Broadcasting and Electronic Media* 36(1): 83–91.

Ferguson, Douglas A. and Elizabeth M. Perse. 1993. Media and audience influences on channel repertoire. *Journal of Broadcasting and Electronic Media* 37(1): 31–47.

———. 2001. Enhanced television viewing with digital video recorders (DVRs): Audience satisfaction in an asynchronous television environment. Paper presented at the annual meeting of the Association for Education in Journalism and Mass Communication, Washington, D.C., August.

Ferguson, James. 1983. Daily newspaper advertising rates, local media cross-ownership, newspaper chains, and media competition. *Journal of Law and Economics* 26(3): 635–54.

Fine, Jon. 1998. Nielsen's fallible system. *Brill's Content.* August. http://www.brillscontent.com/notebook/nielsen_0898.html (June 12, 2001).

Fisher, Franklin M., John J. McGowan, and David S. Evans. 1980. The audience-revenue relationship for local television stations. *Bell Journal of Economics* 11(2): 694–708.

Fiske, John. 1987. *Television culture.* London: Methuen.

———. 1989. *Reading the popular.* London: Routledge.

FitzGerald, Joan. 2002. Site-centric measurement: Can traditional panels meet the new standard? In *Proceedings of the ESOMAR/ARF Week of Audience Measurement Conference: Online,* 43–56. New York: European Society for Opinion and Marketing Research/Advertising Research Foundation.

Fletcher, James E. 1991. Music research. In G. G. Hartshorn, ed., *Audience research sourcebook,* 95–129. Washington, D.C.: National Association of Broadcasters.

Flint, Joe. 2001. Sweeps present firsthand look at what's hot on network TV. *Wall Street Journal,* November 1, p. B9.

Flint, Joe and Bruce Orwall. 2001. Play it again, Goofy . . . Recycled shows are central to Disney-Fox deal. *Wall Street Journal,* July 24, pp. B1, B6.

Foan, Richard. 2001. Certainty in a virtual world—dream or reality? The drive for global accountability for the Web. In D. S. Fellows, ed., *Proceedings of the ESOMAR/ARF Worldwide Audience Measurement Conference and Exhibition,* 121–34. New York: European Society for Opinion and Marketing Research/Advertising Research Foundation.

Foley, Tim, Peter Magnani, and Leigh Terry. 2001. While we "go create," you need to "go measure": Lessons learned while implementing a media strategy for Sony. In D. S. Fellows, ed., *Proceedings of the ESOMAR/ARF Worldwide Audience Measurement Conference and Exhibition,* 55–70. New York: European Society for Opinion and Marketing Research/Advertising Research Foundation.

Forkan, James P. 1986. Nielsen waters down TV forecasters' tea leaves. *Advertising Age,* April 7, p. 79.

Fournier, Gary M. and Donald L. Martin. 1983. Does government-restricted entry produce market power? New evidence from the market for television advertising. *Bell Journal of Economics* 14(1): 44–56.

Fragmentation face-off. 2001. *Mediaweek,* March 12, pp. 26–32.

Frank, Ronald E. and Marshall G. Greenberg. 1980. *The public's use of television: Who watches and why.* Beverly Hills, Calif.: Sage.

Frank, Ronald E., James C. Becknell, and James D. Clokey. 1971. Television program types. *Journal of Marketing Research* 8(2): 204–11.

Frankel, Daniel. 2001. Hitting on a genre. *Mediaweek,* September 10, p. 34.

Freidson, Eliot. 1953. Communication research and the concept of the mass. *American Sociological Review* 18(3): 313–17.

Frutkin, Alan J. 2002a. The content problem. *Mediaweek,* January 28, pp. 10–11.

———. 2002b. Family affair. *Mediaweek,* March 18, pp. 20–22.

———. 2002c. Family shows procreate. *Mediaweek,* June 3, pp. 6–8.

Gandy, Oscar H. 1984. Television audience size and composition. In Brenda Dervin and Melvin J. Voigt, eds., *Progress in communication sciences,* 5:219–54. Norwood, N.J.: Ablex.

———. 2000. Audience construction: Race, ethnicity, and segmentation in popular media. Paper presented at the annual meeting of the International Communication Association, Acapulco, Mexico, May.

Gane, Roger. 1994. Television audience measurement systems in Europe: A review and comparison. In Kent, *Measuring media audiences,* 22–41.

Gantz, Walter and Susan T. Eastman. 1983. Viewer use of promotional media to find out about television programs. *Journal of Broadcasting* 27(3): 269–77.

Gardini, Francesca. 2001. How to predict the success of new TV programs? The efficacy of the reliance on past successful producers as a strategy networks use to cope with uncertainty. Working paper, Annenberg School for Communication, University of Southern California, Los Angeles.

Gelman, Morrie. 1997. At NBC the beat goes on. *Broadcasting and Cable,* July 14, pp. 30–35.

Gensch, Dennis H. and Paul Shaman. 1980. Models of competitive ratings. *Journal of Marketing Research* 17(3): 307–15.

Gitlin, Todd. 1983. *Inside prime time.* New York: Pantheon.

Gold, Fred. 2000. ADS penetration in local markets and the potential overstatement of network cable program audiences: A review of the potential distortion alternative delivery systems have on network cable measurement in local markets. Pamphlet. New York: Telerep.

Goldberg, Marvin E. and Gerald J. Gorn. 1987. Happy and sad TV programs: How they affect reactions to commercials. *Journal of Consumer Research* 14(3): 387–403.

Gomery, Douglas. 1993. The centrality of media economics. *Journal of Communication* 43(3): 198–206.

Goodhardt, Gerald J., Andrew S. C. Ehrenberg, and Martin Collins. 1975. *The television audience: Patterns of viewing.* Westmead, England: Saxon House.

Granatstein, Lisa. 2000. The ABCs of circulation. *Mediaweek,* November 27, p. 44.

———. 2001. ABC's circ for tomorrow. *Mediaweek,* March 19, pp. 34–35.

Green, Andrew. 2002. The end of measurement as we know it? In *Proceedings of the ESOMAR/ARF Week of Audience Measurement Conference: Television,* 69–78.

New York: European Society for Opinion and Marketing Research/Advertising Research Foundation.

Greene, Kira. 2000. TV's test pilots. *Broadcasting and Cable,* July 17, p. 52.

Greenstein, Jennifer. 1999. Plotting a revolution—again. *Brill's Content.* February. www.brillscontent.com/colums/gatekeepers_0299.html (August 18, 2001).

Grotticelli, Michael. 2001. Tech speeds to SVOD: Several server manufacturers seek to capture slice of the action. *Broadcasting and Cable,* June 18, p. 26.

Gugel, Craig. 2001. Caught in the Web: From ad weary to ad wearout. In D. S. Fellows, ed., *Proceedings of the ESOMAR/ARF Worldwide Audience Measurement Conference and Exhibition,* 11–20. New York: European Society for Opinion and Marketing Research/Advertising Research Foundation.

Gunter, Barry. 1993. On the future of television ratings. *Journal of Broadcasting and Electronic Media* 37(3): 359–64.

Gunter, Barry and Mallory Wober. 1992. *The reactive viewer: A review of research on audience reaction measurement.* London: John Libbey.

Gunzerath, David J. 2000. Audience research trends. Paper presented at the National Association of Broadcasters Conference, Las Vegas, April.

Hall, Lee. 2001. "Simplify" now cable's watchword. *Broadcasting and Cable,* March 26, p. 34.

Hallford, Joshua. 2000. Web ratings: Heavy traffic ahead. *Industry Standard,* September 25, p. 104.

Hamilton, James T. 1998. *Channeling violence: The economic market for violent television programming.* Princeton, N.J.: Princeton University Press.

Hanson, Kurt. 1991. Format research. In G. G. Hartshorn, ed., *Audience research sourcebook,* 131–53. Washington, D.C.: National Association of Broadcasters.

Harmon, Amy. 2002. Skip-the-ads TV has Madison Ave. upset. *New York Times,* May 23, p. A1.

Harvey, Bill. 1999. Are higher-rated programs worth a higher CPM? *Myers Report,* July 27.

Harvey, Bill, Tony Jarvis, and Russ Booth. 2002. Better television audience measurement through cable and satellite set top boxes. In *Proceedings of the ESOMAR/ARF Week of Audience Measurement Conference: Television,* 37–47. New York: European Society for Opinion and Marketing Research/Advertising Research Foundation.

Hay, James, Larry Grossberg, and Ellen Wartella, eds. 1996. *The audience and its landscape.* Boulder, Colo.: Westview.

Hayes, Dade. 2000. Predicting box office: Studios find tracking research isn't "perfect." *Variety,* July 10–16, p. 4.

Headen, Robert S., Jay E. Klompmaker, and Jesse Teel. 1979. Predicting network TV viewing patterns. *Journal of Advertising Research* 19(4): 49–54.

Heeter, Carrie. 1985. Program selection with an abundance of choice: A process model. *Human Communication Research* 12(1): 126–52.

Heeter, Carrie and Bradley S. Greenberg. 1988. *Cableviewing.* Norwood, N.J.: Ablex.

Helft, Daniel. 2000. Latin America's credibility gap: The absence of Internet ratings data is making business difficult for everyone. And CEOs are starting to get cranky. *Industry Standard,* September 4, pp. 104–5.

Hemphill, Thomas A. 2000. Doubleclick and consumer on-line privacy: An e-commerce lesson learned. *Business and Society Review* 105(2): 361–72.

Henry, Michael D. and Heikki J. Rinne. 1984. Predicting program shares in new time slots. *Journal of Advertising Research* 24(2): 9–17.

Higgins, John M. 2001. Five blind mice: How the big cable nets lost their way. *Broadcasting and Cable,* June 11, pp. 20–27.

———. 2002. They discovered a business. *Broadcasting and Cable,* June 17, pp. 18–24.

Higgins, John M. and Allison Romano. 2002. Cheaper by the thousand. *Broadcasting and Cable,* February 4, pp. 20–28.

Hirsch, Paul M. 1972. Processing fads and fashions: An organization-set analysis of cultural industry systems. *American Journal of Sociology* 77(4): 639–59.

Hoang, Bruce and Daniel Brechignac. 2001. Using behavioural affinities on Web sites to maximise one's media plan: New on-line targeting tools. In D. S. Fellows, ed., *Proceedings of the ESOMAR/ARF Worldwide Audience Measurement Conference and Exhibition,* 45–54. New York: European Society for Opinion and Marketing Research/Advertising Research Foundation.

Horen, Jeffrey H. 1980. Scheduling of network television programs. *Management Science* 26(4): 354–70.

Howe, Jeff. 2001a. Ready for prime time: No longer considered the enemy, advertisers now see vast opportunities with interactive TV. *Mediaweek,* September 10, pp. IQ10–12.

———. 2001b. BMWfilms.com. *Mediaweek,* November 12, p. IQ5.

How to skin a potato. 2001. *Economist,* May 26, pp. 62–68.

Hudson, Eileen D. 2001. Market profile: Boston. *Mediaweek,* November 5, pp. 12–18.

Hulks, Bob and Gilles Santini. 1994. What kind of audience research will be required in the future? *Marketing and Research Today* 22(4): 269–79.

Introducing meters into nonmetered markets: 1990 through spring 2000. 2000. New York: Telerep.

Ivie, George and Nick Terlizzi. 2001. The MRC minimum standards: The U.S. case for applying consistent auditing standards across different types of media. In D. S. Fellows, ed., *Proceedings of the ESOMAR/ARF Worldwide Audience Measurement Conference and Exhibition,* 135–41. New York: European Society for Opinion and Marketing Research/Advertising Research Foundation.

Ivy Planning Group. 2000. *Historical study of market entry barriers, discrimination, and changes in broadcast and wireless licensing: 1950 to present.* Report prepared for the Office of General Counsel, Federal Communications Commission, Washington, D.C.

Iyengar, Shanto and Richard Reeves, eds. 1997. *Do the media govern? Politicians, voters, and reporters in America.* Thousand Oaks, Calif.: Sage.

Jaccard, James, Robert Turrisi, and Choi K. Wan. 1990. *Interaction effects in multiple regression.* Newbury Park, Calif.: Sage.

Jensen, Elizabeth. 1996. Frustrated NBC mulls creating rival to criticized Nielsen. *Wall Street Journal,* January 29, p. B10.

Jhally, Sut. 1982. Probing the blindspot: The audience commodity. *Canadian Journal of Political and Social Theory* 6(1–2): 204–10.

Jhally, Sut and Bill Livant. 1986. Watching as working: The valorization of audience consciousness. *Journal of Communication* 36(3): 124–43.

Jones, John P. 1995. Single-source research begins to fulfill its promise. *Journal of Advertising Research* 35(3): 9–16.

Jones, Tim. 2001. Revenue quest steadily walling off more Internet content. *Chicago Tribune Online.* April 5. http://www.chicagotribune.com/business/printedition/article/0,2699,SAV-0104050116,FF.html (October 3, 2002).

Jorgensen, Danny L. 1989. *Participant observation: A methodology for human studies.* Thousand Oaks, Calif.: Sage.

Jupiter Media Metrix. 2001. Rapid media consolidation dramatically narrows number of companies controlling time spent on line, reports Jupiter Media Metrix. *Jupiter Media Metrix.* June 4. http://www.jmm.com/xp/jmm/press/2001/pr_060401.xml (October 3, 2002).

Jupiter Media Metrix sold. 2001. *Mediaweek,* October 29, p. 3.

Kalita, Jukti K. and Robert H. Ducoffe. 1995. A simultaneous-equation analysis of pricing, circulation, and advertising revenue for leading consumer magazines. *Journal of Media Economics* 8(4): 1–16.

Kalyanam, Kirthi and Bruce MacEvoy. 1999. Data reconciliation: Reducing discrepancies in audience estimates from Web servers and on-line panels. http://www.lsb.scu.edu/kkalyanam/data-rec/tsld001.htm (December 7, 2001).

Kennedy, John R. 1971. How program environment affects TV commercials. *Journal of Advertising Research* 11(1): 33–38.

Kennedy, Robert E. 2002. Strategy fads and competitive convergence: An empirical test for herd behavior in prime-time television programming. *Journal of Industrial Economics,* 50(1): 57–84.

Kent, Raymond, ed. 1994. *Measuring media audiences.* New York: Routledge.

Kerschbaumer, Ken. 2001. Beyond banners. *Broadcasting and Cable,* October 8, pp. 38–44.

Kieschnick, Robert and Bruce D. McCullough. 2000. *Do advertisers pay more for viewers with rabbit ears?* Working paper, Federal Communications Commission, Washington, D.C.

Kim, Doh-Yeon and August Grant. 1996. The validity of the program type model in studies of television program diversity. Paper presented at the annual meeting of the Association for Education in Journalism and Mass Communication, Anaheim, Calif., August.

Kirkham, Mike. 1996. Measuring the fragmenting television audience. *Journal of the Market Research Society* 38(3): 219–26.

Kirsch, Arthur D. and Seymour Banks. 1962. Program types defined by factor analysis. *Journal of Advertising Research* 2(3): 29–31.

Klopfenstein, Bruce C. 1989. The diffusion of the VCR in the United States. In Levy, *The VCR age,* 21–39.

Koerner, Brendan I. 2001. See and be seen: Does your TV spy on you? *Mother Jones,* July–August, p. 19.

Koschat, Martin A. and William P. Putsis Jr. 2000. Who wants you when you're old and poor? Exploring the economics of media pricing. *Journal of Media Economics* 13(4): 215–32.

KPMG. 2000a. *Logistic regression models of the broadcast license award process for licenses awarded by the FCC.* Report prepared for the Federal Communications Commission, Washington, D.C.

———. 2000b. *Utilization rates, win rates, and disparity ratios for broadcast licenses awarded by the FCC.* Report prepared for the Federal Communications Commission, Washington, D.C.

Lake, David. 2000. A new way to tell who's watching. *Industry Standard,* August 28, p. 75.

———. 2001. Worldwide web domination. *Industry Standard,* July 30, 58–59.

Larson, Christine. 2001. Where we go from here? *Mediaweek,* November 12, pp. IQ1–3.

Larson, Megan. 2001. Digital dollar download. *Mediaweek,* June 18, pp. 9–10.

———. 2002. MTV: Close the cable gap. *Mediaweek,* June 3, p. 5.

Lazarsfeld, Paul F. and Harry Field. 1946. *The people look at radio.* Chapel Hill: University of North Carolina Press.

Leckenby, John D. and Jongpil Hong. 1998. Using reach/frequency for Web media planning. *Journal of Advertising Research* 38(1): 7–20.

Lefton, Terry. 2001. The great flameout. *Industry Standard,* March 19, pp. 74–78.

Lehmann, Donald R. 1971. Television show preference: Application of a choice model. *Journal of Marketing Research* 8(1): 47–55.

Lerner, Preston. 1999. Shadow force: Hundreds of movies have been reshaped as a result of work by Joseph Farrell's National Research Group. *Los Angeles Times Magazine,* November 7, p. 18.

Levin, Harvey J. 1980. *Fact and fancy in television regulation: An economic study of policy alternatives.* New York: Russell Sage Foundation.

Levy, Mark R. 1982. The Lazarsfeld-Stanton program analyzer: A historical note. *Journal of Communication* 32(4): 30–38.

———, ed. 1989. *The VCR age: Home video and mass communication.* Newbury Park, Calif.: Sage.

Lewis, Michael. 2000. Boom box. *New York Times Magazine,* August 13, p. 36.

Lin, Carolyn A. 1994. Audience fragmentation in a competitive video marketplace. *Journal of Advertising Research* 34(6): 30–38.

Lindlof, Thomas R. 1988. Media audiences as interpretive communities. *Communication Yearbook* 11:81–107.

Lindstrom, Paul B. 1989. Home video: The consumer impact. In Levy, *The VCR age,* 40–49.

Litman, Barry R. 1998. *The motion picture mega-industry.* Needham Heights, Mass.: Allyn and Bacon.

Litman, Barry R. and L. S. Kohl. 1989. Predicting financial success of motion pictures: The '80s experience. *Journal of Media Economics* 2(2): 35–50.

Livingstone, Sonia M. 1993. The rise and fall of audience research: An old story with a new ending. *Journal of Communication* 43(4): 5–12.

Lotoski, Adrienne. 2000. The Nielsen local people meter initiative: Implications for Boston and future local markets. Working paper, WCVB-TV, Boston.

———. 2001. Key test for local TV meters. *Mediaweek,* January 8, p. 20.

Lowery, Shearon A. and Melvin L. DeFleur. 1995. *Milestones in mass communication research: Media effects.* 3d ed. White Plains, N.Y.: Longman.

Lu, Daozheng and David A. Kiewit. 1987. Passive people meters: A first step. *Journal of Advertising Research* 27(3): 9–14.

Lynch, Kate and Horst Stipp. 1999. Examination of qualitative viewing factors for optimal advertising strategies. *Journal of Advertising Research* 39(3): 7–16.

Mack, Ann M. 2000. Banner years ahead. *Mediaweek,* September 25, pp. M48–52.

MacFarland, David T. 1997. *Future radio programming strategies: Cultivating listenership in the digital age.* 2d ed. Mahwah, N.J.: Lawrence Erlbaum.

Magazine Publishers of America. 2001. Number of magazine titles. http://www.magazine.org/resources/fact_sheet.html (October 3, 2002).

Mandese, Joe. 1995. Supply and demand, "upfront," ratings points, media fragmentation: Oh how TV has changed. *Advertising Age,* February 28, p. 20.

———. 1999. They didn't get SMART. *American Demographics,* August, pp. 33–35.

———. 2001. CBS, still on the warpath, goes after ad report that compares magazines favorably to TV. *Inside.com.* July 5. www.inside.com/jcs/Story?article_id=34197&pod_id=11 (July 5, 2001).

———. 2002. Ratings box comes out of closet: Ad biz reveals set-top data play. *Media Buyer's Daily,* February 19, p. 1.

Mangalindan, Mylene. 2002. No more free lunch: In the future, the best things on the Web may not be free. *Wall Street Journal,* April 15, p. R6.

March, James G. 1994. *A primer on decision making: How decisions happen.* New York: Free Press.

Martin, David. 2001. *TiVo's data collection and privacy practices.* Washington, D.C.: Privacy Foundation.

Mason, Laurie, Christine M. Bachen, and Stephanie L. Craft. 2001. Support for FCC minority ownership policy: How broadcast station owner race or ethnicity affects news and public affairs programming diversity. *Communication Law and Policy* 6(1): 37–73.

Mattes, John and Joanne Cantor. 1982. Enhancing responses to television advertisements via the transfer of residual arousal from prior programming. *Journal of Broadcasting* 26(4): 553–66.

McAdams, Deborah D. 2000a. Micro-marketing: Research firms ID most likely customers. *Broadcasting and Cable,* July 17, p. 50.

———. 2000b. Eighteen to thirty-four. *Broadcasting and Cable,* October 9, pp. 50–56.

McClellan, Steve. 2000. "Write us down, or we may go dark": Nielsen threatens to delist stations that target diary keepers. *Broadcasting and Cable,* November 20, p. 12.

———. 2001. The graying of the networks. *Broadcasting and Cable,* June 18, p. 32.

———. 2002. War's over but not the battles. *Broadcasting and Cable,* April 22, pp. 6–8.

McClellan, Steve and Allison Romano. 2002. Cable niches get the riches. *Broadcasting and Cable,* June 17, pp. 6–7.

McClellan, Steve and Joe Schlosser. 2001. One and again. *Broadcasting and Cable,* July 30, pp. 18–20.

McCombs, Maxwell E. 1972. Mass media in the marketplace. *Journalism Monographs* 24.

McConochie, Roberta and Beth Uyenco. 2002. Trash and treasures of duplication: Cross media synergy prospects from Arbitron's portable people meters (PPM). In *Proceedings of the ESOMAR/ARF Week of Audience Measurement Conference: Television,* 327–43. New York: European Society for Opinion and Marketing Research/Advertising Research Foundation.

McDonald, Daniel G. and Russell Schechter. 1988. Audience role in the evolution of fictional television content. *Journal of Broadcasting and Electronic Media* 32(1): 61–71.

McDowell, W. and Steven J. Dick. 2002. Switching radio stations while driving: Magnitude, motivation and measurement issues. Paper presented at the annual meeting of the Association for Education in Journalism and Mass Communication, Miami, August.

McGlathery, Donald G. 1993. Does title confusion affect magazine audience levels? *Journal of Advertising Research* 33(1): 24–34.

McGrath, John M. and Chad Mahood. 2001. The impact of arousing television programs on advertising effectiveness: An empirical test. Paper presented at the annual meeting of the International Communication Association, Washington, D.C., May.

McKenna, William J. 1988. The future of electronic measurement technology in U.S. media research. *Journal of Advertising Research* 28(3): RC3–7.

McManus, John H. 1994. *Market-driven journalism: Let the citizen beware?* Thousand Oaks, Calif.: Sage.

McQuail, Dennis. 1969. Uncertainty about the audience and the organization of mass communications. *Sociological Review Monograph 13: The Sociology of Mass Media Communicators,* pp. 75–84.

———. 1997. *Audience analysis.* Thousand Oaks, Calif.: Sage.

Measurecast. 2001. *An analysis of streaming audience measurement methods.* Portland, Ore.: Measurecast.

Media Dynamics. 2001a. *Internet dimensions 2001*. New York: Media Dynamics.

——. 2001b. *TV dimensions 2001*. New York: Media Dynamics.

Mediamark probes consumer psyche. 2001. *Mediaweek,* February 26, p. 48.

Media Metrix. 2001. Understanding measurement of the Internet and digital media landscape. http://www.mediametrix.com/products/us_methodology_long.pdf (December 5, 2001).

Meehan, Eileen R. 1984. Ratings and the institutional approach: A third answer to the commodity question. *Critical Studies in Mass Communication* 1:216–25.

Menneer, Peter. 1992. Apples and oranges: Towards a standardised currency of audience measurement. *Marketing and Research Today* 20(3): 186–93.

——. 2001. Audiometer measurement—Proven currencies? *Proceedings of the ESOMAR/ARF Worldwide Radio Conference and Exhibition,* 203–24. New York: European Society for Opinion and Marketing Research/Advertising Research Foundation.

Menneer, Peter and Toby Syfret. 1994. Toward harmonisation of TV audience measurement. *Marketing and Research Today* 22(4): 231–42.

Milavsky, J. Ronald. 1992. How good is the A. C. Nielsen people meter system? A review of the report by the Committee on Nationwide Television Audience Measurement. *Public Opinion Quarterly* 56(1): 102–15.

Miles, Stephanie. 2001. NetRatings–Jupiter Media deal creates leader in marginal product. *Wall Street Journal,* November 9, p. B3.

Millard, William J. 1992. A history of handsets for direct measurement of audience response. *International Journal of Public Opinion Research* 4(1): 1–17.

Miller, Mark. 2001. With looser rules on who counts as a subscriber, how low will magazines go? *Inside.com.* July 18. www.inside.com/product/productasp?entity=&pf_id=CF257556–3AB3–4318-B7BF- (July 18, 2001).

Miller, Peter V. 1994. Made-to-order and standardized audiences: Forms of reality in audience measurement. In Ettema and Whitney, *Audiencemaking,* 57–74.

Minow, Newton N. and Craig L. LaMay. 1995. *Abandoned in the wasteland: Children, television, and the First Amendment.* New York: Hill and Wang.

Mitgang, Lee D. 2000. *Big Bird and beyond: The new media and the Markle Foundation.* New York: Fordham University Press.

Monistere, Daniel and Krista Zimmerman. 2001. Optimizing local cable: Making qualitative and quantitative data work together. *ADcom Information Services.* http://http://www.adcoms.com/press/articles/Optimizing%20Local%20Cable.htm (October 3, 2002).

Moores, Shaun. 1993. *Interpreting audiences: The ethnography of media consumption.* Thousand Oaks, Calif.: Sage.

Moritz, Meg. 1989. The ratings "sweeps" and how they make news. In Gary Burns and Robert Thompson, eds., *Television studies: Textual analysis,* 121–36. New York: Praeger.

Mosco, Vincent and Lewis Kaye. 2000. Questioning the concept of the audience.

In Ingunn Hagen and Janet Wasko, eds., *Consuming audiences? Production and reception in media research,* 31–46. Cresskill, N.J.: Hampton Press.

Moss, Linda. 2002. Does Arbitron have a better mousetrap? *Broadcasting and Cable,* February 11, pp. 16–26.

MTV Networks–Viacom study of media, entertainment, and leisure time. 2000. New York: MTV Networks–Viacom.

Murdock, Graham. 2000. Peculiar commodities: Audiences at large in the world of goods. In Ingunn Hagen and Janet Wasko, eds., *Consuming audiences: Production and reception in media research,* 47–70. Cresskill, N.J.: Hampton Press.

Murphy, Jeremy. 2001. Study slams stations' sweeps stunting. *Mediaweek,* September 10, pp. 11, 14.

———. 2002. Stations persist with stunting strategies. *Mediaweek,* March 11, p. 11.

Napoli, Philip M. 1997a. A principal agent approach to the study of media organizations: Toward a theory of the media firm. *Political Communication* 14(2): 207–19.

———. 1997b. The media trade press as technology forecaster: A case study of the VCR's impact on broadcasting. *Journalism and Mass Communication Quarterly* 74(2): 417–30.

———. 1997c. Rethinking program diversity assessment: An audience-centered approach. *Journal of Media Economics* 10(4): 59–74.

———. 1998a. Evolutionary theories of media institutions and their responses to new technologies. In Linda Lederman, ed., *Communication theory: A reader,* 315–29. Dubuque, Iowa: Kendall/Hunt.

———. 1998b. The Internet and the forces of "massification." *Electronic Journal of Communication* 8(2). http://www.cios.org/www/ejc/v8n298.htm (October 3, 2002).

———. 1999a. Deconstructing the diversity principle. *Journal of Communication* 49(4): 7–34.

———. 1999b. The marketplace of ideas metaphor in communications regulation. *Journal of Communication* 49(4): 151–69.

———. 1999c. The unique nature of communications regulation: Evidence and implications for communications policy analysis. *Journal of Broadcasting and Electronic Media* 43(4): 565–81.

———. 2000. Perspectives on consumer use of medical information from electronic and print media: A literature review. In Ronald E. Rice and James Katz, eds., *The Internet and health communication: Experience and expectations,* 79–98. Beverly Hills, Calif.: Sage.

———. 2001a. The audience product and the new media environment: Implications for the economics of media industries. *International Journal on Media Management* 3(2): 66–73.

———. 2001b. *Foundations of communications policy: Principles and process in the regulation of electronic media.* Cresskill, N.J.: Hampton Press.

————. 2001c. Market conditions and public affairs programming: Implications for digital television policy. *Harvard International Journal of Press/Politics* 6(2): 15–29.

————. 2001d. The unpredictable audience: An exploratory analysis of the determinants of forecasting error for new prime-time network television programs. *Journal of Advertising* 30(2): 53–60.

National Cable and Telecommunications Association. 2002. *Cable television developments 2002.* Washington, D.C.: National Cable and Telecommunications Association.

National Telecommunications and Information Administration. 2000. *Changes, challenges, and charting new courses: Minority commercial broadcast ownership in the United States.* Washington, D.C.: U.S. Department of Commerce.

National Television Violence Study. 1996–98. 3 vols. Thousand Oaks, Calif.: Sage.

Negroponte, Nicholas. 1995. *Being digital.* New York: Alfred A. Knopf.

Neuman, W. Russell. 1991. *The future of the mass audience.* New York: Cambridge University Press.

Nicholas, David and Paul Huntington. 2000. Evaluating the use of newspaper Web site logs. *International Journal on Media Management* 2(2): 78–88.

Nielsen, Arthur C. Jr. 1988. Television ratings and the public interest. In Jon T. Powell and Wally Gair, eds., *Public interest and the business of broadcasting,* 61–63. New York: Quorum.

Nielsen chastises KSWB-TV. 2000. *Broadcasting and Cable,* December 11, p. 8.

Nielsen Media. 2001. Gemstar–TV Guide International and Nielsen Media Research announce strategic partnership for interactive TV research. April 11. http://www.nielsenmedia.com/newsreleases/releases/2001/TVguidepartnership.htm (June 5, 2001).

Nielsen Media Research. 1999. *TV viewing in Internet households.* New York: Nielsen Media Research.

————. 2000. *2000 report on television.* New York: Nielsen Media Resources.

————. 2001a. *Audience measurement for the twenty-first century.* New York: Nielsen Media Research.

————. 2001b. Q and A's about measuring the ethnic television audience. http://www.nielsenmedia.com/ethnicmeasure/qanda/q+a.html (October 3, 2002).

————. 2001c. Who we are and what we do. http://www.nielsenmedia.com/whoweare.html (October 3, 2002).

Nielsen signs WUNI-TV. 2002. *Mediaweek,* May 20, p. 14.

Noll, Roger G., Merton J. Peck, and John J. McGowan. 1973. *Economic aspects of television regulation.* Washington, D.C.: Brookings Institution.

Nord, David P. 1980. An economic perspective on formula in popular culture. *Journal of American Culture* 3:17–31.

Novak, Thomas P. and Donna L. Hoffman. 1997. New metrics for new media: Toward the development of Web measurement standards. *World Wide Web Journal* 2(1): 213–46.

O'Connell, Fred. 2002. User-centric Internet measurement and its role in media planning. In *Proceedings of the ESOMAR/ARF Week of Audience Measurement Conference: Online*, 57–64. New York: European Society for Opinion and Marketing Research/Advertising Research Foundation.

O'Connell, Vanessa. 2001. Web firms disagree on Internet ad hits. *Wall Street Journal*, November 16, p. B6.

Ordonez, Jennifer. 2000. Hamburger joints call them "heavy users"—but not to their faces. *Wall Street Journal*, January 12, p. A1.

———. 2001a. Arbitron tests meters to count radio audience. *Wall Street Journal*, July 12, pp. B1, B4.

———. 2001b. Music sales hit sour note. *Wall Street Journal*, August 3, pp. B1, B4.

Ofori, Kofi A. 1999. When being no. 1 is not enough: The impact of advertising practices on minority-owned and minority-formatted broadcast stations. Report prepared by the Civil Rights Forum on Communications Policy, Washington, D.C.

Owen, Bruce M. 1999. *The Internet challenge to television*. Cambridge, Mass.: Harvard University Press.

Owen, Bruce M. and Steven S. Wildman. 1992. *Video economics*. Cambridge, Mass.: Harvard University Press.

Page, Benjamin I. 1996. *Who deliberates? Mass media in modern democracy*. Chicago: University of Chicago Press.

Park, Rolla E. 1971. The growth of cable TV and its probable impact on over-the-air broadcasting. *American Economic Review* 61(2): 69–73.

———. 1972. Cable television, UHF broadcasting, and FCC regulatory policy. *Journal of Law and Economics* 15(1): 207–32.

Patchen, Robert H. and Brian Harris-Kojetin. 2001. Latest developments on the portable people meter: The U.S. trial in Philadelphia. *Proceedings of the ESOMAR/ARF Worldwide Radio Conference and Exhibition*, 185–202. New York: European Society for Opinion and Marketing Research/Advertising Research Foundation.

Patchen, Robert and Ronald S. Kolessar. 1999. Out of the lab and into the field: A pilot test of the personal, portable meter. *Journal of Advertising Research* 39(4): 55–68.

Patchen, Robert H. and Beth M. Webb. The future is now: The latest findings from the market launch of the portable people meter in Philadelphia. In *Proceedings of the ESOMAR/ARF Week of Audience Measurement Conference: Television*, 301–24. New York: European Society for Opinion and Marketing Research/Advertising Research Foundation.

Patterson, Thomas E. 1980. *The mass media election: How Americans choose their president*. New York: Praeger.

Pekurny, Robert. 1982. Coping with television production. In J. S. Ettema and D. Charles Whitney, eds., *Individuals in mass media organizations: Creativity and constraint*, 131–44. Beverly Hills, Calif.: Sage.

Peterman, John L. 1971. Concentration of control and the price of television time. *American Economic Review* 61(2): 74–80.

———. 1979. Differences between the levels of spot and network television advertising rates. *Journal of Business* 52(4): 549–61.

Peterson, Richard A. 1994. Measured markets and unknown audiences: Case studies from the production and consumption of music. In Ettema and Whitney, *Audiencemaking*, 171–85.

Petty, Richard E., David W. Schumann, Steven A. Richman, and Alan J. Strathman. 1993. Positive mood and persuasion: Different roles for affect under high- and low-elaboration conditions. *Journal of Personality and Social Psychology* 64(1): 5–20.

Phalen, Patricia F. 1996. Information and markets and the market for information: An analysis of the market for television audiences. Ph.D. diss., Northwestern University, Evanston, Ill.

———. 1998. The market information system and personalized exchange: Business practices in the market for television audiences. *Journal of Media Economics* 11(4): 17–34.

Picard, Robert G. 1999. Audience fragmentation and structural limits on media innovation and diversity. Paper presented at the Second Expert Meeting on Media in Open Societies, Amsterdam, May.

———. 2001a. Expansion and limits in EU television markets: Audience, advertising, and competition issues. Paper presented at the Workshop on Competition in Media and Advertising Markets, Provence, France, May.

———. 2001b. Audience economics of European Union public service broadcasters: Assessing performance in competitive markets. Paper presented at the annual meeting of the Association for Education in Journalism and Mass Communication, Washington, D.C., August.

Poltrack, David. 1983. *Television marketing: Network, local, and cable.* New York: McGraw-Hill.

———. 1988. Living with people meters. *Journal of Advertising Research* 28(3): RC8–10.

Porter, Eduardo. 2001. Measurecast aims to run on-line-radio ratings. *Wall Street Journal,* October 11, p. B11.

Porter, Eduardo and Emily Nelson. 2000. P&G reaches out to Hispanics. *Wall Street Journal,* October 13, pp. B1, B4.

Prag, Jay and James Casavant. 1994. An empirical study of the determinants of revenues and marketing expenditures in the motion picture industry. *Journal of Cultural Economics* 18:217–34.

Puig, Claudia 2000. Putting Hollywood to the test: Who rules in movies' final phase? Test-screen audiences pick flaws and highlights, while studios and filmmakers anxiously listen. *USA Today,* July 21, p. E1.

Purdye, Ken and Bill Harvey. 1994. Focus on broadcast media audience research. *Marketing and Research Today* 22(4): 223–30.

Radio Advertising Bureau. 2001. *Radio marketing guide and fact book*. New York: Radio Advertising Bureau.

Radway, Janice A. 1984. *Reading the romance: Women, patriarchy, and popular literature*. Chapel Hill: University of North Carolina Press.

Rajgopal, Shivaram, Suresh Kotha, and Mohan Venkatachalam. 2000. The relevance of Web traffic for Internet stock prices. Working paper, University of Washington, Seattle.

Rao, Vithala R. 1975. Taxonomy of television programs based on viewing behavior. *Journal of Marketing Research* 12(3): 355–58.

Reid, Leonard N. and Karen W. King. 2000. A demand-side view of media substitutability in national advertising: A study of advertiser opinions about traditional media options. *Journalism and Mass Communication Quarterly* 77(2): 292–307.

Reimer, Eric. 1992. The effects of monopolization on newspaper advertising rates. *American Economist* 36(1): 65–70.

Reinholz, Mary. 2000. Where the boys are. *Broadcasting and Cable*, October 9, pp. 72–76.

Renckstorf, Karsten, Dennis McQuail, and Nicholas Jankowski. 1996. *Media use as social action: A European approach to audience studies*. London: John Libbey.

Rich, Laura. 2001. That's advertainment. *Industry Standard*, June 25, pp. 60–61.

Rodriguez, America. 2001. *Reinventing minority media for the twenty-first century*. Washington, D.C.: Aspen Institute.

Rogers, Danny. 2001. Break free from the bonds of traditional advertising. *Financial Times*, June 5, p. 4.

Rogers, Everette M. 1994. *A history of communication study: A biographical approach*. New York: Free Press.

Rogers, Robert P. and John R. Woodbury. 1996. Market structure, program diversity, and radio audience size. *Contemporary Economic Policy* 14:81–91.

Rogovin, Wendy M. 1992. The regulation of television in the public interest: On creating a parallel universe in which minorities speak and are heard. *Catholic University Law Review* 42(1): 51–102.

Romano, Allison. 2002a. New to Nielsen's numbers. *Broadcasting and Cable*, February 4, p. 29.

———. 2002b. Mohr Sports: The talk of ESPN. *Broadcasting and Cable*, April 1, p. 22.

Rose, Matthew. 2001. To sell ad pages, magazines offer extra services. *Wall Street Journal*, July 9, pp. B1, B4.

Rose, M. J. 2001. Your ad here. *Salon.com*. September 5. http://www.salon.com/books/feature/2001/09/05/bulgari/ (June 17, 2002).

Rosen, Sherwin. 1981. The economics of superstars. *American Economic Review* 71(5): 845–57.

Rothenberg, Jerome. 1962. Consumer sovereignty and the economics of TV programming. *Studies in Public Communication* 4:23–36.

Rowland, Willard D. 1983. *The politics of TV violence: Policy uses of communication research.* Beverly Hills, Calif.: Sage.

Rubens, William S. 1984. High-tech audience measurement for new-tech audiences. *Critical Studies in Mass Communication* 1:195–205.

———. 1989. We don't care about research quality anymore. *Journal of Advertising Research* 29(1): RC3–RC6.

Rust, Roland T. and Naveen Donthu. 1988. A programming and positioning strategy for cable television networks. *Journal of Advertising* 17(4): 6–13.

Rust, Roland T. and Naras V. Eechambadi. 1989. Scheduling network television programs: A heuristic audience flow approach to maximizing audience share. *Journal of Advertising* 18(2): 11–18.

Rust, Roland T. and Richard W. Oliver. 1994. The death of advertising. *Journal of Advertising* 23(4): 71–77.

Rust, Roland T., Wagner A. Kamakura, and Mark I. Alpert. 1992. Viewer preference segmentation and viewing choice models for network television. *Journal of Advertising* 21(1): 1–18.

Sabavala, Darius J. and Donald G. Morrison. 1977. A model of TV show loyalty. *Journal of Advertising Research* 17(6): 35–43.

———. 1981. A nonstationary model of binary choice applied to media exposure. *Management Science* 27(6): 637–57.

Salamon, Julie. 2001. Teenage viewers declare independence: When it comes to TV, coveted adolescents prove to be unpredictable. *New York Times,* March 13, pp. E1, E8.

Sapolsky, Barry S. and Edward Forrest. 1989. Measuring VCR "ad-voidance." In Levy, *The VCR age,* 148–67.

Schiavone, Nicholas P. 1988. Lessons from the radio research experience for all electronic media. *Journal of Advertising Research* 28(3): RC11–15.

Schlosberg, Jeremy. 1993. Kids off TV: What's taking them away from the tube? Parenting style changes are suggested. *Mediaweek,* February 8, pp. 23–32.

Schlosser, Joe. 2000. In the family way: Ad forum to fund kin-friendly script development at CBS, ABC. *Broadcasting and Cable,* November 20, p. 14.

———. 2001. Emeril's test kitchen? NBC. *Broadcasting and Cable,* July 7, p. 19.

Schroeder, Gary. 1998. Marketing research: Behavioral optimization. *American Demographics,* August, p. 34.

Seldon, Barry J. and Chulho Jung. 1993. Derived demand for advertising messages and substitutability among the media. *Quarterly Review of Economics and Finance* 33(1): 71–86.

Shandler, Geoff. 2001. Book scandal. *Industry Standard,* July 9–16, p. 16.

Shapiro, Andrew. 1999. *The control revolution.* New York: PublicAffairs.

Shapiro, Carl and Hal R. Varian. 1999. *Information rules: A strategic guide to the network economy.* Cambridge, Mass.: Harvard Business School Press.

Shaver, Mary A. 1995. Application of pricing theory in studies of pricing behavior and rate strategy in the newspaper industry. *Journal of Media Economics* 8(2): 49–59.

Shoemaker, Pamela J. and Steven D. Reese. 1996. *Mediating the message: Theories of influences on mass media content.* 2d ed. White Plains, N.Y.: Longman.

Silk, Alvin J. and Ernest R. Berndt. 1993. Scale and scope effects on advertising agency costs. *Marketing Science* 12(1): 53–72.

———. 1994. Costs, institutional mobility barriers, and market structure: Advertising agencies as multiproduct firms. *Journal of Economics and Management Strategy* 3(3): 437–80.

Sills, David L. 1996. Stanton, Lazarsfeld, and Merton: Pioneers in communication research. In Everette E. Dennis and Ellen Wartella, eds., *American communication research: The remembered history,* 105–16. Mahwah, N.J.: Lawrence Erlbaum.

Simon, Herbert A. 1976. *Administrative behavior: A study of decision-making processes in administrative organizations.* 3d ed. New York: Free Press.

Smith, Ken. 1995. Intermedia competition for advertising in small daily markets. *Journal of Media Economics* 8(4): 29–45.

———. 1998. Advertisers' media selection in small newspaper markets. *Newspaper Research Journal* 19(1): 30–44.

Smythe, Dallas W. 1977. Communications: Blindspot of western Marxism. *Canadian Journal of Political and Social Theory* 1(3): 1–27.

———. 1981. *Dependency road: Communications, capitalism, consciousness, and Canada.* Norwood, N.J.: Ablex.

Sochay, Scott. 1994. Predicting the performance of motion pictures. *Journal of Media Economics* 7(1): 1–20.

Son, Jinok and Maxwell E. McCombs. 1993. A look at the constancy principle under changing market conditions. *Journal of Media Economics* 6(1): 22–36.

Soong, Roland. 1988. The statistical reliability of people meter ratings. *Journal of Advertising Research* 28(1): 50–56.

Spalding, John W. 1963–64. 1928: Radio becomes a mass advertising medium. *Journal of Broadcasting* 8(1): 31–44.

Spence, Michael A. and Bruce M. Owen. 1977. Television programming, monopolistic competition, and welfare. *Quarterly Journal of Economics* 91:103–26.

Sprenger, Polly. 1999. Cable boxes see what you see. *Wired News.* http://www.wired/com/news/print/0,1294,19132,00.html (October 3, 2002).

Stanley, T. L. 2002. Prime time for sale. *Mediaweek,* May 13, pp. 33–38.

Stations resist people meters. 2001. *Mediaweek,* October 9, p. 3.

Steiner, Gary A. 1963. *The people look at television: A study of audience attitudes.* New York: Alfred A. Knopf.

Steiner, Peter O. 1952. Program patterns and preferences and the workability of competition in radio broadcasting. *Quarterly Journal of Economics* 66:194–223.

Stinchcombe, Arthur L. 1990. *Information and organizations.* Berkeley: University of California Press.

Stipp, Horst and Nicholas Schiavone. 1990. Research at a commercial television network: NBC 1990. *Marketing Research* 2(3): 3–10.

Stockley, John and Tim Farmer. 2001. RAJAR respondents: A re-contact survey.

Proceedings of the ESOMAR/ARF Worldwide Radio Conference and Exhibition, 57–71. New York: European Society for Opinion and Marketing Research/Advertising Research Foundation.

Stoddard, Laurence R. Jr. 1986. Will single-source data change media planning? *Journal of Advertising Research* 26(2): RC13–15.

———. 1987. The history of people meters: How we got where we are (and why). *Journal of Advertising Research* 27(5): RC10–12.

Stoughton, Stephanie. 2001. Watching you watching them: Your electronic friends—car, TV, and cellphone—may soon be the key to letting almost anyone peek into your private life. *Boston Globe,* July 9, p. C4.

Stucke, Maurice E. and Allen P. Grunes. 2001. Antitrust and the marketplace of ideas. *Antitrust Law Journal* 69(1): 249–302.

Sunstein, Cass R. 1993. *Democracy and the problem of free speech.* New York: Free Press.

———. 2001. *Republic.com.* Princeton, N.J.: Princeton University Press.

Surgeon General's Scientific Advisory Committee on Television and Social Behavior. 1972. *Television and growing up: The impact of televised violence: Report to the Surgeon General, United States Public Health Service.* Washington, D.C.: GPO.

Surmanek, Jim. 1996. *Media planning: A practical guide.* 3d ed. Chicago: NTC Business Books.

Surowiecki, James. 2002. Ageism in advertising. *New Yorker,* April 1, p. 40.

Takada, Hirokazu and Walter A. Henry. 1993. Analysis of network TV commercial time pricing for top-rated prime-time programs. *Journal of Current Issues and Research in Advertising* 15(2): 59–70.

Tam, Pui-Wing. 2002. Ethnic media muy popular in California. *Wall Street Journal,* April 23, pp. B1, B4.

Tasca, Eileen. 1998. The business of films: More science than art. *Video Age International.* January. http://www.videoageinternational.com/archive/jan98.html (February 8, 2002).

Tavakoli, Manouche and Martin Cave. 1996. Modeling television viewing patterns. *Journal of Advertising* 25(4): 71–86.

Taylor, Catharine P. 2002. Web disconnect. *Mediaweek,* September 9, pp. Q26–Q30.

Terranova, Joe. 1998. Ratings wars: SMART versus DART is shaping up to be the battle of the eyeballs; who can you trust to do the measuring? *American Demographics,* October, pp. 31–35.

Thomas, Laurie and Barry R. Litman. 1991. Fox broadcasting company: Why now? An economic study of the rise of the fourth broadcast "network." *Journal of Broadcasting and Electronic Media* 35(2): 139–57.

Thompson, Maryann J. 2001. Pop-ups pay off. *Industry Standard.* July 16. http://www.thestandard.com/article/0,1902,27898,00.html (August 22, 2001).

Thompson, Maryann J. and David Lake. 2001. Playing for keeps. *Industry Standard,* May 14, pp. 54–55.

Thompson, Maryann J., Stacy Lawrence, David Lake, and Mark A. Mowrey. 2000. The danger of trading on ratings. *Industry Standard,* July 24, pp. 172–93.

Thomson, Lynn M. 1990. The impact of audience information sources on media evolution. Ph.D. diss., Northwestern University, Evanston, Ill.

TiVo, Inc. 2001. White paper submitted to the Federal Trade Commission, Washington, D.C.

Trigoboff, Dan. 2002a. Nielsen's new tech banished in Boston. *Broadcasting and Cable,* April 22, p. 15.

———. 2002b. A majority of one: May sweeps with lone Nielsen-rated station in No. 6 market. *Broadcasting and Cable,* April 29, p. 18.

———. 2002c. Arbitron, Nielsen want to wait on PPM. *Broadcasting and Cable,* June 10, p. 15.

Trugman, Alan. 2002. Has media measurement kept up with the changing consumer media landscape? Remarks before the Radio and Television Research Council, New York, March 11.

Turow, Joseph. 1997. *Breaking up America: Advertisers and the new media world.* Chicago: University of Chicago Press.

TV ad buyers: The BIG spenders. 2001. *Broadcasting and Cable,* November 11, pp. 35–36.

Twyman, Tony and Chris Mundy. 2001. Mixed research techniques for a mixed economy. *Proceedings of the ESOMAR/ARF Worldwide Radio Conference and Exhibition,* 13–33. New York: European Society for Opinion and Marketing Research/Advertising Research Foundation.

Underwood, Douglas. 1993. *When MBAs rule the newsroom.* New York: Columbia University Press.

U.S. Census Bureau. 2001. Income 2000. http://www.census.gov/hhes/income/income00/inctab1.html (September 20, 2001).

Veronis, Suhler, and Associates. 2001. *Communications industry forecast.* New York: Veronis, Suhler, and Associates.

Vickery, Lisa, Kelly Greene, Shelly Branch, and Emily Nelson. 2001. Marketers tweak strategies as age groups realign. *Wall Street Journal,* May 15, pp. B1, B4.

Vogel, Harold L. 1998. *Entertainment industry economics: A guide for financial analysis.* 4th ed. New York: Cambridge University Press.

Vranica, Suzanne. 2002. Ad giant Interpublic shops for literary, talent agencies. *Wall Street Journal,* June 14, pp. B1, B4.

Wakshlag, Jacob J. and Bradly S. Greenberg. 1970. Programming strategies and the popularity of television programs for children. *Human Communication Research* 6(1): 58–68.

Waldfogel, Joel. 2000. Preference externalities: An empirical study of who benefits whom in differentiated product markets. Paper presented at the Telecommunications Policy Research Conference, Alexandria, Va., September.

Walker, James R. 1988. Inheritance effects in the new media environment. *Journal of Broadcasting and Electronic Media* 32(4): 391–401.

Waterman, David. 1986. The failure of cultural programming on cable TV: An economic interpretation. *Journal of Communication* 36(3): 92–107.

———. 1987. Electronic media and the economics of the first sale doctrine. In Robert Thorne and John D. Viera, eds., *Entertainment, publishing, and the arts handbook,* 3–13. New York: Clark Boardman.

———. 1992. "Narrowcasting" and "broadcasting" on nonbroadcast media: A program choice model. *Communication Research* 19(1): 3–28.

———. 2001. The economics of Internet TV: New niches versus mass audiences. *Info* 3(3): 215–29.

Waterman, David and August Grant. 1991. Cable television as an aftermarket. *Journal of Broadcasting and Electronic Media* 35(2): 179–88.

Waterman, David and Michael Z. Yan. 1999. Cable advertising and the future of basic cable networking. *Journal of Broadcasting and Electronic Media* 43(4): 645–58.

Web Characterization Project. 2001. Size and growth. http://www.wcp.oclc.org/stats/size.html (November 21, 2001).

Weber, Rene. 2001. Prognosis methods on television viewing patterns for target audiences. Working paper, Institute of Psychology, Berlin Technical University.

Webster, James G. 1985. Program audience duplication: A study of television inheritance effects. *Journal of Broadcasting and Electronic Media* 29(2): 121–33.

———. 1986. Audience behavior in the new media environment. *Journal of Communication* 36(3): 77–91.

———. 1998. The audience. *Journal of Broadcasting and Electronic Media* 42(2): 190–207.

Webster, James G. and Shu-Fang Lin. 2002. The Internet audience: Web use as mass behavior. *Journal of Broadcasting and Electronic Media* 46(1): 1–12.

Webster, James G. and Gregory D. Newton. 1988. Structural determinants of the television news audience. *Journal of Broadcasting and Electronic Media* 32(4): 381–89.

Webster, James G. and Patricia F. Phalen. 1997. *The mass audience: Rediscovering the dominant model.* Mahwah, N.J.: Lawrence Erlbaum.

Webster, James G. and Jacob J. Wakshlag. 1983. A theory of television program choice. *Communication Research* 10(4): 430–46.

Webster, James G. and Ting-Yu Wang. 1992. Structural determinants of exposure to television: The case of repeat viewing. *Journal of Broadcasting and Electronic Media* 36(2): 125–36.

Webster, James G., Patricia F. Phalen, and Lawrence W. Lichty. 2000. *Ratings analysis: The theory and practice of audience research,* 2d ed. Mahwah, N.J.: Lawrence Erlbaum.

Weiss, Michael J. 2001. Trying to clean up sweeps, the silly seasons of TV programming. *Inside.com.* http://www.inside.com/jcs/Story?article_id=30400&pod_id=11 (May 19, 2001).

Weissman, Rachel X. 1999. Broadcasters mine the gold. *American Demographics,* June, pp. 35–37.

Wells, Melanie. 1997. New fall shows disappointing advertisers. *USA Today,* November 17, p. 7B.

Werbach, Kevin. 2000. Syndication: The emerging model for business in the Internet era. *Harvard Business Review* 78(3): 85–93.

Westin, Av. 2001. The color of ratings. *Brill's Content,* April, pp. 82–85, 129–31.

White, Kenneth J. 1977. Television market shares, station characteristics, and viewer choice. *Communication Research* 4(4): 415–34.

Wildman, Steven S. 1994. One-way flows and the economics of audience making. In Ettema and Whitney, *Audiencemaking,* 115–41.

———. 1998. Toward a better integration of media economics and media competition policy. In M. E. Price and R. G. Noll, eds., *A communications cornucopia: Markle Foundation essays on information policy,* 573–93. Washington, D.C.: Brookings Institute.

Wildman, Steven S. and Theomary Karamanis. 1998. The economics of minority programming. In Amy Garmer, ed., *Investing in diversity: Advancing opportunities for minorities in media,* 47–65. Washington, D.C.: Aspen Institute.

Wildman, Steven S. and Bruce Owen. 1985. Program competition, diversity, and multichannel bundling in the new video industry. In E. M. Noam, ed., *Video media competition: Regulation, economics, and technology,* 244–73. New York: Columbia University Press.

Wildman, Steven S. and Stephen E. Siwek. 1988. *International trade in film and television programs.* Cambridge, Mass.: Ballinger.

Williamson, Oliver E. 1985. *The economic institutions of capitalism.* New York: Free Press.

Wilson, Clint II and Felix Gutierrez. 1985. *Minorities and media: Diversity and the end of mass communication.* Beverly Hills, Calif.: Sage.

Wingfield, Nick. 2001. Entertainment firms sue SonicBlue over features of new ReplayTV device. *Wall Street Journal,* November 1, p. B2.

Winston, Brian. 1986. Survival of national networks in an age of abundance. *Intermedia* 14(6): 30–34.

Wirth, Michael O. and James A. Wollert. 1984. The effects of market structure on television news pricing. *Journal of Broadcasting* 28(2): 215–24.

Wood, William C. 1986. Consumer spending on the mass media: The principle of relative constancy reconsidered. *Journal of Communication* 36(2): 39–51.

Yan, Michael Z. 1999. Audience segmentation in network broadcasting: An empirical analysis. Paper presented at the annual meeting of the Association for Education in Journalism and Mass Communication, New Orleans, August.

Yorke, David A. and Philip A. Kitchen. 1985. Channel flickers and video speeders. *Journal of Advertising Research* 25(2): 21–25.

Youn, Sug-Min. 1994. Program type preference and program choice in a multichannel situation. *Journal of Broadcasting and Electronic Media* 38(4): 465–75.

Zeitchik, Steven M. 2001. More pay, less play? *Industry Standard.* May 23. http://www.thestandard.com/article/0,1902,2473200.html (August 22, 2001).

INDEX

value, 96–97, 103–110, 121–124;
as predictor of purchasing
behaviors, 107–108
flow, 148
measurement industry; data
gathered, 26; and financial
considerations, 162; and fragmentation, 154–64; monopolies
in, 18–20; response rates, 70
research, 12, 185n5; areas of inquiry,
6; criticisms of, 8, 22
audiences
factors affecting value of, 4, 12, 98–
110, 121–123
measurement of, 5, 18
as product, 2–5, 13; components of,
29–35, 170; perishability of, 20,
30–31; production process, 23–25
Audimeter, 71–72, 89, 99
effects on programming, 198n23
strengths and weaknesses of, 74
Audit Bureau of Circulations, 19,
and paid circulation criteria, 103
Audits of Great Britain, 20, 73

BIA Research, 114, 119, 195n21
Big Four broadcast networks, 52, 56,
57, 189n15, 195n29
Big Three broadcast networks, 52, 53,
59
decline of, 136, 138
and UHF handicap, 193n3
Billboard magazine, 93–94
Blockbuster Video, 152, 178
BMW, 152
Bolton Radio Research, 189n3
Bookscan, 192n31
Boston, MA
and local people meters, 74, 155, 156,
163, 198n21
broadcast radio
audience measurement, 72
pretesting of content, 43

revenue streams, 4, 17
value of AM versus FM audiences,
101
broadcast television
revenue streams, 4, 17
syndication, 81
value of station audiences, 101
Broadcasting and Cable, 53–54
Brooks, Garth, 94
Bulgari, 153

Cable Act of 1992, 198n27
cable television
advertising sales, 3–4, 176
and audience measurement, 84–85,
89, 160
and audience prediction
CPMs, 109
and electronic data interchange
(EDI), 139–140
pricing strategies, 3
revenue streams, 17
caller-ID, 70
Cambridge, MA, 165
Castaway, 153
Cat Fancy, 187
CBS broadcast network, 10, 52, 53, 57,
59, 62, 63, 98, 108, 136
and "cradle-to-grave" strategy,
187n4
and David Letterman, 194n11–12
demographics of, 18, 125
and program testing, 152
CBS/Viacom, 18, 152, 187n2
channel repertoires, 8, 186n9
Clear Channel Communications, 27,
163
Cleveland, OH, 198n25
"Click-through" rates, 38, 171
Clinton, Bill, 177
CNN, 92
Coca Cola, 152
Comcast, 161